Jersey Sure

by
Gilbert Van Wagner

authorHOUSE™

1663 LIBERTY DRIVE, SUITE 200
BLOOMINGTON, INDIANA 47403
(800) 839-8640
WWW.AUTHORHOUSE.COM

© 2005 Gilbert Van Wagner. All Rights Reserved.

No part of this book may be reproduced, stored in a retrieval system, or transmitted by any means without the written permission of the author.

First published by AuthorHouse 09/07/05

ISBN: 1-4208-6926-4 (sc)

Printed in the United States of America
Bloomington, Indiana

This book is printed on acid-free paper.

DEDICATION

Welcome to my yesterdays

Mom I miss you. Every single day

Dad I am you. More every single day

Sis I envy you for your sense of family and your success in life

You are my George Bailey. Watch the damn movie!

Jack I love you. Although we never say it

Sharon and the kids Your turn is coming. Be afraid. Be very afraid.

The people of Keansburg, then and now. Be proud. See you on the Boardwalk.

To Jersey Folks No matter what exit you are from, you are special

This book is as true as they come. Mostly true. Some not. From the heart, but with poetic license. I have poetic license in 13 states, for I am a storyteller and this is my story. A collage of events mixed with other events, but all based on life. I love my life, and the days in Keansburg made my life what it is. I hope you enjoy the story as much as I enjoyed writing it and living it. Hopefully, you will find yourself reflecting on your own life and realize that your cast of characters and your adventures were just as entertaining. We are all connected in that regard. Be proud of who you are. Be proud of who you were. For like it or not, they are intermingled more with each passing day. Let the 10 year old inside of you out to play once in a while. It is fun!

Prologue

New Jersey is not just a state; it's an attitude. A defensive offense against a lifetime of put downs and jokes. Toxic waste jabs. New York cast-off comments. What exit inquiries. It seems all Americans feel the right to slam New Jersey. Even the ones in shitty states like Ohio and Kansas. George Washington most likely glibbed he would rather fight Hessians than remain in Jersey. Locals would have been surprised had he not. Then told him to shove his wooden teeth up his ass when he did. Loving him all the while.

This small state, wedged between colossus New York, dwarf Delaware, and enigma Pennsylvania, has no gimmicky attraction. California touts its sunshine, with nair a mention of the ever-present fault waiting for eventuality. Florida boasts of its beaches but glosses over the "next stop—Death" population. New Jersey claims little but denies nothing. If the Garden State were an amusement park, which it can be actually, the main attraction would be the natives.

Garden States folks have a chip on their collective shoulders, and it simultaneously endears and enrages non-Jersians. Jersey folks look adversity in the eye and say take your best shot. Sometimes they lose. But they never quit trying. It is always one hell of a ride.

New Jersey was my universe as a child. Keansburg, specifically. Oasis on the Raritan Bay. Actually a beachfront, much mellower version of the Big Apple, visible distantly across the bay. One square Mile. The Keansburg of my youth had a population of just over a thousand people year round, which tripled when summer filled the bungalows as New Yorkers claimed this blue collar Rivera. We had the beach on the bay as one border and Highway 36 as the other. To the East, East Keansburg. To the West, West Keansburg. Early pioneers were not very creative when naming villages. This was my universe. Froth with adventures and fun.

Keansburg was NYC minus the sky scrapers, traffic, social life, hustle, bustle, and millions of people. It was suburbia before we knew what that was. The City, and the glitz and grim of the Port Authority, was a bus ride away but seemed all around me. It lived in the people. Brooklyn in the form of my mother and most of the neighbors. The smells of little Italy from the houses of the non-Irish. We had the cosmopolitan air of a community of mixed marriages. Dutch married Irish like my own father and mother. Italian and Irish, a culinary combination doomed for failure, merged in matrimony. A mostly European mix of Micks, Guineas, and Polacks living in friendly animosity. Catholics right along with pagans. Somehow we survived.

Everyone in Keansburg started in the city, except those of us like me who actually started in the Burg itself. Some came just for the summer. Some stayed behind but kept the City alive in their actions and words. All were changed by exposure to Jersey. Maybe it was the radiation. Who knows?

My house, technically my Mom's and Dad's but this is my story, was on the corner of the street named for the tree in my own front yard. Big. White. The house, not the tree.

It was the only place I ever knew as home. The big corner house, as it was and is still called, was the center of my universe, narrow in scope but without compare. My only frame of reference. Zero-zero. The spot used to measure distance to all others. New York was forty minutes by bus. Cape Cod a long and often painful car ride with a sober, and therefore angry, father at the wheel of a used Cadillac or Buick. Other areas of the world were merely things on TV or in textbooks.

New Jersey was my world until I turned eighteen and ran away to join the circus called the United States Air Force. While many of my so-called peers headed north by the light of their burning draft cards, I was off into the wild blue yonder. That is a book unto itself, which you will have to read after I write it. This is the story of life in the Garden State. Life in a simpler time. Life begun in the 50s, lived in the 60s, and better understood after a century turned. Life viewed via the rear-view, fun house quality, mirror of time. Warning—stories may actually be larger than they appear.

As we age, strange things happen with memories and photographs. They meld into a blurry blend of truths and half-truths. Do I really remember being bundled up for the snow as a two-year-old as my father shoveled snow to free his car or did the photo I saw many times morph into a memory? Maybe it really was a black and white snowsuit. Then again, perhaps not. Early memories can be questionable. More altered history than fact. But stuff that happened when we were ten is admissible as evidence in courts, at least in parts of Mississippi and Alabama. So let's begin there. (Not Mississippi or Alabama. When I was ten. In New Jersey. Stick with me here! I write. You read. Remember?)

Almost School Days (Boredom and Lawn Fires)

At ten, all things centered around school. The calendar may begin on January 1st for the world, but not when your world is a decade old. The year was the school year, the pre-school year, school holidays, and summer, when there was no school. The new year was a few weeks away but seemed further as well as closer. Nineteen Sixty Four may have a few more months on the calendar but the school year that straddled it and the following year was about to begin, so '64 was about over for us kids. Happy New Year. The lazy, hazy days of summer eased into uniforms and new books.

I sat on the stoop and thought about it. The mailman was due any minute, so it was a good place to be. I was Occupant. Occupant thought of school and its looming beginning less than two weeks away. Fifth grade straight ahead.

Fifth Grade is big stuff. The year before sixth when they split up the boys and girls in Saint Anne's. I think I knew why. It had something to do with Annette and her swell sweater. I watched the Clubhouse for two reasons, and both of them were on Annette. Mickey was cute, but

Annette was, well I was not really sure what she was but whatever it was, it sure captured my attention. Perhaps by sixth grade, I would know why, but for now, it was a sweet mystery. Girls and boys were different and we got a bit differenter about the sixth grade. We had a few girls in fourth that were already pretty different. Fifth promised to be even better. I liked girls. Not sure why, but they sure caught my eye. Always did. Hoped they always would. Just wish I really understood why.

Fifth Grade would be great. Same kids. Just bigger and older. Small towns do not change much except we all got older each year. Rare to see a new face in the crowd. Pimples came and went. Growth spurts happened for some and not for others. Changes changed, but not all things. Each year the pack formed more and more. Dumb kids hung out together. Readers pushed the SRA limits as a group. Jocks itched to be with other jocks. The field jostled a bit each year, but not too much. After all, we were dumb or we read or we were jocks last year and would be next year and the year after that.

Fifth grade would find me in the middle again. I was an in between kid and that made things different. Not in-between as born in the middle but in-between in stuff like names and height. Names and height were pretty important in school since names and height got you to things faster or kept you from them longer, sometimes good and sometimes bad in both situations. Us in-betweeners were always after someone else. The mind noticed when you were never first in line. In-betweeners loved lines of one. I knew I did. Lines of more than one reminded me I was an in-betweener.

On line, I was far from the tallest and a few away from the shortest. Being short had some distinct advantages. Especially for a boy. Most of the people in line with me when aligned by height were girls. Girls were more fun than boys. Something about them and all that softness that

Jersey Sure

made it fun to be even near them. By the time sixth grade arrived, I fully intended to know why. Short or not.

There were two boys in class shorter than me and I envied them a bit. After all, if you gotta be short, be short. Be Tom Thumb short. Be freak show short. Short people had their own little sub-culture. Clothes made for younger people fit us. We rarely had to duck. Hide and seek was our domain since the tall kids stuck out wherever they went. We blended into a group almost to the point of hiding. There were advantages to shortness. Shortness was cool. I am sure tallness was cool too, but unless I moved to Munchkin land, I would not know that first hand. So I settled for short, but envied the two boys in the class who got to be shorter than me.

The Alphabet did not do much to help my stature either. V is a tough letter. There were a lot of letters between A and V. Most of them, in fact. The 22nd letter of a 26-letter alphabet was pretty much the end of the line. That dreaded phrase, "line up alphabetically, children" had me just head to the back of the room and wait. All the Adamses, Agars, Appletons, and God knows who else came first. Us alphabetically challenged kids waited our turn. It was a long wait. A through U came before us folks with Vs and Ws as well as those even rarer X, Y, Z families.

Sometimes, not too often though, we lined up alphabetically, starting at the back of the alphabet! That was way cool but even then, the V got me away from first place. There are lots of W's out there. Wilsons. Wheelers. Whalens. Wheatlys. Williamsons. Warrens. Damn them all for being behind me in the alphabet. If I had to be at the end of the alphabet, at least I could have been at the very end of it. I guess it could be worse. Heck, half the class would be after me if I lived in China or one of those other countries that use the entire alphabet. The alphabet, forward or backward, made me an in-between.

No sign of the mailman yet, so I spread out on the stoop. Felt good not being between others. On the stoop at that very moment, I was not last. I was not second. I was first. Being first was better than being third, so I enjoyed being first for the moment in my line of one that took a break on the stoop in my own little parade. I wondered if the two kids shorter than me did lines of one as well in the summer when we were not made to be in lines of more. A few more weeks and, unless the shorter kids had some freakish growth spurt like the one kid who looked like a bean pole and stooped to look shorter, and I would be third again.

Being third is not always bad. Line up by height for shots, (why height had anything to do with shots always eluded me) and there were several others who got poked first. Someone may like needles, but it sure the heck wasn't me. People praised good old Salk and his polio magic. I personally wanted to thank the guy who figured out how we could take it via a sugar cube inside of a puncture to the skin. Now, there's a hero! Medicine-one, Needles-nothing. Needles never made my list of good things. So I used my place in line to my advantage. I watched the reaction of the kids in front of me to determine if this was a good thing or a bad and figured by the time they got to the third one of us on anything, they worked out the kinks. Being third was not all bad.

Red The Mailman crossed Main a few houses down. Mail on the way. Red had been our mailman for as long as I could remember. In fact, I think he was always our mailman. He brought my birthday cards, but that was months away. He brought tons and tons of Christmas cards, but that was months away too. At Christmas, Mom and Dad gave him booze. Not to drink that day, but to take home. To wherever he lived. I did not know where he lived. Mailmen were like that. They came into our lives with stuff and then went back to their lives until it was time to bring more stuff into

Jersey Sure

our lives. I wonder if Red had to deliver his own mail or if someone brought stuff into his life like he did into ours.

He saw me and smiled. He headed for the mailbox that was not the mailbox but the box for mail that Red sorted and then brought to houses. It was a storage space. On the lot by the bus stop on the corner of Maple and Main, only we were on Maple and the box was on Main. All by itself. Well, it and a bench, but that was it. I crossed over the front yard to watch.

Red smiled again and went right to work. He did not mind me being there. If he did, he would have said so. He worked silently and knew things about mail that were really cool. There were always stacks of things in that box, and he knew how to sort them. Magazines and letters folded together in first meeting before final destination. He squatted and sorted. His leather bag smelt like a saddle. Used and loved. Lots of miles toted. The strap was newer and stuck out as not quite worthy of the bag yet. But it would not take long. Straps came and went quickly. Bags stayed. I know. Red had that same bag for as long as I can remember.

He filled the bag and tested the load on the ground. I liked how well he did it. Like a pro. He was, as my father would say, a damn fine mailman. He rose with the bag linked to his shoulder so it came up with him. He locked the emptied storage box and turned to Maple. The mail in his hand was ours. He handed it over with a "There you go, sport". I was usually sport to him. I was Occupant to the stuff he handed me. I liked how he handed it over to me, even if there was only Occupant junk that day. Red was a mail whacker. He bent the mail, carefully though, with advertisements and magazines folded over letters and bills, and he whacked it on his hand. As if he tested the weight or something. Whack. "There you go, sport." Sometimes a double whack. Whack. Whack.

He headed up Maple, and I headed in the house. Occupant got crap that day, but there were bills and stuff for Mom and Dad, so I put them on the sideboard and wrestled with what to do for the day. Only a few more days before school began. Better use them wisely. I wanted to school to start soon, but knew I would regret that idea just a few weeks later. Fickle is the word for it. Bored is another word. I was bored this day, and there were very little to do. So I sat to figure out what to do.

Sometimes I just liked to sit in the living room. No TV. Not tempted to cross the room, turn the knob, let the test tubes heat up, and, twenty five seconds later, watch whatever was on. Just sit in the living room. On the couch in Dad's spot. Feet on the TV table, after sliding the ashtray with the little, muscular guy pouring molten steel from a pipe shape shovel thingy to the side so the feet could rest. Uncle Larry gave us that. It had something to do with Bethlehem Steel and was made of it. I think. I put my hands up behind my head like Dad did when he thought heavy thoughts, and I thought my own version of heavy thoughts.

Would this be my living room someday? What would it be like to have this living room or my own? What will my very own living room be like? Hmmm. It would be bigger. It would be better. One of those color TVs like my brother, Jack, had in his new place. Even commercials looked good on a color TV. The shows all looked better "in living color!" I would have a color TV in my living room. A living room like Ward Cleaver's, with my own den off to the side. Bookcases. Bookcases have class. We did not have bookcases in the house on 1 Maple Avenue. I would have bookcases. Maybe even a picture on the wall. Framed. Landscape. Running water or ocean or mountains. Something really classy. Yeah, that's the ticket. I could see

Jersey Sure

the whole house. Brick thing. Two story. Columns. Yard with mowed grass and flowers. Someone to mow it, even. Why not? I am a big executive or something like that. Yeah. The family looks like it should be in a photograph. Damn, I aged well. Distinguished. Loafers. A smoking jacket. A pipe. Very scholarly, as they say. See the love in my woman's eyes? See the way the kids look at me? I like this house. I like this life. I smiled and took a deep breath. To capture it. Ah, life was good. I was much more than Occupant now.

The living room was really quiet. Seemed sorta small, too. Outside beckoned. I called Greg. Outside alone did not beckon. Outside with friends did. Or friend. Greg would do. He usually did. He was my best friend. I knew his number by heart. The operator was there with her standard "Number, please."

"May I have Keansburg 6-2109 please?"

She let me have Keansburg 6-2109, and I was pleased. Greg answered right away. He was grounded, so I wished him well and opted for a day alone. Sometimes a day alone can be fun. Even if you didn't expect to be alone.

JoJo was under the side table, the one with two shelves, one lamp, and a bunch of old magazines that was in the corner and that he called his sleeping spot. JoJo was our dog. Family members rarely slept under the side table. JoJo did a lot. I smacked my leg and said, "Let's go for a walk, JoJo."

JoJo only knew a few words. Walk was one of them. He bolted for the door and I let him out. Not exactly Timmy and Lassie, but we did alright.

I made it as far as the tree in the front yard. Sometimes walks were like that. Just mundane. Life can be mundane. Sometimes. Sometimes not. But mundane is, and we get used to it. As a kid, mundane was rare, but I did not know it at the time. I thought nothing of climbing a tree because it was there. No plans. No schedule. Look, a tree! Up I went. In fact, the tree in my front yard became known. As this one became known even more today, JoJo drifted off to conquer mundane himself. I was a flat leaver and he did not even growl. Good dog.

There were several trees in the yard. Three, but only two were climbable. The big maple, for which the street was named, was not really climbable since the lower branches were not really lower at all. Even at ten, I knew that if climbing involved a ladder, it was not really climbing. It was something else. Something structured. Something not so much fun.

The other two trees, the good, climbable trees, were evenly distributed. One in the front yard. One in the back. Someone planned their plantings long before I called this place home. Smart tree placement by someone now well planted. Two outta three climbable and well placed. Wooo hooo. The tree in the front was mine. The one in the back my sister's. Not marked, but claimed nonetheless. She claimed hers the hard way. A few years ago, she climbed it with two future thugs. She did not climb it well, but she sure did climb it high. She fell from just about the top to just about the bottom. The thugs helped break the branch she was on, and she headed South quickly. Limbs on limbs. I was younger at the time, too young to be in the tree with two thugs and a sister who routinely beat the shit outta me. I saw her fall. Through the limbs. Crack. Plummet. Crack. Thud. Shades of Batman. I reacted in the manner befitting my station, as well as my age. I ran in circles and yelled, "My sister. My sister. She's dead!" The cycle repeated and repeated. Not the her falling part. That only happened once. The me running in circles part was the thing that repeated and repeated. She was out cold for a while, but

Jersey Sure

there were no ambulances or hearses involved. We did not have to call two medics, paramedics as it were, nor even any adults. She lived so we all did. Had she not, well, it would not have been a good thing for anyone. She, being the corpse, would have gotten off easy.

The tree in the front yard that was not the maple tree for which the street was named was mine. I was a much better tree climber than my sister. After all, my body never careened from limb to limb and ended up a listless sack of near death with siblings running in circles claiming the end was here. My tree was nicer to me than hers was to her.

The trunk had some gnarls. Gnarls were important to the art of tree climbing. For a gnarl was a rung on the ladder otherwise called the trunk. The trunk was the major factor in if a tree was climbable or not. Novices thought the limbs were the priority. Veterans knew it began and ended with the trunk. Access and egress, without surrender to gravity and the breaking of bones and spirits. My tree had a grand trunk that led me to the first Y and heights limited only by the limbs that then became important.

My tree was a nestler. It offered several spots where the climber could just nestle. Nestling in a tree is a sweet thing. At least in good nestling trees. For nestling spots offered a hard wood seat, back support, and the all-important but often overlooked advantage of camouflage. I nestled in the tree, about half way up, and settled in for a while. Sometimes people passed directly underneath and did not know I was there.

There was power in that. A crow's nest. A look out. A place where you surveiled secretly. Secrecy can be nice. It can be peaceful. It can be nerve-racking. When nestled really well, one achieved a trance-like state. There, but mind far, far away. Treed to someplace where thoughts frolicked. Consequently, there were times when the first hint that there were other living beings was when they passed directly underneath my vantage point.

This was an exciting return to reality, but that startled jolt back to the here and now was sometimes physical. That feeling adults got when they dozed for a second, or several seconds, or minutes, behind the wheel of a two-ton object traveling 60 miles an hour. Jolt! Jolts at 60 miles an hour scared you. Jolts at 20 feet in the air nestled in a tree did as well.

The trick was to jolt and not move so the person below remained blissfully unaware of the eyes overhead. If not, the process went Jolt, move, slip a bit, and the amazing jolt transfer. For the person below heard the slip and, in turn, jolted. They almost always ducked. Silly people always clung to life and hoped to miss the bird, the plane, the superman, whatever the hell it was that was about to crush them from above. When the adult realized it was kid in the tree, they went from scared prey and potential victim to falling aircraft and space aliens, to a pissed-off neighbor pretty quickly. A matter of seconds. Expletives of relief that they were still alive. Strange relief, but what the hey.

I stayed in the tree for hours at a time. Sometimes only minutes. Sometimes not for weeks on end. But it was my tree. I knew the gnarls and sometimes shared them with kids, only everyday friends, since sharing a favorite tree was a bit of an intimate act. My branches hosted them. They could, not that they would, decide to climb the tree on their own sometime. We both knew that would be wrong, but it was an eventuality that had to be considered. Trees were pretty personal.

I sat for a while, nooked and comfortable. JoJo was not down there. At least not where I could see. So I sat. Picked a few leaves apart and let them drift to the dirt in pieces of what they were. Fall came early for a few within my reach. My thoughts drifted as the former shaders ceased shading.

Jersey Sure

Drifting thoughts only get you so far when you are ten. Reflective did not look good to a young mind. At least today. One of the last days of summer before school, and I spent it sitting in a tree? I think not. So down I went. A swing and a jump from tree to whatever lied ahead. Boredom was real, but movement trumped boredom most times. Boring bored me. So I headed down Maple Avenue without a clue of what to do. A clueless and bored ten year old was not a good thing to be.

Boring can be dangerous. It ended up dangerous this day. Boring and creative made for a spiral of events. This day spiraled. My walk from the house only made it as far as the tree. My walk from the tree only made it as far as Chuck Brown's house. Three houses down. Chuck was on his front porch, bored. He saw me. I saw him. We were both bored, and there was no one home at his house except him. It went downhill from there. Fate had plans that day, and the two of us were along for the ride.

I joined Chuck, and we went into his house. I was not sure where the adults in his house were, but I knew where they were not. They were not there, so we had the place to ourselves. We read a bit. He showed magazines of World War II and pointed out a photo of a bomb taking out a bridge that was about as big as a shoestring. At least a bridge that looked about as big as a shoestring from where the bomber guy was. I am sure it was a much bigger bridge before he bombed it into the water it used to cross. Chuck liked things like bombs, planes, ships, and things associated with wars. He had magazines and books all about wars, but he seemed to like World War II the best. I think it was because his dad fought in it. Had his name on the monument by the firehouse on Carr Avenue and everything. Not Chuck's name. His Dad's name. Although technically, it was Chuck's name as well, since Chuck was a Junior. Guess seeing your own name on a monument about World War II made you interested in it. Nice that Chuck's Dad's name was on the monument for just fighting, and not for dying. Otherwise, there would not have been a Junior, and I would not be in his house reading his magazines or playing with his World War II models.

Chuck had a heck of a lot of models about World War II. Ships of all shapes and sizes. Destroyers. Frigates. Loved that name. Sounded like a curse. PT Boats. Real cool now, due to PT 109 and all. Aircraft carriers complete with little planes on deck. Chuck had tanks, trucks, halftracks, jeeps, and even motorcycles. Models, that is. His favorite, though, seemed to be airplanes. Fighters. Bombers. All gussied up with decals and logos and bombs. Chuck was a good model guy. I guess that made him a modeler. Or whatever you call a guy who is good at building models. My models ended up a bit lumpy with excess glue and paint bumps. Chuck was quite the expert, and we moved from pictures of World War II things to models of World War II things.

That started it. We played with his models. His really cool airplanes dive-bombed his really cool ships and tanks. Zoooooooom. Booooooooooom. Ah Ah Ah Ah Ah. The rat-tat-tat of machine guns and ack-ack filled his room. We flew missions deep into enemy territory. We strafed ships on the floor from our really fast blue planes with the folding wings just like in the John Wayne movie. Hell Cats Leathernecks of Iwo Jima or whatever it was. We flew from wall to wall and dogfought like veterans. Targets became carnage. Chuck and I were deep into World War II in his room that day.

Unfortunately for Chuck, and for his models it turned out, the room was small so we expanded to the yard. The Brown's yard was anything but brown. It was the envy of the neighborhood. Mister Brown did not just cut the grass and hope for the best. He fertilized, edged, mowed, raked,

Jersey Sure

to the point of manicure in a neighborhood of cut it and forget it yards. Mister Brown was very, very proud of his front yard. The same front yard that his son and I converted to the Sea of Japan. I am not sure when it got out of control. Were we ever sure when things got out of control? It started out slowly and innocently. Two boys. Lots of models. Even more energy. Even more creativity. Basically, a recipe for disaster.

Rat-tat-tat. Boom. We dove. We fired. We sank things. Then I remembered what Lou Wood did with his models. Lou was a modeler, too, but did some things to with his models that Chuck had not tried. Cotton and paint became flames and contrails on Lou Brown's models. Loony Louie, as we called him, mastered special effects. He inspired me. We did that for Chuck's models. That held for a while. But cotton flames lacked something. Something fundamental. Heat. Fire. We needed real flames. Screw cotton flames. Real flames were much better. That creative thought led to matches that we ignited and dropped as bombs on the models. It was a blast. But not literally. Yet. Somewhere along the way, we decided the matches needed a chance to actually ignite something. That brought out the lighter fluid. That little edge that helped the matches become real incendiary devices. Soon models burned. Bombing runs resulted in hits. We were in the zone. In the war zone. Tanks blazed. Ships burned. Planes augured in after taking a hit. It was glorious. It lasted a long time. Chuck had a lot of models. Most of which melted quickly in the summer sun with help from some lighter fluid and matches. Molten wrecks filled the Sea of Japan.

The Sea of Japan became the front yard again as soon as Mr. Brown turned into the driveway. He did not make it all the way up the driveway. He did not pause at his mailbox to see if Red left him any good stuff. He exited the car before it even came to a stop. Unsafe for sure, but something had his attention other than safety.

"What the?????" The sentence was not complete but we caught its meaning right away. He headed for the little masses of burning plastic that littered his prize lawn. Chuck stopped right away and froze to the spot.

Mr. Brown was as mad as I ever saw him. Poor Chuck. I bet he would be grounded for the rest of the summer. He was lucky there were only two weeks of it left. If he set his models ablaze in June or even July, he would have been grounded for months instead of weeks. School would save him when it started. Good for him. I had to go home. This was not going to be pretty. The Sea of Japan burned and smoked as I walked to the sidewalk and wished Chuck well.

I wonder what was for dinner.

Catholic School (Ladies in Leather and the Story Teller)

Those two weeks flew by, as did the first two weeks of school. Never did see Chuck again that summer, and not much since back to school. Chuck was a few years older and went to high school. If he was not still grounded. Oh well, I had fifth grade stuff to learn. Chuck had to fend for himself.

The newness of the clothes eased away as we adjusted to the subtle changes in people over the summer. Homework became routine. Summer became memory. Back to the grind but now at the fifth grade level. In Saint Anne's school.

Saint Anne's parish was the home to my church and school. The concept of parishes sometimes confused non-Catholics. Catholics were confused as well but, more often than not, feigned understanding. Simply put, parishes were outposts in primitive lands. Outposts for Mother Rome and the One, Holy, Catholic, and Apostolic Church. Back in Rome, the Pope and his team, the Cardinals, hoped and prayed their minions in the hinterlands reached the natives.

In the primitive lands, in this case the wilds of the Garden State, the missionaries hoped and prayed that Rome did not leave them in New Jersey forever.

The priests and nuns of Saint Anne's were somewhat typical in their approach to life in our parish. They worked hard, prayed daily, and pondered what they had done to deserve the trials and tribulations of Keansburg. Each day, they swore they would be better and begged for forgiveness and freedom.

To the locals, these missionaries were far more than visitors doing penance for their sins. In parishioners' minds, the priests and nuns were Bing Crosby, Ingrid Bergman, and the entire crew from "The Bells of Saint Mary's". Purity embodied. Justice personified. Christian brotherhood and sisterhood in the flesh. Examples sent from high on how to be. These marvels of creation taught, guided, and ruled.

Meanwhile, the priests peered through the safety of the Rectory windows and saw "Wild Kingdom", although the natives did not have bones through their noses. The nuns taught the heathen offspring during the day and hid behind the doors of the Convent at night, while they pondered the evil afoot beyond the locked barricade.

Saint Anne's had the clergy and the rabble. The clergy worked to save the rabble via the technique outlined by Rome Central and mirrored after the feudal system of fiefdoms. In the secret manuals of the Catholic Church, still hidden deep in the catacombs and guarded by two dogs, Fido and Butch, this process for working with the rabble was called "Masses and Classes". It enforced separation of Church and State, but more for reasons of sanitation and non-infiltration rather than some higher code.

Rectories and Convents were castles without the moat. The elite lived and hid inside. The serfs and subjects rarely visited. Priests reached out and touched during Masses where they spoke in Latin and dressed in garb far different

Jersey Sure

than the natives. Nuns girded their loins, and all other flesh except that necessary for sight and breath, in habits, wimples, rosary beads, veils, and leather belts as they headed for classes with the native children. Seems there was some small print in the bible. "Go Forth!" (Be careful what you touch and be sure to wash thoroughly afterwards.)

The rectory, the convent, and the school made up the core of Saint Anne's parish. Why Saint Anne's one place and Holy Cross somewhere else? Which was named for the Sacred Heart and which for one of the Apostles? That decision was the choice of the Bureau of Official Names, referred to by those in the know as Boon. Boon was located deep in the sub-basement of the Vatican itself, turn left at the Cappuccino machine. This vital function was wedged between the Office for Alien Autopsies and the Center for Sainthood Certification. In a carefully guarded screening process, the priests in this office, Booners as it would be, hand-picked from a secret sect thought to trace back to the glory days of the Inquisition, selected categories of authorized names for parishes worldwide.

Saints' Names? Yes. After all, Saints were political forces in the history of the Church. They were canonized, and to be canonized was not a walk in the park. Canonization was the act of sainthood approval. Why canonized and not saintized? It was named for the better odds of sainthood if the candidate was shot point blank by a cannon while saving a multitude of orphans. Churches were named after Saints. They were always dead. No one survived being shot point blank by a cannon. Churches were named after them though, and I guess that made it alright. But Churches were not only named after Saints. Churches were also named after Christ's earth family. Mary and Joseph were big on the parish name circuit. So were the Apostles. Although that was tricky since most knew only 4 or 5 and there was that one guy with the silver pieces and all. Booners named a lot of Churches after the Apostles.

The well-kept secret is that the Booners were suckers for anything associated with the Lord himself. Those names moved through the otherwise cumbersome process with great speed. A body organ? Make it the Sacred Heart of Jesus and you were in. Mere terms like Redeemer or shepherd? Put the magic name of Jesus in front of it and print the stationary. You were home free.

In Keansburg, we had Saint Anne's. For the uninitiated, Saint Anne was the mother of Mary, the mother of Christ. For the initiated, Saint Anne was the mother of Mary, the mother of Christ. The connection with Jesus made using the name of Saint Anne's almost a given. Who could turn down naming a parish for Jesus' Grandma? Not someone in the Bureau of Official Names. (Boon)

Catholic School was heaven for parents, hell for the students, and the purgatory of my childhood. For my formative years, hundreds of stories, and dozens of narrow escapes, Saint Anne's school was the institution of my youth. Saint Anne's was all brick, all business, and mostly nuns when I was amongst the student body. Unknowingly, I dodged the bullet of parochial education for the first grade and attended Keansburg Public School, home to the heathens, right across the street from Saint Anne's. I sometimes watched that Catholic School playground and pondered what it would be like. Uniforms. Nuns in black rushed to and fro in the schoolyard to squash the first sign of fun.

Second grade marked the cross over. I departed public school and entered that strange land thus far seen only from across the street. There was the tie that bore SAS and a sports coat and slacks and the days of Catholic School were upon me. I would never be the same again.

The second grade is a foundation point in the evolution of any student, especially those in the Parochial School system. For if not properly shaped while in this class, the likelihood of molding the student dropped exponentially each year thereafter. The Roman Catholic Church and the parish of Saint Anne's turned to Sister Cornelia for this Herculean effort. She was my second grade life and shaped me even as a fifth grader now. She was that kinda teacher. The scary kind that stuck with you, as sure as a fluffernutter did to the roof of your mouth.

Sister Cornelia was a legend in Saint Anne's School. She was much more than just a nun. Everyone in Saint Anne's knew her. Even the kids in public school across the street from Saint Anne's knew this strict nun. She was famous. My brother and my sister had her for their formative years in the all important second grade. They knew her regimentation and discipline. They knew her ability to break even the most wayward of children. Sister Cornelia was known and feared. She relied on energy, a garrison belt, rigid structure, and the Iscabibilator.

The Iscabibilator was as much a part of the Sister Cornelia legend as she was. My brother heard of it ten years before I did, when he was formed into a stalwart Catholic boy at the hands of this nun of note. My sister spoke of the Iscabibilator with hushed tones when she survived her year with its inventor. For the Iscabibilator was the weapon of last resort in discipline. Sister Cornelia had her stare, which usually quieted even the rowdiest student. In the few cases when that did not work, she moved to the more traditional "standing in the corner" or "writing this sentence 100 times" approach for the more errant boys and girls. The Sister of Shaping had been known to use that garrison belt, but largely as a swinging in the air to scare the shit outta them way rather than actual abuse. From the smoke coming out of her nostrils when she waved it, you knew she really wanted to lay into them once or twice. The thing Sister Cornelia used last was the mere threat of the Iscabibilator. It was her nuclear weapon for student compliance.

The Iscabibilator was mentioned so seldom that the entire room hushed with fear and reverence when it was. Rumor had it that even the classrooms next door quieted when Sister Cornelia spoke of the device. For the Iscabibilator was a living legend. Some said it was a torture device left over from the Inquisition. Straps and levers to slowly and painfully kill bad boys and girls. Others thought it more contemporary with images of a Frankenstein, science fiction invention with electric pulses and lightning bolts to shock would-be delinquents into compliance. In her twenty-two years of teaching, Sister Cornelia never actually took anyone to the dreaded device. My brother knew of it from his day under her rule, and my sister did as well. They heard the same, very effective, threats and saw the compliance that followed. The Iscabibilator worked without ever actually being used on a student. That is, until the year Sister Cornelia and her machine of death encountered none other than yours truly.

I did not mean it to go that far. It was simply a day of mischievous innocence gone awry. A sugar high from a candy ladened lunch drove me to waywardness. As with most calamities, it started small but spiraled out of control rapidly. Funny faces. Laughter. Chastisement. She corrected me, and I quieted down for a while. A small period of quiet, and then more funny faces. Words were exchanged, and Sister dispatched me to the corner of the room. Far back. Away from her and the students. She intended to isolate the problem, and the problem was me. It worked for a bit. The fly in the ointment was her own work at the blackboard. While she diligently did cursive things

Jersey Sure

or something just as vital, her back was to me. I sensed it. A window of opportunity. A chance for the class clown to play to the crowd. Despite the odds. Despite the location. Draw attention from those who should be looking at the board. Draw the laughter and love of classmates while isolated in the corner. I accepted the challenge. Soon, more than a few heads turned to see what I was doing. She wrote on the board, and I grabbed the attention of a few more kids each time. The psssts spread. Soon, more watched me than her. I hammed it and entertained the crowd. Sister Cornelia taught away. Penmanship or something of the sort. The board was her medium. She wrote. I joked. She wrote more. I joked more. Soon, she lost a room full of kids' attention to a smart-ass ineffectively isolated at the back of the room. I played the crowd and forgot I was in trouble. Fate did not let me forget for long.

The events turned quickly. Almost a blur. Sister Cornelia turned. She pivoted. Her feet planted. Right there. Close to the chalkboard. She did not move, but that did not stop her reach. She transformed into the fifth of the fantastic four. Elasto-Nun. Her finger pointed. It reached from the front of the room, across rows of desks seven deep, and hovered an inch from my nose.

The room quieted. All except for the boom of her voice. A voice that echoed in my ears for years to come. "THAT'S IT!". Pause. Echo. Echo. Echo. "THAT'S IT!" Pause. Echo on echo for a reverb effect achieved only through equipment not yet invented or in caves deep within the earth's core. The noise stopped, and she said words that, until that fateful day, had never been spoken. "YOU ARE GOING TO THE ISCABIBILATOR!". There was a mass intake of breath as my life flashed, not just in front of my eyes, but in front of all the eyes in the room that day. I went from smart-ass to toast very quickly.

21

Gilbert Van Wagner

Sister Cornelia snapped. Otherwise, she may have heeded my pleas for life. She may not have swooped, one of the finest examples of swooping I had or would ever see, to the back of the room and grab my earlobe. But swoop she did. Her feet never even touched the floor as she swooped. My feet did not touch the floor as she dragged me from the room via an organ intended for hearing, not for lifting.

Earlobes are quite amazing assemblages of cartilage. Earlobes can sustain the weight of a human body. While the dangling human may wish the earlobes would rip from his head and end the pain, the sturdy little muscle mass failed to ease me from my misery that afternoon. Sister Cornelia was anything but sympathetic as she guided me to my doom.

We left the room, with me knowing it would be my last view of that classroom and the life therein. She carried me down that hall. Although my ear was somewhat occupied by the intense pain, my other organs worked full blast. My mouth opened wide and let the screams out. My eyes darted all over to determine where we were going. The answer was a few doors down. The Boiler Room. The cast iron blast door hid who knew what. That is where she kept it! The Iscabibilator was therein, and we headed to the door. Sister Cornelia opened the door with her free hand and we entered, in tandem since I was merely along for the ride.

Captured prey, my eyes darted around the room. No escape. Windows too small. Boiler to the left of us. Door closed by an evil nun pushed over the edge. Somewhere in this chamber was the device she built herself that was about to taste of me. I looked for it, barely noticed my now stretched to dumbo-like proportions ear. Failed to notice she let it go. I looked for the device of doom. Where was the it? Left? Right? Where? There was something in the shadows behind the boiler. Perhaps. I stared.

Jersey Sure

In those shadows was quite a surprise. In the darkness of Saint Anne's boiler room was a milky way of stars. An entire constellation of brightness I saw for the first time when sweet Sister Cornelia, the dedicated and religious spirit vowed to live as a Bride of Christ, cold-cocked me.

I'd been hit before, and would be again, but Sister Cornelia set a standard that day. She knocked me back a few paces and was gone by the time my eyes stopped bouncing from the blow. My ear liked it, though, for its level of pain diverted to my face where the imprint of a Nuns hand tattooed most of it.

I was stunned, and not just physically. Emotionally, the reality of what happened reassured. She was gone. I would live. A good belt to the face and I would live? There was hope in that dank and dour furnace room. My face stung, but my heart sung with death defying joy. My tears still flowed, but there was less sobbing now. It eased to sniffles and growing belief that tomorrow would still count me amongst the living.

Then she returned. I instinctively winced and cowered a bit, although that part would not make the story told in years to come. She approached and extended her arm, no fist this time, although that possibility was the first thing my mind imagined. Instead, she held a peace pipe in the form of a bottle of Coca Cola. Opened. Chilled. Ready for me.

"Drink this." A command for sure but one easy to obey so I did. The sips came between sobs and tears, but it was still soda and still tasted good. I drank in silence, a bit confused at the offering and the actions that preceded, but figured a soda was a soda. She watched as my sobbing ceased and the bottled emptied. She held her hand out, and I returned the glass case of air that used to be a nice cold Coke.

She reached out with the other hand and did the pinchy thing adults do to kids faces. That "oh, look at how big he is getting" thing kids hate. Sister Cornelia did not pinch to inform of cuteness. She pinched to focus head and thus eyes on hers as she leaned in a said in the firmest whisper I ever heard:

"If you ever tell anyone there is not an Iscabibilator, I will make one just to use it on you. You are to go back to that room and let them feel your fear and NEVER tell anyone there is not an Iscabibilator. Understood???"

The "Understood" was really not a question. I knew it. She knew it. Bear in mind that at this point, she could have commanded me to speak Latin for the rest of my born days and I would have said, "si" or whatever the hell yes is in Latin. So I pledged my allegiance of silence, and we returned to the room. Her with one slightly better behaved student and me with a story to tell for years to come.

That happened in second grade, and I was still alive now in the fifth. Not a year went by, though, without some mention of the Iscabibilator. Someone always asked. Sometimes a new student. One time, it was even a new teacher. I reported of the boiler room and how the Iscabibilator hurt, made you see stars, and cry. Facts only slightly distorted. The necessary truth versus the actual truth. I smiled inside as I told the tale. For the legend was safe. Sister Cornelia would not track me down and make the Iscabibilator. The Iscabibilator was still quite effective. It helped me since the legacy grew each year, as did the now legendary sole survivor. Made for a nice story that I happily told upon request. Sometimes even before a request. Stories became a bit of a trademark for me in school.

Now that I was in fifth grade, there were even more stories to tell. The Iscabibilator was merely one of them. Some stories based on fact. Others based on other things.

Jersey Sure

Some blends of both. The sources were many and varied. Saint Anne's School was a story unto itself.

Saint Anne's was a Catholic School. Catholic Schools mirrored their pagan counterparts with classes, textbooks, recess and the like, but there were significant differences. Public Schools, in the days before bussing, were microcosms of the local community. The facility matched the population mix almost exactly. The result? Irish taught Irish and Italian taught Italian. Students lived in little models of their own town when in the classroom.

Catholic Schools were abominations of nature. In those hallowed halls lurked creatures found nowhere else in the world. Nuns! Sister Cornelia and her kindred were beings unlike any others on the face of the earth. The very concept of nuns defied the laws of nature. Motherless Mother Superiors. Unmarried Brides of Christ. Childless nurturers of children. Bastions of virtue draped in black. The nuns of Saint Anne's belonged to the Order called the Sisters of Mercy. Ironic, since the Sisters of Mercy accentuated the traditional black habit with a leather garrison belt that shaped many a young mans' mind, and other parts, over the years.

These Sisters of Mercy were teachers. Teachers directly influenced by daily garb of black leather. They taught with a vengeance. Nuns big on memorization. Evidently, they memorized things under penalty of death or torture, so we did likewise. Prepositions. From, about, and after, all the way to up and with crammed into our brains and proven via drills and public chastisement. Conjugate the verb "To Be" or you will not be. There were a few easy ones like the limiting adjectives. Loved saying The, A, and An when the next kid in line got the propositions to spout. Nuns did not limit their quest for us to memorize to just Grammatical things. History was good with "We, the people, put forth this document for all to memorize". Founding Fathers be damned, memorization was not included in my personal pursuit of happiness. But the Nuns found it joyous. It gave something to ask during the most dreaded event on the Catholic School kids daily calendar, the grammar drill.

It did not take much. Some poster board with the parts of speech listed, as well as the parts of the sentence. Some letters to signify tense, kind of ironic that it did indeed always make us tense, gender, case, etc. Things we were taught so they could be used against us later. No Fifth Amendment Rights in Grammar class. If we could be beaten over the head with learning the Bill of Rights word by word, Grammar drill could be run with Gestapo tactics. It was. Especially in the fifth grade.

The nun eased the poster board, the same one that loomed in the corner of the room as sure as death standing watch, to the center of the room and announced, with a gusto that spoke volumes of their sadism, "Grammar Drill!" It was only missing the Achtung!

We cleared our desks of all materials and stood, ready for drilling. Drilling is not a fun word. This was fully justified. Dentists drill. Harsh military Sergeants drill. Nuns drill. Ouch. Ouch. Ouch. However, for a student and a storyteller, this was not all bad. Students of Saint Anne's did indeed learn. Or else! As for the storyteller, the territory was ripe with material. Drilling. The quest for memorization. Women from hell who ruled with an iron fist in the name of Jesus. It fed my imagination and fueled the most requested story in my grammar school days.

"Gil, tell him the story." That was usually all it took. A light to an eveready cauldron of stories. Danny was a new kid. New kids were rare in Keansburg. He joined us this year from all the way up in New Hampshire. Part of me thought it was cool that he lived somewhere else before

Jersey Sure

coming to St. Anne's. Most of me wondered why the heck anybody would move. Go somewhere else and it must be pretty much the same all over. Wherever you go, there you are. Why take all your stuff, leave all the people you knew for years, and be the new kid somewhere? It just did not make sense to me. Heck, my folks moved from the City, and all they talked about was how great it was. Why the hell did they leave in the first place? If we moved from Keansburg, I would still be me, and would most likely be telling everyone how great it was. So I decided to stay put, be me, and not have all that turmoil with moving and stuff. Besides, it took a long time to make everyday friends and, if I moved now, it would take forever to make new friends.

New kids did come in handy though. A new audience. A rarity in our town, and even I tired of telling my same old stories to the same old audience. Almost everyone I knew heard about the Iscabibilator. They did not ask of it again. Most heard my story of how Catholic School first started but they knew I added a bit more to this tale with each telling. It became known as "the story" and improved with age. The kid from New Hampshire was fresh meat. A valid excuse for the telling. A quick glance around the school yard showed the Nuns occupied elsewhere. The coast was clear.

The Nuns would not have liked parts of the story so I had to be a bit cautious. A crowd gathered as I began my tale of how Catholic School started. Some regulars settled in to enjoy the show. That made me feel good. The showman in me knew a repeat audience was a good thing. To know the show and sit through it again anyway? Hadda be good.

With only slight variations each time, the story of how Catholic school started went like this. My German accent, copied from movie Germans, improved each time.

"It begun in the olden days when the Church, das Holy Roman Catholic Church, vas struggling because the peasants learnt to read. The Bishop of Hofenpepper was not hoppy. Bishop Bismarck called the priests together.

'Das been a dark day! Peasants to vead?? Was is los in the Hofenpepper? Ve vead. They listen. Ve speak. They shut up and listen. To vead?? Nix! Nix! If they vead, they vill think! If they think..................Das is nix good!!!!'

Danny chuckled. They all chuckled. Some more that others, but they all chuckled. Bismarck and the Hofenpepper was always good for a laugh. I eased into the story and hammed it up even more. I eased them into laughter.

"Bishop Bismarck knew things." A shake of my fingers and hands emphasized it. Play the crowd, I thought instinctively. "He knew of this people. He knew of these peasants. He knew vhat they needed. His priests knew because he told them. Over and over and over."

'Peasants Are Really Only Capable and Happy If Always Led!'" This part of the story needed body language. A snap of the heels and SIG HIEL body language. I goose stepped a bit as Bismarck.

"Peasants Are Really Only Capable and Happy If Always Led!" The crowd was laughing now and a few watched for the Nuns. They knew the story. They knew the consequence if my personal history of Catholic School was revealed to the Nuns.

"Ve must lead these peasants. They vhant to vead? Ve will let them vead. Vhat? Vhat ve say. Vhat ve vant." Bismarck always got a bit hyper here and paced and threw his arms about wildly.

"Ve must have schulls. Good Schulls. Vhere ve will break them. Vhere ve will mold them. Our va. Our va. Our va. Maria." The Maria was good for a pop laugh since it was a surprise.

Jersey Sure

"Ve vill have ladies teach them. Not just any ladies. Brutal ladies. The meanest of the mean. Ladies who understand ve must not let the peasants think. Ve must teach them to think as ve vant them.

Ladies in black. Harsh black. Let these peasants know these vimen but vonder if they are vimen or machines. Hide the pretty parts. Hide all the pretty parts. Give them leather. Ooooooooooooo, leather." Bismarck always drooled here.

"Are these vimen? These are not like any vimen the peasants ever saw. Nun! Nun like these vimen. These vimen scare. These vimen break. These vimen rule.

These schulls will be rigid. March to class. No pansy wansy valking. In line! In line! Alvays in line! Sit the same. Stand the same. Think the same. They vill vear the same things. Look the same. Be the same. Good little peasants."

"Ah, but Bismarck was not alone. He had priests. One of these priests dared to voice vhat the others only dared to think" A brave priest. Father Ballsee.

'Heer Bishop. Vill these vimen like Nun other not scare the peasants? Will the leather und da marching und da yelling not scare these peasants?'

Bishop Bismarck of Hofenpepper was not accustomed to being questioned. All the other priests stared as the good Bishop Bismarck shot daggers at this Ballsee Father Ballsee.

Bismarck did not speak but he stared and it spoke for him. Priests standing around Ballsee moved away. Ballsee let the silence linger and then he spoke.

'Bishop, ve can make them come villingly. Come to us villingly to do our bidding. They vill vant to cum if ve do it right.'

Bismarck softened. Just a bit but enough to speak. 'Tell of this, Vather....'

'Ballsee, Sir.'

'Ya, Father Ballsee. Tell me of this.'

So Ballsee did,

'Ve name this schulls after Saints. Saints are nice. Saints are good. Saints do not scare. Ve let them hear nice names for this schulls.'

'Hmmmm, a good idea, Heer Father. Tell me more. Tell me more of this plan of yours.'

'Ve teach them better than the pagans. Our peasants will be smarter and better and ....'.(Ballsee always paused for effect her), 'vicher! Vicher to give to our church, Bishop.'

'Hmmmmm, excellent.'

Bismarck even caught the idea of this deception.

'Vhat do we call these schulls, Heer Father? Vith these vimen like nun other who yell und scream und beat vit them sticks und straps und bare hands? Vith das marching und das uniform clothing.......'".

The story usually went on to explain that the name Parochial was actually from the Bishops own belief that "Peasants Are Really Only Capable and Happy If Always Led". I did not know to call it an acronym, so usually explained to the crowd that it came from the first letter of each word in the saying. The story usually ended with Bismarck and all happy about the nuns, the school, and the Master Plan. Usually. This day the story ended when my ear stretched to the sky and Sister Celeste ended story hour. The same ear never fully recovered from the long ago trip to the Iscabibilator.

My crowd vaporized quickly since my eyes filled with tears. Sister Celeste dragged me to Principal's Office, with my feet well off the ground.

I was not a stranger to the Principal's Office, but to be dragged there less than three weeks after school began set some sort of record. Even for me. Sister Anne Bernadette, the Principal and Queen of All in Saint Anne's, knew me and I knew her. She was short, stocky, and mean. Sister Celeste deposited me in a chair and began her report, eager to rat me out. She did not get far, since the Principal looked over at her prey and said, 'Ah, Mister Van Wagner. Welcome back." She turned to Sister Celeste and asked, "What did he do this time? The how Catholic School got started story?"

Sister Anne Bernadette smirked with a knowingness that frightened. What else did she know? How much did she know? She watched. I squirmed. She savored. How much did she know? I knew the answer. She knew too much. She and Sister Celeste closed the door of Sister Anne Bernadette's inner office and left me in a chair, alone and afraid. The future was not completely unclear though. It would involve me memorizing something and result in a story to tell.

The Haircut
(Barber Shops and New
Chevys)

Even haircuts were adventures as a youth. Sometimes the adventure was in what the barber did with that strange disarray of cowlicks. Other times the adventure was in the trip to the barbershop itself. For in childhood, there was no such thing as a straight line. Childhood was commitment to the moment. Everything meandered. Whim just was. Time meant very little. Distance meant even less. With good purpose, I headed up Main Street with money in my pocket and a firm order from Katie, although I never called Mom Katie to her face, to get that mop cut. Almost four weeks after the obligatory back to school haircut, it was time to pay attention to appearances.

Nature, the ultimate slight of hand artist, diverted my attention as sure as the best magician. It began at the milk machine. Not that the milk machine was natural. It was anything but. This blink on the timeline of technology nestled, albatross like, in some hedges just off the sidewalk on Main Street, back dropped by a vacant field. There was an urban-ruralness to it. Machine meets nature. As

Jersey Sure

if someone saw a field and said, "Hey, I have an idea, let's run some power and stick a milk machine in this empty area." For that is exactly what they did. This oversized refrigerator of a machine did just what the name implied - it held milk. Fresh from the teat to a metal cube in your neighborhood. A sort of metallic cow that milked us for money to get the juice therein. Thirty cents for a quart and sixty cents for a half-gallon. Pricier than the stores, but far more convenient. After all, purchasing milk while in the middle of an otherwise vacant lot was something right out of the World's Fair Futurama. State of Abstract Art so to speak.

Bizzaro quality aside, the milk machine was a must stop for me on any trip uptown. It was not the humming machine that drew me to it each time, but the wooden planked platform just in front of it. It was the treasure hunt it promised. For once, and it only took once, I found a quarter in the dirt below that platform. For the mere investment of a stick, some gum, and fifteen minutes of time, I was a quarter richer. That glorious day transformed the milk machine into a ray of hope, so that each day that followed drew me to the machine as sure as the pits drew the miner in hopes of another strike. The milk machine, turned slot machine, held no cash cache this particular day but mother nature did, in the form of a hubcap wide anthill that straddled the underbelly of the platform and the sidewalk.

In childhood, an indefinite delay at an anthill was fully justified. This particular anthill was a doozy. Ants are cool. There were thousands of them on this mound of life, getting very personal with each other. After all, they were climbing all over each other, butts on heads and God only knows what else. How more personal could you get? Insect hygiene and relationships aside, their work was impressive. Closer inspection, achieved as I laid prone on the now forgotten platform and looked Gulliver-like at their efforts, showed the details.

Scurried is the word for it. All of them scurried. As Mother Nature intended. Chipmunks scampered. Elephants lumbered. Penguins waddled. Ants scurried. Drunkeningly perhaps, but scurried nonetheless. This anthill impressed with its commonality to all anthills. Work, work, work. Ants never took it easy. Ants were urgent. Ants never just meandered. Look at any anthill on the face of the earth, and you never saw an ant on smoke break. There was never one just leaning on a twig contemplating their navel, or lack thereof. Ants were indeed insects with a purpose. Hither and yon. To and fro. Perhaps they were all born late and spent life catching up. Maybe Nun-ants watched for the slightest sign of idleness, the gateway to hell. If idle hands were the devil's workshop, ants had a potential industrial park of evil with all those legs and stuff. Perhaps they all liked coffee. Way, way too much. Whatever it was, ants never just kicked back. There were no break rooms or lounges on ant farms. Ants raced against some time clock only they saw. These ants honored the ant code and worked feverously, little maniacs using each moment to do something. Anything. Just do it fast and run while you do it. Then do it again. Even faster this time. Teamsters must hate ants.

I laid there in awe of their efforts. They industriously moved bits and pieces of something from on high to down below. The focus was on dismantling, for they carried small chunks, small to me but often several times bigger than the ant carrying it, across the pile of their brethren and into their earthen abode. "Coming through. Watch out. Heavy load here. Stepping over. Hey, watch it. Nice butt. Doing anything after work? Ouch. Hey, give me a leg here will ya? Damn, we need a union.". Feeling quite Olympian

Jersey Sure

from my vantage point on high, I followed their path to see the object of their attention.

It was, and was is the optimum word, a Devil Dog. Less than a quarter of the Drake's cake but a mountain of sweetness and creamy filling for a community of ants. Basically a chocolate cake the size of a NYC bus for these industrious insects. It took me a minute to determine what it had been, and I knew the whole Drake's line intimately. The Devil Dog was fundamentally a tubular Yankee Doodle. Both the cupcake shaped Yankee Doodle and the Devil Dog shared a particular, overpowering trait. They were dry. Beyond dry. Have-milk-in-your-hand-ready-to-drink-before-taking-a-bite, dry. Conversely, Ring Dings and Yodels could be consumed sans liquid. For their nice chocolately coating moistened the entire cake. There was also the infamous coffee cake, two sizes. Neither size drew my attention much. I always headed to the Dark Lord of chocolate when selecting from Drake's line. Chocolate made almost anything better. Evidently the ants agreed since they thoroughly enjoyed the former Devil Dog that laid a few inches from my mesmerized face. A Devil Dog in name only since it was mummified via an undulating mass of insects that methodically dismantled the discarded taste treat. No ten-second rule rational here, this chocolate delicacy was beyond saving by any standard, except insects. It now nourished my admiration for ants. So I stayed. Watched. Savored. Time succumbed to the magic of a child in the zone of education/entertainment/awe in the schoolhouse of life. Cool. Way cool.

Cool enough to attract the attention of Timmy Pulaski as he walked by. In my life, Timmy was one of those kids you know. There are many levels of kids in kiddom. Kids that are "everyday friends". I had a few of those, like Greg and

Jimmy. "Everyday friends" were friends, well, everyday. Even on days when you did not see each other, they were still your friends. You knew the inside of their houses. You ate dinner at their homes, or at least lunch. Sometimes even with their parents' permission. They reciprocated in kind. They were kinda like family. You liked them even though you knew things about them you did not like. They liked you, too, despite some of the things they knew about you. "Everyday friends" were honest to each other yet remained friends. Everyday friendship was earned. Everyday.

There were also kids there were "sometimes friends". Those gravitated into and out of the circle of friendship but were not really "everyday friends". Alright people, but not part of the fiber of your life. Sometimes you would see them for many days in a row, but both of you knew it was temporary. "Sometimes Friends" were the Canadians of friendship, while everyday friends were Americans. "Sometimes friends" looked the same but were not really the same. Same language. Same looks, sorta. But there was always something a little different about sometimes friends, and you could only take them in small doses. They would cross the border and be fun for a while, especially if everyday friends were away. Other times, they were up North, easily forgotten, and that was quite all right. You had a lot in common with "sometimes friends". Just not enough.

"School friends" made up the next level down in the kid's friendship hierarchy. Those kids you knew in class and on the playground but rarely, if ever, saw outside of school. The bond of being in the same class, especially in a Catholic School, was strong, but did not really transcend the environment that brought you together. Akin to being on the same cellblock. Prisoners know prisoners. Cellblock mates have common screws. Sometimes literally. However, just like ex-cons who meet on the outside, "school

Jersey Sure

friends" outside of the classroom or playground had very little linkage. The school was the bond, and without it, you were basically strangers with common ground. You acknowledged, perhaps even chatted for bit, but moved on quickly since you were both fish out of water in regard to things in common. In fact, if you spoke at all, you spoke of school, exhausted the subject quickly, and pressed on. Awkward acquaintances.

Next level down were "kids you knew". This, the most fluid of levels, was a holding area for friends on the way down the hierarchy, as well as candidates for promotion. "Everyday friends" who had a falling out became "kids you knew". "Sometimes friends" who had a falling out became "kids you knew". "School friends" who had a falling out became "kids you knew". Kids falling from or ascending to any category ended up in the purgatory category as "kids you knew". This level for descent and ascent was essential, since being a kid involved a lot of falling-outs. Some kids were placed here based on the possibility of moving them to the preferential status of "sometimes friends" or, if they proved themselves truly worthy, even "everyday friends". Moving up the hierarchy was akin to dating. The two parties got to know each other and decided how much they really liked each other. A dance of sorts to determine how, when, and if friendship levels changed. It was usually a laborious process. Unless there was a pool involved.

The surest way to jump from a "kid you know" to an "everyday friend" required the installation of and full sharing of the holy grail of friendship, a backyard pool. Keansburg had exactly ten pools, none of which were in the back yard of the big white house on Maple Avenue. I don't think my sister or I even dared to ask. Even dared to think of asking. It was beyond the realm of feasibility. Mom somehow convinced us of that without ever saying it directly.

Gilbert Van Wagner

Perhaps there was a recording device in the walls of our bedrooms in the house on Maple Avenue. A recording device that only played at night with subliminal messages. Messages in the voice of Katie the Omnipotent. "Pool? Don't even think about it!" Messages that varied with the season. "See the Macy's parade in person? I think not!' "An English racer for you?? Get real." "Cash? Kids don't need no stinking cash." Whatever it was, it worked, for we dared not even think of our own pool. Instead, we focused on the ten pools in town.

Two public. One salt water and the other chlorined to almost blinding levels. The other eight pools were people's pools. Other people. Those people known far and wide as "people with pools". As kids, we knew of these "people with pools". They may have worked for the Borough. Perhaps they commuted to The City each day. Maybe they were Doctors. Or Lawyers. Or Indian Chiefs. They could have been three men in a tub but we knew them only as "people with pools". Pools we tested in person, at least once. Usually with mixed results, although the chase afterwards made me appreciate the art of running. For without exception, these "people with pools" did not welcome us with open arms on those dark of night summer forays.

Sadly, only three of the ten pools were associated with "kids in my class". Consequently, my odds of frequent pool access were drastically diminished. The two pools closest to my house belonged to snot-nosed, would be upper-crust, punk kids. The likelihood of these kids jumping from "kids I knew" to "everyday friends" was very slim, since they did not share their pools to our particular network of kids. Hence, they were forever banned from being my "everyday friends". Somehow, they lived on, blissfully unaware of this missed opportunity.

The next level down on the kids' hierarchy was a dreaded but very influential level. "Kids you knew of".

Jersey Sure

"Kids you knew of" were the kids you saw but hoped not to actually encounter. You knew of them because they were tough. These were the thugs. They may have even done time. Yes, done time. After all, this was Jersey. Eddie Haskell was a wuss compared to the "kids you knew of" when you and the "kids you knew of" lived in the Garden State. Reformatory schools in the third state to declare independence from England released their venom back to real world. Venom that then walked the streets armed with a reputation and an attitude. These kids usually hung out together, drawn by common disinterest. There were areas in town ripe with them. The Flamingo Bar wall. Manny's stand. A few other areas most of us carefully avoided. For good reason. "Kids you knew of" thought the idea of any other kid in town alone a great amusement. They did not see kids, they saw prey. We knew of them. We avoided them whenever possible. All part of kiddom.

There was actually another level on the hierarchy of friendship for kids but it was almost a non-level. It was "all other kids". For kids were kindred spirits even if they never met. The experience of being kids linked all of us. It was a universal thing. So much commonality. Parents. Bedtimes. School. Matinees, movie ones. The annual cycle of holidays. Cartoons. Things that transcended locale and time. Farm kids. City kids. Rich kids. Poor kids. West coast kids. East coast kids. Landlocked kids. Island kids. Fat kids. Skinny kids. Kids who climb on rocks. Tough kids. Sissy kids. Even kids with chicken pox. They not only liked hot dogs, they knew what "all other kids" knew. We were a community linked by commonality and experience. We knew things that all the others of us knew. That was why the hierarchy worked wherever you lived. We all had our place on it in different lives.

Gilbert Van Wagner

On my hierarchy, Timmy was one of "those kids I knew". He went to the same school but was in a different class. We chatted and said hi but did not really hang out together. The anthill drew us together this fine day, and we enjoyed each other's company. We watched for a while and what mesmerized one quickly bored two. He asked what I was up to and I mentioned the haircut. Then Timmy introduced the crossroad of honesty when he asked me which barbershop. There were only two Barber Shops in town. One was cool. The other was definitely not.

Joe's was the cool one. Up on Church Street, it was Floyd's with a Jersey twist. Comics and Field and Streams. Baseball pictures, Yankees. Mantle hitting number 500. That Ruth guy. Elston Howard. Black and white players in black and white pictures. Passionate talks of sports and players and numbers that awed us kids. There was always Yankee talk. Keansburg was a Yankee town. Joe's was a Yankee barbershop. Even though they lost the Series in seven games this year to the Cardinals and last year to the Dodgers in less than seven. Way less than seven. As less as seven as a World Series could be. Damn that Koufax guy. We knew it would pass. They were the Yankees, not the Red Sox. People in Joe's talked of the Yankees and how they would come back next year. Barbershops and sports were linked.

Joe's was manly before we understood what manly was. The fragrance of Barbersol. Hair piled like soft debris. Combs of all lengths and sizes stored in water for reasons no one ever really understood. A array of bottles and lotions to cover eventualities few could imagine. That even fewer wished to imagine. The buzz of the razor. The burp of liquid splashed on necks so everyone smelled good for a while. The chairs themselves. Joe's Barber Shop had three chairs. Three Barber Chairs!

Jersey Sure

Barber chairs were not like any other chairs on the face of the earth, or other planets for that matter. Barber chairs came with their own hydraulic system. Hydraulics put to the test with each customer. The chair lowered for ease of sitting and then raised to levels decided by the man himself. For the all powerful and omnipotent barber decided how high or how low customers were while in their shop. Barbers ruled all in their magical chairs. Chairs that adjusted the world to them. Short barbers. Tall barbers. Drawf barbers. Even Barbers with chicken pox. It did not matter. The Barber was the standard for size in all he surveyed.

Barbers were destined not to stoop. It was written somewhere in the Barber Code of Ethics. Thou shall not stoop!. Not a foot for the little ones. Not an inch for normal sized ones. There is not "to stoop or not to stoop". There is only "not to stoop". Stooping would be stupid. Barbers did not go to Barber College to be stupid. Clowns went to Clown College to be stupid. Although class reunions at Clown Colleges were a helluva lot more fun, barbers did not stoop. Leave stooping to the clowns. Barbers had very special chairs just for the purpose of not stooping. What did clowns have? Wild hair that screamed their lack of respect for barbers. Barbers knew clowns were jealous. Ask anyone of them. Barbers were, in fact, anti-clowns. Call any barber a clown and see what happens. Make sure you are not on their magic chairs when you do. It would not be pretty.

Barbers were artists. Clowns entertained and amused. Barbers had squirt bottles. Clowns had flowers that squirt. Barbers stood tall and erect as they mastered their craft. Clowns crammed into tiny cars with all the dignity of ants on a Devil Dog. Barbers were better than clowns. In fact, barbers knew the only thing that kept some men from being

Gilbert Van Wagner

clowns was their haircut. Barbers were society's last best defense against a complete clown takeover.

Barbers also did not tippy-toe to work on a customer. No ballet looking shenanigans for men with magic chairs. That would be akin to wearing floppy shoes and slipping on banana peels. Thanks to hydraulics, men who dared to think themselves larger and thus possibly more important than barbers were quickly put in their rightful place. Thanks to the only chair with a pole for legs, barbers were omnipotent. They dressed like Doctors in smocks. They carried sharp objects all day. They decided, with a push of their powerful foot, if they towered over or merely looked down on all in their domain. They were self-imposed gods armed with scissors and leather shaving straps. The chair was their source of power. Joe's had three of them. Chairs as well as barbers.

Joe's was not just a Barber Shop, it was an event. You went there as part of history since they knew your father and your brother. You went there fully knowing they remembered the first time you squirmed and cried as they took cutting tools towards your body parts. You went there for the dialogue and banter. You went so they could ask of you and your life with a welcoming sort of non-judgmental care. You went to let them know you were all right. It was much more than a haircut. It was part of the social fiber of manhood in small town America. Joe's Barber shop had all that and lollipops to boot.

Then there was Ben's. His shop was much more clinical in nature than his brethren up town. Sure, Ben had magazines. A few even had bits of the cover still attached. No comics. No pictures on the wall. No talk. No nonsense. No lollipops. In and out. No clowning around at Ben's. Sit and wait your turn. Ben had one chair and it rose and lowered more like a jack than a hydraulic wonder. If we named his shop for his less than state of the

Jersey Sure

art barber chair, Ben's would be Ben's with the shitty chair. Instead, we nicknamed Ben's based on his artistic ability with haircuts. He was Ben the Butcher. Ben had the good fortune of all bad barbers. Ben did not have to cut his own hair. His customers did not have the same good fortune. However, Ben had two things going for him that made him my mother's barber of choice. He did crew cuts, and he did them for 50 cents.

When it came to haircuts, Katie allowed any haircut as long as it was a crew cut. Cootie prevention. Lice exposed before school officials picked at your head and confiscated your combs. Although I was actually the only one in the family with a crew cut, it would not have shocked me if Katie pushed for all to have that buzz thing going on. She was that serious about us remaining "cootie-less". A town talked about "cootie people" and my Mother would not have the Van Wagners become one of "those families". We had a better chance of becoming "people with pools" that we did of degrading to one of "those families". Those poor, desperate "cootie people". Crew cuts were her insurance against such indignity. Ben's was her choice for my haircut since it was quick and a quarter cheaper than Joe's.

Now that Timmy asked which Barber I was headed for, the problem was to be uncool with the answer of Ben's or to lie. I lied. After all, Timmy knew people I knew, and word would get out.

We headed uptown. Timmy lived in that direction, and I was headed for the barbershop. My mind already figured I could head for Joe's after leaving Timmy and then double back to Ben's for a cut and run. No problem.

Timmy was a cool kid. Intelligent. Polite. Sporty. A bit of a jock but not in the "I can beat the shit outta you" kinda way. A likable kid, just not an everyday friend in my part of the universe. We chatted and walked. Along the way, Timmy shared something about himself that increased his coolness. Timmy had a set of drums!

Drums were cool. Not pool cool but cool nonetheless. Timmy even offered to show me the drums, an offer no kid could refuse. Ironically, Timmy lived around the corner from Ben's so it worked out nice. It was nice when a plan worked out. Even when it wasn't even a plan. We headed for Timmy's house and a set of drums.

We never really went into the house. For some odd reason, the drum set was banned to the garage. Go figure. Timmy opened the door and there they were. Real drums. Not kenner. Not plastic. An entire set of real drums just like on TV and stuff. The snare. The big round one with the foot thingy. The other one that was not the snare and not the big round one with the foot thingy. Cymbals. Two of them. I walked to the drum set and stared, openly awed. Timmy sat down on the little round seat that was adjustable and took real drumsticks and started to play.

He may have sucked really bad, but he sure sounded good to me. Bang. Clash. All sorts of noise. He clanged, boomed, and bashed with abandon. I was awed. Real drumsticks hit real drums. We jammed. Well, he did, but I was there so I was cool by association. Then Timmy asked a question that birthed the inner musician in me. He asked if I wanted to try, and then he held the sticks, real drum sticks, in my direction. A quick gosh later, my butt eased onto the already warmed, ewwww, stool. Once the sticks were in my hand, I realized I had no real idea how to hold them. That did not stop the percussionist in me. With bravado unique to ten year old beings, I started off tentatively with a touch of one drum and then another. But tentative gave way to something new. Something wild. Something free. Show time!

Jersey Sure

Badda Boom. Boom Boom Ba Boom. Crash! Loved those cymbals. My hands were alive and one with the sticks of joy. One drum. Bruuuuump. Another drum. Bruumppp. Back. Brumpp bump bump bump. Foot-pound. Cymbals! Foot thingy.

I was in the zone and went where natives and big band orchestras lived in harmony. The land of music and musicians that bridged time and space. I was one with the cosmos of harmony and joined the ranks of composers, singers, musicians, magicians, and entertainers of all shapes and sizes. These were real drums. These were real drumsticks. This was my debut of talent. My head bowed, uncut hair and all, as I bent for harder hits. Not taps. Body blows. Hard meant loud. Loud meant good. Harder meant better. I was the best I could be quickly that fateful day. Boom. Boom. My foot did not merely tap the foot thingy. It jammed it to the ground with enough force to shatter concrete. I pounded while my hands whirled dervishly from drum to drum and then cymbal to cymbal. This first time encounter with drums unleashed a beast in me that broke the cage of restriction and then did not know quite how to handle life in the real world. Crash. Boom. Oops. Crash. Real crash. The demon-possessed drumsticks lashed out but the cymbal dodged the manic sticks as the cymbal fell to the ground. With skill normally reserved for the sports field, I reached to right the cymbal but found only air. Too much air as the drum previously before me became the drum underneath me and then the drum behind me. A tuck and roll later, the drum set scattered. I was on the concrete.

The natives and orchestras no longer lived in harmony. The cosmos dissipated with a speed directly proportional to the growing astonishment on my host's face. Timmy was quite aghast. For drums are round and drums rolled when plummeted onto their sides by a flaying body turned projectile. Timmy dodged them but you would think he did not for how upset he was. Even after I helped pick up the pieces, he was noticeably cool towards my musical debut. We talked a bit afterwards but it was as awkward as awkward could be. Besides, I had to get to the haircut, so I departed. My laughter held until well out of sight of the scene of the crime but when it came, it was deep and pure. Snot out the nose pure. I knew instinctively that Timmy would not be moving up my hierarchy of friends. By his own choice. I just hoped he never got a pool, for the drum debut would cost me dearly if he did.

Timmy lived right behind a soda factory. Although it was really just a store that sold soda, well actually soda and beer, but only soda and beer versus chips and stuff. It was known as the Soda Factory. Sold it by the case. Had lines with rollers and stuff to custom select bottles for each personalized case of soda. No Pepsi and Coke here. This was generic before we knew what generic was. Their cola sucked. Tasted syrupy. Their claim to fame was the broad array of other flavors. Root Beer. Birch Beer. Cream. Orange. Grape. Lemon-Lime. They had a flavor called Coco-Cream that achieved a taste only duplicated if you took a piece of chocolate, a big sip of generic cola, and then burped. Not sure how they bottled it but it was quite impressive. They even had Celery Soda. Celery? Tried it once. On a dare. Seems a large portion of their flavor research was based on indigestion. It tasted like a celery burp. Even at ten years old, I knew they did not sell much Celery Soda.

I paused and watched as cases of soda rode rollers from storage area to truck. A reassuring sound. An assembly

Jersey Sure

line of sweetness. Fountain Ford. It captured my attention as sure as roadwork. At least it did until two other events drew my attention from the bubbling efficiency of the Soda Factory. First, the obligatory "hey, get out of here, kid". As common as background noise to any inquisitive kid. The other sound was different. It was out of the ordinary. The Soda Factory blipped into a sea of nothingness as I turned towards the new attraction. Music and garbled words filled my ears. Sounds from a pick up truck with a loudspeaker thing on top riding down Main Street. The one vehicle parade had me quickly forget the "get out of here, kid". Even the one who said it forgot it as he moved to the door, not to chase me but, to determine what that noise was. The pick up truck drew both our attention.

The vehicle was not alone. It pied pipered over a dozen kids, some on bikes and others on foot as it moved slowly and announced something of epic proportion. After all, you did not have a loud speaker on top of your car just to wish folks a happy Saturday. The sight of kids behind it assured me it was not one of the political things, for kids did not care about politics. We had no vote. We had no rights. We had no money. We did have a thing for pick up trucks festooned with crepe paper and banners. This one was a doozy. Bumper to bumper everything; it was white trash on wheels. A Chevy Banner flew like a flag of triumph overhead. The words had that garbled, you really had to listen, quality, so I joined the impromptu parade to hear what the heck it was all about.

The driver, a trivial detail in such an extravaganza, drove well below the speed limit so we could keep up. He would have to be dressed as a clown to even be noticed. Cars passed him but did so slowly to hear of the attraction firsthand. Bikes passed as well, but then looped back in a sort of perpetual parade. People exited houses and stores on the route to see the truck and its promise of joy. The cavalcade inched on with me in the crowd.

There was a repetition to the announcement. Enough to translate another few words each time. Ten times through equaled understanding. I focused with an intensity teachers long to inspire, but seldom do. If all teachers taught while parading down Main Street with loudspeakers on their heads, our education system would be the envy of the world. We followed and focused to catch it all. Passed shops and homes. The shoe repair man moved from his hundreds of sole searching shoes to his window to see. He was alone, as usual. Shoe repair is not a spectator sport. Others left their chores and activities to see what the fuss was all about. The impromptu crowd watched as the throng thronged.

In the mass, I saw none of them. I followed, but focused on the words to decipher where we headed. A few more words each time. We marched oblivious to newcomers and onlookers. Half way to a whole message, the truck turned from Main to Manning Way, so we made the right as well. Ben's Barbershop well behind me when I finally pieced together the puzzle of the almost inaudible announcement. "The New Chevys are in. See them for yourself at 2 O'clock. Hot dogs for the kids. Drinks. Be the first to see the 1965 models. Come to Trenary Brothers now. The New Chevys are in. See them for yourself at ......"

Holy Mackerel! The new Chevys were in. This was huge. The wait was over. Trenary Brothers was our local, and only, car dealer. As a kid, I did not know, nor did I care if the Trenary Brothers were really brothers, or if they were even really people. The siblings were less real to me than Aunt Jeminia and the Quaker Guy on the round cylindery thing of bland cereal. For that happy, sweet-faced lady and that pious gentleman had faces and context. The Trenary boys were just a name. Be that as it may, the Trenary Boys, like all their counterparts, were far more than automotive

Jersey Sure

dealers. They dealt in Chevrolets, but they really sold sex in metal form. These two pimps enticed in ways that rivaled any prior or since. A basic premise that worked so well. Don't let the public see, and they will want to see.

To a ten-year-old boy, and to many far older, the annual arrival of the new models paralleled the never-ending quest for sex. In a marketing process so diabolical, it changed people for the rest of their lives, car dealers around the country built up such an aura about the new models, people lusted for days. Impalas wantonly invaded consumers' dreams. Caprices basked with drivers on island sands, with sheen aglow. Corvettes, the ultimate dream machines, spent more time in dreams than in garages. Would be Vette owners woke exhausted and spent. This fetish for metal and chrome began with the models hidden behind butcher paper.

Weeks in advance, the windows to the Trenary Brothers display room on Church Street went from panes of visibility to pains of secrets. Just after Labor Day, as if car dealers honored the school calendar, and almost up until Election Day, butcher paper foiled would-be gawkers. Paper and tape was all it took. The word went out quickly. New Model cars coming! Promises of soon to be joy and bliss. The new Chevrolets. There was mystery. There was intrigue. We peeked to no avail. Butcher papering those windows was an art for it had to conceal and conceal it did. No hints. No rips. No hope of sneak peaks. But it did not stop with the torment of blindness. Even the arrival of the sacrosanct Chevys was marked in secrecy. Unloaded in the dark of night, some plotted to be there to see them rolled in the cloak of dark just to be the first. The date was promised but the showroom was masked. All to build to this day. The day worthy of loud speakers on a pick up truck.

The truck eased to the dealership and inched through an impressively large crowd to park on the side street off of Church Street. The followers stopped following and became part the multitude. An impressive multitude it was. Church Street itself was packed with people and Trenary Brothers was the draw. There was a grandstand bracketed by some bleachers in one of the parking spaces that usually held a used car. A good one at that, since it was so close to the showroom door. The back spaces usually held the "buy at your own risk, it used to be really something but has lived well passed it date of planned obsolescence" vehicles. All conspicuously absent this red letter day. Instead, every space in the lot not dedicated to fanfare and festivity held a good used car, soaped clean and then soaped over with a special marked down price. Each vehicle decorated with crepe paper in our country's colors, in tribute to the nation of their birth. For these vehicles were made in the good old USA. They flew the colors like badges and touched the buying public in their patriotic pocketbooks. It was a great day to be an American. American car dealership in an American town. American colors on anything that didn't move and a few things that did. American salesman pushed American iron to American consumers salivating for American cars, used and new. The American theme carried over to the grandstand itself as well as the bleachers in the form of red, white, and blue bunting. Right alongside of those bunted wonders, I saw the best our land had to offer. Tubular wonder food! Hot dogs distributed as fast as they were grilled. Was there anything more American than an hot dog? I thanked God for the land of my birth and excitedly eased towards free food.

The excitement of the moment caught everyone. Spirits were lighter, and it permeated the mood that fine, fall afternoon. The free dog was handed with a smile. A minute later, the second one was as well. The third one

Jersey Sure

challenged the master chefs patriotic spirit so I ate it slower and explored the gathering a bit.

On the stage in the primo parking space, someone made a speech. The tithers of laughter a clear sign that it was not an exceptionally good effort. I could not see who it was. Folks watched the speaker. Others spoke over the noise. From my vantage point, it was either one of the Trenary Brothers, Aunt Jemina, or the Quaker Oats guy. Blinded by the lack of visibility and interest, I people-watched instead. This gathering was well suited for the under-appreciated art.

This gathering was diverse. It was spontaneous for some while orchestrated for others. An interesting hodge podge of pop-in and planned. As cross-cultural as white, Anglo-Saxon, protestant, and Catholic, Keansburg could muster. I spied Mister Brown, my neighbor and Keansburg's Borough Manager, the last politician I would ever like. There were a few policemen with that "I am here in an official capacity but would rather be somewhere else" look about them. Several adult faces from school, church, and some of the bars. A few I knew from all those places. The atmosphere was friendly though because there were a lots of kids. Free Hot Dogs drew kids like nuns to novenas.

The air of expectation as thick as some of our nun's thighs. Everyone politely mingled and chatted, but all eyes were on the butcher-paper encased showroom. Several speeches, two sodas, and three hot dogs later, the waiting was over. A band Sousafied the afternoon air and then rolled some drums, not literally as I had done. The crowd oo and ahed. The butcher paper was strip-teased from the windows to reveal the gleaming, seemingly intergalacticly beautiful Chevys. Two of them. A snow white Impala and a sea blue Nova. The gathering hushed and watched lustfully.

The unveiling itself was a bit anticlimactic. Almost literally. A foreplay of sorts, without any chance of completion. Lots of longing. Equal amounts of lust. People wished. People hoped. Then the moment of truth came. The long awaited and much touted beauties were there. All made up and ready for action. Sleek. Shiny. Glistening. With those come-on headlights. Curves you usually only saw on TV. Extras that made you remember the flaws in the model at home. You saw. You gently caressed waxy surfaces. But you knew in your hearts of hearts, you could not have.

This day, and annual events like it, set the stage for a life of passion for vehicles. Tormented beings lusted for metal for the rest of their lives. They longed for the curve of fenders and fondled steering wheels with disturbing but lingering passion. Americans loved automobiles. A love programmed by Trenary Brothers and those like them all across this great land. A love reinforced with torment and tantalizing teasing each new model year. We coveted. With all our hearts and souls.

A little touch of metal, a few wishful sighs, and that sense of resignation germane to window shoppers the world over, and the afternoon eased to a close. Folks dispersed slowly. The crowd lost momentum as it lost mass. The energy drained as the numbers dwindled. It was palatable. I rode the flow of dissipation to the grills and ate another hot dog. My teeth sank into it but not my heart. Parades and new car unveilings were good but the crash afterwards drained. Listlessly, I eased up Church Street towards Main Street and home.

People straggled with little purpose. They looked at shops. They enjoyed their time together after an annual outing to see Detroit wonders right in Keansburg. They eased back to reality gently after the bright, elusive butterfly of hope migrated away for another year. I fluttered with

Jersey Sure

them. Shuffled a bit. Checked out the Methodist Church, from the outside, of course, since going in meant eternal damnation. My hands eased into my pockets and I walked. My surprised fingers felt coins there. Quarters? How did I get quarters? No deposit bottles as of late. My hand took the coins from the pocket to confirm their reality. Sure enough, two quarters. Hmmmmmm. How did I get money?

The ten-year-old mind is an amazing thing. For the moment the reality of what those two coins meant registered, my reaction was cartoon-like. It could not have been any more animated if I was Ruff N' Ready's close friend, the stupid kid who forgot about the haircut. My eyes bugged out, a foot or so, with a Booooing, once I saw those two coins for what they were and jumped straight into the air as I did. Only a few feet but I hovered there and then exited, stage left, without touching the ground. Whhhhhhhfttt. Cartoon lines and a puff of smoke that would do Hanna Barbarra proud as I ran to the intersection of Church and Main and whirled around the corner as papers and people flew in my wake. I loony-tooned it to Ben's.

My mind raced as fast as my feet. Raced with hope. Hope that befitted the day. For I longed that Ben's would still be open as sincerely as those poor saps hoped to own those new Chevys. With an equal chance that it would actually happen. Pleeeeeeeeeeeeeeeeeeeeeeeeeeeeeeee eese. PLEEEEEEEEEEEEEEEESSSSSEEEEE. Pretty, pretty, pretty pleeeeeeeeeeeeeeeeeeeeessssssssseeee. With whipped cream and a cherry on top. Pleeeeeeeeeeeeesssss sssseeee. With a whole jar of cherries on top. Pleeeeeeeee eeeeeeeeeeessssssssseeeeee. I ran. I hoped. I prayed. But I knew. It was fruitless. The day was almost over and Ben would be where ever Ben went when he was not butchering hair. But still I ran. A race against death. Death at the hands of Katie as she noticed the non-hair cut. Death as the hands of the woman who could ask "Where the hell have

53

you been" in a way that made convicts convert. I ran for my life. I ran with urgency. I ran with great speed.

Not fast enough. Ben's was closed. My pounding on the door did not change it. My pleading there at his window did not change it. My prayer to God and all the angels and saints for a miracle did not change it. Ben's was closed. Lights out, gone far away, no haircuts until Tuesday, closed. Ben closed his shop while I ate hot dogs. Ben closed his shop and ended any hope I had to live. Damn you, Ben!

The walk from Ben's was that terrible walk of a kid headed home to death or worse. Excuses careened to life in my head but died quickly in the harsh reality of shaggy hair and closed barbershops. My steps were listless. My hopes few. Each step a step closer to execution. All because of the new Chevys.

That was when the would-be writer in me tapped the creative spirit. The cause of the problem could also be the alibi. With some minor modification of reality. I smiled. A "I think I may just live through this thing" smile. A little creative spin to the events was all that was needed.

Plan B kicked into motion. The plan formulated with each step towards the big white house on the corner of Maple and Main. The steps accelerated, for the pace had to reflect the mood of the day for me to pull this off. This required some theatrics. A life or death performance. I crossed the lawn with steely resolve and headed into the house. With a bound. An actor headed to the stage with a very critical audience in the house.

"Dad! Mom! The new Chevys are in! Dad! Mom! I got to see them!"

They were both sitting at the Dining Room table. She noticed the haircut, or lack thereof right away. I saw it in her eyes. My mind raced. Offense, damn it. Offense. Defense would not work against such a formidable foe.

Jersey Sure

"Dad! You gotta see them. Two of them! A nice white one and a blue one, too. There were hot dogs and soda for free. Every one was there, Dad. Even Ben closed his shop to be there. It was way cool. They had music and speeches and lots of people. They even had a pick up truck with a loud speaker, and it rode around town. I saw Mr. Brown and even a few of the guys from school. It was a blast."

While my mouth spewed forth words, my nimble mind focused on her. Mid-stream in my torrent of babble, I spied to see if she picked on the oh-so-clever mention of Ben and his closed shop. It seemed like she did, but the most daring part of my plan was yet to come. The part of the plan that would confirm if she did and if it appeased her. I reached for my last best chance of living through this Chevy induced dilemma. The two quarters. Money to appease the potentially vengeful god I called Mom.

With a cavalier bluster that impressed even me, I reached across the table and placed the quarters there for both to see. Strategically positioned before Katie, as if in tribute.

Nonchalantly I said, "Here is the money for the haircut, Mom. I will have to get a hair cut next week".

Back to babble, quickly. Offense! Offense! The rest of the conversation was something about the cars and how many hot dogs I ate. I rambled. With freedom. With joy. With gusto. With bravado. All part of the master plan. A master plan I pulled off. Life would go on. Katie confirmed it as soon as she cupped the quarters and eased them into her pocket. Without a word of complaint or even an evil eye of "I know better, boy".

The rest of the evening was inconsequential. Washed up. Ate dinner. Watched some TV or something. It mattered little. A day with an anthill, a drum debut, new cars, free hot dogs, and outwitting Katie was tough to beat.

Gilbert Van Wagner

Fifth grade was cool. I never could have pulled this off in the fourth.

Cub Scouting—With a Jersey spin
(Cupcakes and Pinewood Heartbreaks)

Scouting builds men. Just ask the Boy Scouts of America (BSA). BSA was far more than a Hitler Youth look-alike association. The uniforms, para-military rules, and secret codes sometimes confused outsiders as they watched the boys march in parades and sell things door to door. The Boy Scouts of America was actually easy to explain. A group of adult men dressed in Boy Scout Uniforms took boys into the woods to teach them things. It was a time to test character and develop habits that shaped boys into the men they would become. It lived up to the concept of being the Boy Scouts of America since it was present in every state of this great land. The Garden State was no exception when it came to supporting the BSA and its ambitious credo. Just as with anything else, Jersey interpreted things a bit differently. After all, in my neck of the urban woods, rope play and knife use were practiced by most would be cubbies before they even joined the cubs. We were a group of child prodigies in that regard.

Cub scouting, the prelude that all forwent before they were entitled to bounty of fun in the Boy Scouts, was traditionally a time of innocence. Plays. Craft projects. Team building. Macramé. Young boys harnessed that seemingly endless energy under the close supervision of someone's Mom. Usually, right after school on days when latchkey kids were but didn't know they were. Plus, there were cupcakes. All in all, a good deal for everyone involved.

St. Anne's Church sanctioned Cub Scout Pack 105 and its sister unit, Boy Scout Troop 105. Boys in our class joined in groups, some would say gangs, and looked forward to adult-sanctioned lessons in starting fires and tying things up. We knew from word of mouth that all the good stuff happened in Boy Scouts but stood ready to tolerate our days as Cubs. Fifth grade was the time most of us moved from cubs to Boy Scouts. Some never made the leap. Rumors were the Boy Scouts did not have as many cupcakes as the cubs. A few of my brother cubbies were in it just for the snacks.

As promised, cupcakes happened. That in and of itself was payment enough to tolerate the pablum in Cub Scouts . Evidently, the authors of Dick and Jane wrote the Cub Scout books. It was propaganda in its purest and most insidious form.. Books so far removed from the reality of life in New Jersey as to seem more like fiction. I read them and enjoyed them, though, just as I did Tom Swift and his many adventures. Tom and his electric grandmother was one of my favorites. Cub Scout books entertained and amused with their flights of fancy. Lily-white, Aryan-like Scouts, with perfect uniforms and television teeth, lived in those pages and nowhere else in our universe. Those books whet our appetite for things like campouts and jamborees.

Jersey Sure

The reality of New Jersey did not quite match the images promised in those lying, cheating, over-promising Cub Scout manuals.

Only rich pansies got to attend Willowbrook, the summer, weeklong, scout camp hidden in the New Jersey Hinterlands. We heard about it though. Canoes. Archery. Singalongs. The rich kids probably rode there on their English Racers. Bastards. Hoped they got poison ivy where the sun didn't shine. However, even us urchins went to the daylong festival in that big stone building, The Convention Center, in beautiful Asbury Park. A day of competition and fun. A day of crafts and speed. The one and only, Pinewood Derby!

The Pinewood Derby was as much a tradition as it was an event. It was a process versus a Saturday gathering. It was far more than hastily assembled wooden cars riding down an angled track with gravity as the only propellant. The Pinewood Derby was art as well as science. Boys learned of aerodynamics. Weight and Balance concepts became part of their vocabulary. Some of the cars were prepared on lathes and measured to centimeters for exact dimensions. Vehicles were sometimes airbrushed and hand detailed for beauty. We were told of all of this. We heard we could take a trip to Asbury Park. Woo Hoo!

Preparations began months in advance. You had to register. So we did. Even before school began, we registered for the fall Pinewood Derby. You had to order the pre-approved, specially made, and hand selected materials for your Official Pinewood Derby Race Car well in advance of race day. So we did. Back in the middle of summer. Albeit after quite a bit of begging and pleading to our folks because the Official Pinewood Derby Race Car cost money. Money in addition to the already exorbitant 10 cent weekly dues we paid adult Cub Scout leaders my parents knew as the "price grubbing bastards". We pleaded. We begged. We longed. We persevered. We ordered. We swore we could not wait. Eagerly, they distributed the materials for the Official Pinewood Derby Race Car. Then we forgot about it. Weeks to wait distracted even the best of intentions at ten years old. Make it months and we were not just reminded, we were surprised at the long forgotten project.

Finally, the day arrived. A crisp fall day that promised winter. Just six weeks before the now forgotten Pinewood Derby. We met in a garage. Unheated, yes but it was inside, so we did not complain. Our gathering point was a picnic table carefully positioned over an oil stain. We saw the bags in a box and immediately knew what they were. Mrs. McGrath, our Cub Scout den mother, (we normally added another word to this title, not because she was, but because we liked the sound of that better) taunted us a bit with the materials. Not in the "leather clad, whip cracking, you low life scum bucket" manner but more in the "I have the goods and you can't have them until I say so" manner. She placed the box of materials on the table, within our reach, and told us not to take them until she said it was alright. Basically, she abused her power. Perhaps I should say she attempted to abuse her power. Heck, we dealt with nuns everyday. Mrs. McGrath was bush league. We smiled at her and attacked the box in mass.

Instant bedlam. Kids grabbed bags from the quickly crushed box. Materials flew hither and yon. Voices screamed in excitement. Struggles ensued over a particular bag although all held the same things. Cubs shoved other cubs aside to get their bags. Elbows wedged eyes. Hands grabbed hair and neckerchiefs as we jockeyed for position. Less aggressive scouts fell to the ground, helpless victims in the stampede. As the dust settled, Mrs. McGraph comforted one boy covered in footprints and huddled under

Jersey Sure

the table in tears. Another scout sulked and cowered in the corner. One of the smarter wimps eyed the maylay from the distance and shrewdly crammed cupcakes in his mouth. Most of us headed for neutral corners and surveyed the contents of the hard won bags of goodies.

A block of wood for the chassis. Some wheels. A few pieces of wood and metal to connect the wheels to the chassis. A book of rules. (There was always a book of rules). The Pinewood Derby became a reality with the touch of the wood in our hands.

Mrs. McGrath repaired the battlefield, tended the wounded, and had us gather around the table for instructions. We listened with the halfhearted efficiency of youth and headed home for the actual preparation of the Official Pinewood Derby Racing Car.

For many cub scouts, the Pinewood Derby was a father/son project. A time to bond while working on a car they remembered for the rest of their lives. The two drew out their vehicle with the boy's cartoon based knowledge of racing and the father's real world experience with automobiles. They weighed the wood. They converted pounds to grams. The father taught the boy about tools like lathes and electric drills. He emphasized safety and precision. The boy heard "measure twice, cut once" and added the phrase to his vocabulary for life. Father and son took their design from paper to reality with hours of sanding and sculpting. The Pinewood Derby became a topic of conversation at the dinner table and all family gatherings. The two seemed obsessed by it. Two generations linked with the passion of building a winning machine.

My Official Pinewood Derby Racing Car was a different story. It was constructed the day before the race, and I did it alone. It was quite easy and involved a butter knife, a can of paint left over from some house project, and some Elmer's Glue-all.

Gilbert Van Wagner

The intent of making an Official Pinewood Derby Racing Car was to take a block of wood and shape it into something streamlined. Although the butter knife chiseled away some chips and such, my resolve weakened before the block of wood took any shape other that a gnawed appearance. Another factor in an Official Pinewood Derby Racing Car was a show-case type look. Although white house paint, in the hands of an skilled craftsman, could approach that look, my patented drop-the-wood-in-the-paint can-and-fish-it-out immersion technique left a lot of room for improvement. Attaching the wheels to an Official Pinewood Derby Racing Car was a vital matter since the choice of medium had to be highly effective, but not weigh down the vehicle. My choice of Elmer's Glue-all seemed quite fortuitous at the time. It was off to the races.

The Asbury Park Convention Center was a mammoth venue to a youth. Cavernous yet chock full of humanity as Cub Scouts from around Monmouth County gathered to compete in a nationwide tradition. They picked this venue for many reasons. One of which was autumn at the shore. No oppressive heat and humidity. No tourists. Basically nothing going on so the Convention Center was available. Cheap. Good time for community activities. When the money train rested in the city until spring. We bussed in and filled, the other than summer, emptiness of Asbury Park.

I carried my creation in a bag. Seeing the other cars there, I left it in the bag for a while. These Official Pinewood Derby Racing Cars looked like miniature versions of something that could win at Monte Carlo. All shapes and sizes. Rounded. Jet shaped. Bullet like. They had decals. Flames. Numbers. Names. Color schemes that rivaled anything Detroit ever imagined. They did not resemble anything like the blocks of wood from whence they came.

Jersey Sure

The races themselves teamed with excitement as fathers and sons cheered while their cars screamed down the track. There was comaradie and competition everywhere. It was exhilarating. It was intimidating.

In the bag, my car waited. White. Chiseled and chipped. The missing link in the evolution from block of wood to the race cars all around me. I knew it was missing something and the sight of the decals and paint schemes inspired me. It needed a number! Surely that would make it go faster. I scrounged a pencil and headed to a workspace, also called a stall in the boys' room. As the car first saw the light of day in the restroom, it did so with one set of wheels off. There was a twinge of panic, but the glue was still sticky so I placed the errant wheels on the car and pressed with all my might. As my hand gingerly eased away from the car, so did the wheels. Undeterred, I stenciled the car and held the wheels in place so the glue could take hold. That was the plan.

Ah, but what number? Decisions, Decisions, and so pressed for time. It was as if the actions were in the pit at Indy and had to be quick. In a panicked scrawl, my Official Pinewood Derby Racing Car became Number 2. The piece of shit number though I did not think of it at time. Off to the races!

The trip from the rest room to the racetrack was a time of mending as I held the wheels to the glue. There was a crowd at the starting point so I waited and willed the wheels to hold. Finally, it was my turn and the adult turned to me and asked my name and my cub pack number. I informed him and handed him my handicraft.

This particular adult was not a poker player of any caliber. His face displayed disbelief. The eyes bugged noticeably, framed by eyebrows that almost left his forehead as they raised. A strange mix of shock tainted with pity for all to see. He shook his head softly and handed the car back to me. The wheels fell off as he did.

A nervous chuckle later, I replaced the wheels and placed my hope at Cub Scout legend on the track for its moment in the sun. There were six cars in this particular heat. Six tracks. The steepest hill at the very beginning to allow momentum as well as competition. Cars rested against the bar that would be lifted so they could sail down the track at breakneck speeds. Six scouts standing by. Anxious. Nervous. Eager. The adult in charge said some things, ensured all was ready, and then raised the bar.

Most Pinewood Races lasted from 10 to 20 seconds. Mine was much shorter. In less than half the time of normal races, I knew the outcome. Just under 5 seconds into the race, my car finished. Not the race. Itself. The wheels fell off the chassis and careened to the floor. One set of wheels went further than the rest of the vehicle ever would. Number 2 laid on the track helpless and listing. The other vehicles raced to the finish. I quietly picked up the pieces of my notable racing machine and placed them in the bag. Sure was glad I was headed to the Boy Scouts soon. The Pinewood Derby was for kids.

Operation Halloween (Bums and the invention of the nano-second)

Halloween was an avenue to candy unparalleled in my childhood. Manna in the form of M&Ms and Milky Ways. Lollipop loot for the asking. Chocolate delights with no strings attached. For everyday existence, my parents fed us the staples. It was the law, except in parts of Mississippi. But sweets?? On a blue-collar budget already stretched to the limit with beer and other necessities? My parents, as well as all my friends' folks, neither kept candy in the house nor flittered away spare change on such luxuries, despite numerous pleas to the contrary. They were cheapskates of conviction. Hope for sugar deprived youth came in the form of All Hollow's Eve. This fall celebration offered a treasure trove of opportunities to stockpile sweets. We, affectionately known as the greedy little bastards throughout the town, planned for it weeks in advance with a gusto akin to the preliminary stages for the Invasion of Normandy.

But this year, the effort took on epic proportions. This year was extra special. We had but a day to capitalize on an event that happened once a decade, so, thanks to mathematics and the calendar, only a single time while still of Trick or Treating ages. A Halley's Comet of sorts in All Hallow's Eve. Unless you had absolutely no pride and pandered for candy well into your teens and beyond, which has happened. This year, Halloween fell on a Saturday! A full day of begging. Uninterrupted by school, which normally sucked away eight hours or more with seemingly sadistic glee. Our plan started last year, school year wise, as fourth graders with a vision. We saw the calendar in January and the idea of a blitzkrieg of mooching festered as the school year progressed. Summer diverted our attention but once we started school, my co-conspirators and I began our campaign strategy. September moved to October quickly after that. So much to do. So much candy to get.

We mapped the terrain thanks to free maps of Keansburg courtesy of Borough Hall. The map supported the genesis of our plan. We gathered around the display of streets we knew so well that we could highlight flaws in the product. Sure, it was a chinsey mimeograph sheet drawn by someone clearly not destined for a career in cartography, but it was official paper from an official source. It made the effort seem real. Arrows and timetables sprang forth with a naturalness that the Pentagon would envy. The debate over start time ended in compromise. Although Greg's spirited push for two hours earlier made lots of sense, Operation Halloween would begin at 9 o'clock. We knew the houses closer held more potential and targeted them as first strike opportunities. This eliminated the spiral back to base plan which supported an earlier H hour. Besides, crossing town and pushing back to base camp involved passing places we could hit and run. Not something we saw as even possible. An empty treat bag was a terrible thing to waste.

We mapped routes, planned re-supply stops to consolidate loot and replenish essential supplies of bags, and calculated our time clock. We found every possible moment

Jersey Sure

of trick-or-treat opportunity. It took hours but we invested our time. After cub scout meetings. In the playground. On weekends. Whenever we could, we planned for this special Halloween. We re-visited the plan several times as the calendar inched to the end of October. All this from life forms who forgot trash day each week.

The issue of costumes presented an easy dilemma. We would be whatever we could be for free. That equated to bum. Over the years, I developed an affinity for that word. It encapsulated so much in three letters. Especially when spoken with a New York/New Jersey accent. Ya bum! It could be endearment or high insult. Perhaps low insult is the right term. Bum could be the ball player who miffed a vital play. Even a not so vital one. The Yankees were bums when they lost the series two years running. The bums! An un-employed, boozing, neer do well relative or someone who took the last Superman comic was a bum. Bum was also the costume of choice for urchins with parents who never bought a "store bought" one.

Old pants. Preferably with both knees gone. A torn shirt and tattered jacket. Dirt on the face. Little different than how we looked after a hard day at play. We were ready for Halloween year round. The price was right. We were natural bums.

Some kids got the pre-fabbed customs. Shiny skeletons complete with glitter and plastic masks. Witches with coned shaped hats and flowing black robes. Us bums goofed on the little pansies but inwardly wished we could afford such blatant luxuries. We were too smart to wear these "kick me signs" of costumes. I often wondered if the kids who wore these costumes were brave or just stupid. Most likely, just stupid.

These seemingly rich kids paraded proudly in plastic decadence. Blatant targets for candy piracy. Stores should have offered warning labels on the boxes.

CAUTION-The Surgeon General warns that wearing this costume can result in mugging, humiliation, and loss of all candy in your possession. It is recommended that this costume never be worn without a parent present. The manufacturer is not responsible for beatings incurred as a result of wearing this costume publicly.

Thugs' entire Halloween plan consisted of waiting for kids in store-bought costumes and beating the shit out of them. Not a very sophisticated approach, true, but efficient nonetheless. No costume. No knocking on dozens of doors. Very little walking at all. A few verbal taunts, a punch or two if required, and Viola! Bags of goodies. They let the primadonnas do the work. These vultures, willing to attack weaker prey, struck with brutal efficiency. They left their victims with little candy and even less dignity. These carrions of the night then savored someone else's booty with little regard for the emotional scars they inflicted. Most of them destined for careers in public service or political office.

Bums were safe. Thugs were unsure of kids in bums' costumes. They equated poor with tough. Not sound logic, but they were thugs, not brain surgeons.

The day itself arrived and we assembled at my house one hour before H-Hour. My mother was at work and my father was sleeping it off so we had the run of the yard. We paced like caged animals. The sensible kids in us knew that knocking on doors prior to 9 o'clock would incur wrath of a nature not suitable for young ears. We knew because our parents warned us not to be "begging" before nine. At the stroke of the hour, we ran for the treasure. A gluttonous

Jersey Sure

display unparalleled in recorded history. Or at least a spectacle worthy of note by any eyewitness.

The campaign was a model of efficiency. Actual interchanges delayed stops at the early houses. Neighbors commented on things ranging from costumes to the time of day. All tolerated since these stops normally had a secret reserve of goodies for the kids they knew. "A bum again? Weren't you a bum last year?" "You guys really have grown." "Isn't it kind of early for trick or treating, boys?" We took it all with a grin and hoped against hope for the Holy Grail of Halloween candy. The full size candy bar. If there was a chance for this blue moon of treats, it was at these early stops. In neighborhoods where we were merely greedy little faces in the crowd, the chance of anything even close to a full sized candy bar dropped to slightly less than our odds of winning the Irish Sweepstakes and being hit by lightening at the same time. In fact as the day progressed, the quality of candy dropped dramatically. Items distributed ranged from countless apples to a single grain of candy corn. Almost always accompanied with a not so quiet cry of "cheap bastard"

The plan was masterful. We moved through the town like Sherman marching to the sea. Knock. Beg. Loot. Move. Repeat. We moved with passion as the sun raced across the sky.

An entire day of trick or treating yielded some dilemmas uncommon during years where it was measured in minutes. We returned to base camp and dumped the booty as the bags grew in weight. A nice problem for ravenous moochers but an issue nonetheless. The overabundance of payola forced us back to home base three times. We headed out in a different direction each time since many of the houses closer to home were quite literally "picked clean".

It was physically demanding. This did not deter us. No time to rest. Fueled occasionally by sugar from the very bag we filled, we came as close as any scientist in history to perpetual motion. The entire operation was a thing of beauty.

It was on this Halloween that the nanosecond was born. Serendipitously, as were most major discoveries. The day eased into night. Most respectable trick or treaters long since declared the Holiday a success and went home to wallow in rotten apples and undersized candy. A stalwart few remained. It was still October 31st on the clocks and the calendar even if the sun toiled on the other side of the planet. We would not be deterred. Despite numerous signs to the contrary.

Dark houses. Slammed doors at the ones still lit. Nasty looks. Verbal abuse. Evidence to the contrary, we did not let the day end. Close to bedtime, with severe verbal abuse awaiting our obviously late return home, Greg and I were about to declare victory when a voice in the darkness called forth. The moment froze in both our minds.

"Boys. Oh, Boys." We looked around and saw nothing. Chills ran up my spine. Greg's bug eyes said his spine was more than just cold. The sound came again.

"Boys."

Evidently, the source of this call sensed our confusion and guided us. "Up Here, Boys. Across the street."

There, on a darkened balcony of a darkened house, was a woman. More shadow than person in the night, she waved to draw our sight.

"Come here, Boys. I have a bunch of candy, and no one came Trick or Treating. I do not want it to go to waste."

Greg looked at me and me at him. My mind raced and his did as well. Years of lessons about not taking candy from strangers returned in a single, yet dramatically clear rush. Countless lectures on staying away from dark houses played as if taped and reviewed. All this as two greedy kids with limited access to sweets weighed societal conditioning

Jersey Sure

against the odds of such an opportunity ever again. That was when the nanosecond was born. For a nanosecond was how long it took us to weigh all the factors and race headlong across the street. In the darkness we let the female stranger in a dark, dangerous house fill our bags with candy meant for dozens.

We thanked her and headed home. Subdued. Both slightly guilty about our dismissal of rules intended to protect us. But the inner youths were joyful our battle plan worked.

The butt chewing was there when I entered. But it was half hearted. Even though they were parents, they understood. It was our candy lottery. We seized our once in a lifetime shot at a day long Halloween. Besides, it was Saturday and there was no school tomorrow.

I added the last of the loot to my impressive pile but I noticed something as the pile grew. My greedy eyes peeked through the euphoria and saw what was not there. My stash was smaller than when left. Some chocolate bars. Understandable. Dad had a sweet tooth. But some of the crappy stuff too. Dry Bit of Honeys. Dum-Dums. Closer review showed almost one-fourth of my hard begged throve gone. I asked my Father, and he merely smiled and said ask your mother. She matter-of-factly admitted she used my stuff for trick or treaters to our house. The indignity! The humiliation! The inhumanity!! All that hard work, and she gave it away! With the sense of any child who values life, my words were a muffled but distinct protest. The best shot dared in my household. My mother, the heartless candy-giving-away unquestioned power in this exchange, cut to the quick. "You have plenty. Besides, that stuff will rot your teeth."

The air oozed from my balloon of victory as Dad helped himself to another candy bar. A full sized one.

The City
(Bus Rides and Accordians)

Mom got a wild hair and I got to cut school. Yippee! She decided that she and I were going to The City. New York City. The Big Apple. A bus ride away. On a school day. Just me and her. She did not put it to a vote. She asked, but it was one of those questions she knew the answer to before she ever spoke it. One of those, "Would you like a cookie?" type questions. Duh! Of course I would like a cookie. Duh! Of course, I would like to skip school and go to The City. She and I bounced, alright I bounced but there was a spring in her step as well, to the corner and waited for the bus.

The New York-Keansburg-Long Branch busline was our connection to The City. Right from our own corner. Well, OK, across the street to head into The City but we got off right at the corner when coming home. Right at the spot with the bench and the mail storage box Red used. Our very own personal bus stop whenever we wanted it. Buses passed several times everyday. The morning ones were pretty full with lucky folks who got to ride to The City everyday. The middle of the day ones were less crowded but they passed anyway. Sometimes I did not even notice them.

Jersey Sure

Most of the time I did though. Wishfully. The City was big and gritty and dirty and awesome. It was skyscrapers and taxies and more buses and movies months before they ever got to Keansburg. The City has escalators and elevators and subways. City people cursed in public. Cops rode horses in the City. New York had stuff that surprised me every time. There was always something.

We hopped on the bus and I grabbed the window to watch stuff. The way buses swayed was a bit like sailing the seas, at least I thought so because I never really sailed the seas, but saw movies and stuff and was sure you swayed when sailing the seas. We sailed right through town, onto Highway 36, made a few stops, and then hit the Parkway.

There were two main roads for travel in the Garden State, the Parkway and the Turnpike. Sure, we had lots of Highways and roads but those were everyday things. The Parkway and/or the Turnpike meant a trip. I loved that feeling. That going on a trip feeling. The Parkway fueled it, but so did the Turnpike, although the two were completely different.

The Parkway was green. The Turnpike was concrete. Not literally. Feeling wise. The Parkway was smooth and had green all around in the form of trees and grass and bushes and, sometimes, even flowers. It was countrified. We took the Parkway to get to the Turnpike to get to the City. The Parkway was comforting. Efficient. Personal. It meandered through scenic New Jersey. It reminded travelers this was the Garden State. Even the tollbooths enhanced the Parkway experience. Tollbooths placed every so often to take your toll. Dad always went to the booths with the people, even when he had the exact change. He figured they needed the work so who the hell was he to throw it in a bucket and put the poor schmuck out a job. The Parkway was a nice road to travel. A vacation travel kind of road. Trucks were not allowed. Buses were, but the

Gilbert Van Wagner

Parkway people watched to ensure the buses did not taint the ambience. The Parkway had image. People trimmed the grass and kept it pretty. It was like driving through a really nice back yard.

The Turnpike was in your face. Concrete. Everywhere. Bridges. Overpasses. It was as anti-green as anything could be. Everything about it was harsh and metal. The Goettles Bridge looked like it was made from a black erector set. No graceful curves. Girders and rivets, take it or leave it. The only types of plants on the Turnpike were industrial ones complete with stacks and pillars of fire. If they saw green on the Turnpike, they cemented it over and put up a sign. One tollbooth when you got on. Another when you got off. No lollygagging on the Turnpike. The Turnpike was there for one reason and one reason only. Mass Transit. Trucks. Lots of them. Turnpike planners meticulously avoided any scenic areas. Industrial parks? Go right through the middle. Abandoned urban blight? Let's stick a rest stop here. Fill it with vending machines and perhaps a few Stewart Sandwiches, but only if beyond expiration date. Airports? Alright, but only if directly in flight paths. Toxic Waste sites? If you don't have one, will you put one in for us? Tire graveyards? Please, and light them ablaze now and then. Yes-Sir-re-de, the Turnpike was the underbelly of New Jersey. It invigorated. It paved the way to the Lincoln Tunnel and New York City.

I saw the skyline from the Turnpike. The Empire State Building over it all. The Chrysler Building and its distinctive spire. Cubes of other less famous edifices blocked the horizon with mans tribute to horizontal construction. Building after building. So close, it was more wall than skyline. It was tall. It was strong. It was unlike anything on the face of the earth. It scared the living the shit outta me. I loved it.

Jersey Sure

We passed through the tunnel. Loved the idea of a road buried in bedrock under a river linking two states. What could man not do? I watched close for the tiles that marked the state line. When we emerged, it was right into the grittiest, grimmest, smelliest, place on the face of the earth. The Port Authority. Yahoo! We were in the City!

The Port Authority was the ultimate introduction to New York City. Buses from all over the United States converged on this multi-storied building each day. Noisy buses that drowned out all other sound. Buses that filled the air with noxious and distinctive smells and coated everything in a film of soot. You stepped off the bus and were absorbed into a machine of transportation. It shook all within and a few without. My mother grabbed my hand, we dodged a few Greyhounds, and ran inside.

Escalators. Even when we did not need to ride them, escalators were the ultimate. Moving stairways. Like a free ride. If Mom and Dad put an escalator in our house, I would fight to bring up the laundry and stuff. Riding escalators was cool. I pleaded. She gave in quickly. She stood at the bottom of the escalator and let me ride it. Four times. Then she grabbed my hand and offered hints of more later if I was a good boy.

The dirt and grime of the Port Authority foretold things to come. Forty Second Street. Dirt of a whole different caliber. It stood between the Port Authority and the rest of The City. The Gauntlet that separated the bus station from safety. Something to be crossed. We could go several blocks in the other direction but that took time. We could take a taxi but that cost money. We could have done several things but it was our City and we would not be kept from it by 42nd Street. Mom took my hand, held her head high, and headed up one of the sleaziest areas on earth with a bugged eyed ten year old in tow. Xs Everywhere. People handed passer-bys flyers, like it or not. Flyers right from Happy

Harry's magazine collection concealed in his security booth in CBS back in the Burg. Flyers of things usually hidden not so proudly under mattresses. Flyers right there for the taking on beautiful 42nd Street. Welcome to New York City, pretty lady and little man! Mom avoided eye contact of any sort and plowed ahead. A kind of screw you attitude. Part Bravado. Part pride. Part defense. Part Offense. All native. Meanwhile, I bobbed and weaved but knew there was something very bad about this cultural experience. Something I tried not to miss. Mom did her best to make sure I did just that. Mothers could be so uncool at times.

We made it to Times Square without our pockets picked and with our morals in tact. Times Square! It was worth the Gauntlet. I stood and gawked. The term gawk was invented for just that moment. A ten year old from rural-urban, God knew what, New Jersey stood, mouth open, and tried to grasp the sheer magnitude of New York City on the corner that the world knew as Times Square. Theater marques as big as most theaters in small town America. Lights ablaze in the middle of the morning. Hundreds of people everywhere when the rest of the world was at school or at work or somewhere. Where did they all come from? Where were they all going? Buildings towered and blocked the sun. I was amazed. I fell in love with NYC each time I visited.

Times Square. That spot captured it all. The City was there and it consumed all therein. Over you. Around you. Underneath you. The senses tried to absorb it, with mixed success. The place throbbed. Jack Hammers. There were Jack Hammers all the time. Jack Hammers. Taxi cabs. Were there any taxies left anywhere? All things in Times Square. The Allied Chemical Building reported the news in state of the art, wrap around, ticker tape. I rode the news around the corner. Eyes on one word as it traversed the side of the building and curved into nothingness. Then another

Jersey Sure

word followed. A bump from the crowd broke my eye on the words of the day.

Someone bumped me but most in the mass eddied. I was an island in the middle of river rapids. People in a rush to be somewhere else, it seemed. People of all shapes and sizes. Big ones. Little ones. Black ones. Lots of black ones. For a white kid from a white town, NYC was pure color. A kid from New Jersey was part of the big Apple at that moment. Another face in the crowd. I gawked. It simply amazed.

Mom let me gawk. She understood. Sometimes you just had to stop and take it all in. This was one of those times. I was not sure but I think she gawked a bit as well, even though she was raised in Brooklyn. Manhattan was something different. Times Square was Manhattan cubed. Mom sensed it as well.

We gawked, and then it was time to explore. I knew what I wanted and why. New York had movies that would not reach Keansburg for many months. I wanted to see one and brag for a long time about how lucky I was. The movie was right there. Elvis in "Roustabout". On a big marquee. Opened mere days earlier for the Holiday rush that would begin in a few weeks. A brand new Elvis movie and his last one, "Viva Las Vegas" had yet to make it to Keansburg. This new one would reach the Casino Theater in the Burg late next year, if not the year after.

Movie rules were very strict. Play in the big cities for months. Head for the small cities for weeks after that. Perhaps then, let the rubes in places like Keansburg see the show. As for TV, the movie rules were even more restrictive. TV only after even the rubes saw the show and maybe not even then. A movie on TV had to be black and white or wait until everyone in the cast died. Unless of course, you were Bob Hope or John Wayne. Then your movie could make to the NBC in prime time as a special feature but not

Gilbert Van Wagner

the late, late show. New York City was movie central for us and Elvis' latest was right on there on the marquee, begging me to see it. Today! Months before the other kids. Right now. "Maaaaa!"

The pleading began. I just hadddddd to see that movie. It would be sooooooooo cool. To see it months before anyone else. I just hadddddddd to see that movie. Mom smiled that smile that showed my pleading amused but was not effective. But Maaaaaa..... She had a counter suggestion. Something about Radio City Music Hall and a movie and a stage show. "But Maaaaaaaa..." Radio City? Radio was so yesterday. Who the heck wanted to see someone hitting cups on a table to sound like a horse? Stage show? When we could see a first run movie months before anyone in the Burg? Stage show? There were not any bragging rights with a stage show. I pleaded. She played the trump card. The "Trust me, I am your Mother" card. Right up there with the "Because I say so" card. She trumped. I sulked a bit. We walked.

Sulking was tough in so lively a city. We explored. It was cold and overcast and I was glad. Cold and overcast in The City meant a quest for heat. In most places in the world, heat was inside. Shelter was inside. That was true in New York City as well, but in the Big Apple, inside was not the only option for heat and shelter. We walked and used the alternate options.

Subway Grates heated. Especially when the trains blasted by in fits of warmth and power. Store entrances offered shelter as well as window-shopping of the very best caliber. We walked from opening to opening, heated our bodies, and fueled our lusts for stuff.

One shop had every camera every known to man. The very picture of photography perfection. They even had the little spy camera just like on the back of the comic books but you didn't have to send away for it. They had a camera

Jersey Sure

with lens so long it would take pictures of the moon and let you see inside the craters. Heck, that would have to be the case since the lens was so long it would be inside the crater when you took the picture. The store next store had purses and ladies shoes. Borrrrring. I moved next door while Mom delayed a bit at spiked heels and evening clutchy things. Toys! A whole store of toys. Cheap plastic things from Japan. Crap that would break soon after purchase, but looked big and gaudy and dangerous. More crap than any store in the Burg. Plus, this store had a display window. Some of the toys whored themselves. One robot laid on its side and humped as the key bumped him up and down now and then. He looked sad and lonely. Another bumped into a box and then headed back to bump into the one he bumped into less than a foot away. Then he repeated the process with eyes that pulsed and twinkled but did not see how stupid that was. There was even a model of Supercar just like the show. I pictured it flying into my bathtub and exploring the depths with me at the helm. Mom grabbed my hand gently but eased me to another opening as we covered New York City, one store at a time. Made a guy hungry.

One of the doorways was the gateway to the Automat. We ate there. The Automat was unique in dining experiences. Food on a room sized, rotating display. Sandwiches. Soups. Deserts. Juices. All of it. Behind each door, a joy. Wow! This was state of the art. We didn't have anything like this in Keansburg. Wooo. Hooo. We ate in contemporary fashion in the City that never sleeps in the middle of school day, and it was all Mom's idea. Way, way cool.

We ate Automat Delicacies, took our trays to the garbage cans, and headed back to the streets. We did not stay on the streets for long. Doorways were cool for only so long on cold, overcast days. Besides, it seemed colder and less pleasant outside now that we eaten pre-heated, plastic wrapped food from behind glass doors. We headed for the subway.

A ride on the train in the ground in NYC was part of the routine. A subway ride was part of being in the city. As sure as heading for the top of the Empire State Building or hoping to be part of the audience at Radio City, the subway was part of the show.

I was not sure what numbered or lettered train it was, nor which station we began in, nor were headed to. It seemed we were not there for efficiency. It was not about mass transit or the from and the to. It was about the ride. The platform. The people. The grit and the grime.

People were often blinded by dirt. They dismissed dirty things as if dirt, grime, grunge, and all variations thereof were bad things. Evil things. Dirty, in a much different sense of the word, things. But from dirt came some very wonderful things. Miners were dirtiest when they brought heat and light to the multitude. Babies were at their slimmest when coated with a bloody goo that exited the cocoon with them. Sadly, we sometimes lost the ability to see the beauty behind the grit and grime.

I had that ability on that filthy subway platform that gritty day. Graffitied trains whizzed by, and I drank in the warm breeze. My eyes matched their pace and saw the words and messages in the urban art. My feet felt the amazing skatability of greasy concrete. Without the grime, the NYC subway was not the NYC subway.

The subway experience was best on days when crowds moved in frenzied disarray. Hither and yon. To and fro. Bump and grind in a different sort of way. Less dirty in all that dirt. I stood. I savored the dancing crowd while my mother and I waited for our train. Not a train. Not the train. Our train. The one we would ride together from a place I

Jersey Sure

was not sure of to a place I can't remember. Wherever it was and wherever it went, it was at that moment our train. Our train was due at a time she knew but I did not so I watched the crowd. Almost all of whom towered above me, sometimes two fold and sometimes less, with a few even mores.

The subway experience that day was like all the others with my mother. I assumed the Statue of Liberty stance and watched. I looked a bit like that iron lady in the harbor, only I felt the promise of safety versus making it. My mother held my hand and arm high, with an unbreakable iron grip. A very special grip that assured safety as sure as any allegiance ever oathed or treaty ever penned. A grip that told everyone, myself included, I was not going any place not of her choosing nor anyplace without her. I loved the feeling. It was safety. It was the bondage of protection that did not suppress but freed.

My mother stood above me. I noticed her stance and actions. Her purse, already linked to her body via a strap, was further cradled in her bent arm like a winning football by an about to score player. There would not be any fumble today. She scanned the crowd, sentry like, with her valuables secured. She must have brought a lot of cash to the city because she protected things with a vengeance whenever we were there together. One word described her posture, her attitude, her entire countenance at times like that moment on the subway platform. Vigilant. She was a stalwart protector and all within her presence knew it. It felt wonderful. Warm. Secure. I hoped everyone had someone vigilant in their life. As for me, I used the freedom my mother gave me to watch the people.

Some in the crowd did not partake of the subway experience. They missed the world while reading of world events. They nodded to their inner world and Rip Van Winkled the subway moment away. They moved through it, blinded by their focus on the next thing. They saw their watch and missed the scenery. It was hubbub of the moment, and they contributed but did not partake. People going to and from places with urgency and movement that energized the hole in the ground as much as the third rail. Suits stretched as the occupant almost ran. Dresses flowed as the ladies, I think they were all females and rounded up and assumed all ladies, cascaded in to the day. Legs and torsos all around and seemingly all in motion. It was then, through those torsos and legs, that I saw her. She appeared and disappeared like a badly animated cartoon as the crowd framed her into and out of my sight rapidly.

She stood out as she sat with her back against the wall on the grimy subway platform. Perhaps it was the Viking Horns, the only set I saw that day. Perhaps it was the accordion she played, the only one I saw that day as well. Perhaps it was something else. Whatever it was, she became the center of my attention as the train that was not yet there remained somewhere else. I stopped scanning and focused.

Her accordion was in her lap, its case opened at her feet with money it in that filled the emptiness. Her head was bowed. She seemed somewhere else. The clothes that warmed and disguised her form chameleoned to the environment. Dirty. Subdued. Lackluster. Functional. I could not tell what color they were nor what color they had been. Her Viking horned hat concealed the bulk of her hair and almost all of her eyes. It seemed more sombrero at siesta than Norse war gear. She hunched in posture and played, almost drowned out in that cavern of transportation. You had to stop to see her. You had to pause to hear her. It took effort to hear her instrument above the fray. I switched to receive mode, audio-wise, and heard. Although not a connoisseur of accordion music, I could tell she was second rate. But something told me it was not about the music.

Jersey Sure

The crowd continued to do what it needed at the pace it decided. No one noticed this grimy loser with an oft-ridiculed instrument in a forum not designed for concerts no one requested. She was just there, and it did not really matter. So it seemed. Then I saw that a few people did notice.

A few, turned, noticed, smiled, and continued into the day. She played on. Some looked and disapproved. I saw it in their quick smirk. In the shrug of their shoulders. In their shake of the head. She played on. A select few paused, reached into their pockets and placed some coins, one even did a bill, most likely a single, in the accordion case. Seemingly simple acts of charity to one less fortunate. Happened too seldom but routinely nonetheless. But that day I saw things others sometimes missed. That some never saw. Perhaps it was because of the vigilant lady that I saw. Perhaps it was something else, but the boy on the platform saw clearly that day.

There was a process there that the coin-givers may not have been able to describe, but surely felt. For they did not merely place coin of the realm in an upturned instrument box. They offered of themselves as surely as if that money was ushered in wicker baskets to an altar. They paused, donated, and then took away. For she did not merely play. For those few who connected, she subtly, so subtly it was almost an imperceptible movement, acknowledged. My vantage point did not let me see how, but I sensed it and its effect. For the givers gave and paused, sometimes mid-step, and warmed. No words exchanged. No signals. Just energy. Warmth. Connectedness. Belonging. Community. A nanosecond of love. The givers took it and walked away all the better.

I smiled at the process and knew it was special. Then my mother urged me forward. Seemed that train of some number or some letter came from wherever it was and was about to take us wherever we were going. We headed into the subway car. As we crossed the threshold and outside became inside, I turned back to the dirty, mediocre accordion player. She looked up from under her Viking Horn sombrero and winked.

It was not just a wink. It spoke of understanding. Of awareness. Of just plain knowing. A wink that said she saw with full knowledge that I witnessed and knew the truth behind the process. A quick drop of an eyelid that transmitted insight and the power of that insight.

The subway car doors closed and took her away from me but that wink stayed. It tattooed her to my brain. To my heart. To my soul. She was out of sight forever as we went to wherever the heck it is we went that day. Visibility was limited when we see with only the eyes.

Poets, philosophers, and artists pondered of what if God was one of us. The seemingly sacrilegious blaspheme with the query of if He, the Almighty, Yahweh, The Big Kauhna, Art in Heaven, were just a slob like one of us. I knew at that moment the answer was yes. Sometimes He is. Sometimes He is a She. Sometimes She wears Viking horns and plays the accordion on NYC subway platforms.

But could that really be? Would She choose that particular, peculiar apparition? Would God Almighty choose to flash from a subway platform artist to my almost eleven year old soul in the blink of an eyelid? As we entered the subway, I knew. This was not about Mom and me. This was something bigger. Something that would last a very long time. I knew I would remember that moment. Well after the hand that held the hand was no more. Well after the hand that was held in turn held another and that another and that even another, I would remember as long as I could remember. I would tell of it someday. On a different keyboard and at another time. I would share that

Jersey Sure

wink. God was that powerful. Even when in Viking horns and playing the accordion. New York was such a cool city.

The subway ride ended somewhere around what Mom wanted to see while I still wanted to see a movie that she decided she would not see. It seemed a little less important now. We went to the place to see a movie of her choice and some kinda stage show that she chose. Mom had her way, and I was kinda okay with that. It might have had something to do with that lady in Viking Horns ,but my mood was alright as we entered Mom's choice for entertainment.

The Music Hall Theater place was warm and full of people even though this was weekday. Mom brought the tickets. I looked around. The people gave off a vibe. As if linked by being there. Connected. A common experience. It touched me. I let it.

Radio City is quite a place. Old but really, really classy. Up scale and it felt it. There was Flash Gordon architecture and rails. It was a heck of a lot different than the Casino, my benchmark for movie theaters. Mom came and we walked hand in hand up a really grand staircase. Carpeted with a pattern that said a heck a lot more than any throw rug ever could. The banisters were brass or chrome or some kind of metal. When I saw my fingerprints, I quickly rubbed them away. It was that kinda place. It hushed you like Church.

Mom let me have popcorn and candy. We headed for our seats. Almost every one of the seats in this really big auditorium was full. I leaned up to see down below better.

People settled in. The seats filled as I looked at a ceiling unlike any other I ever saw in all my born days. It looked like it was waxed, it was so shinny. It curved downward in circle things that got smaller and smaller and took your eye to the stage. A pretty big one, for sure. Bigger than the Casino's. Bigger than Saint Anne's auditorium. Even

Gilbert Van Wagner

from up here, it looked big. Those curtains musta weighed a ton. Made Mom's plastic drapes look sorta trashy but I just thought it and did not share that with her.

They started the Movie. "The Sword in The Stone". Already a bit old but it was not bad. It was Disney. Disney was not Elvis but Disney sure was Disney and that seemed right at the moment. Somewhere between the kid pulling out the sword, some dancing something or other, and a mouthful of popcorn, I fell asleep. Mom woke me when the movie was over. Time to go back to the City. So I thought.

Mom said not yet and that we needed to stay in our seats for the stage show. I was kinda tired but watched the curtains and waited for whatever the heck was about to happen. There was music, but it sounded sorta disjointed. Like folks practicing or something. I asked Mom what is was, and she had that smile. The I was about to learn something smile.

"That's the Orchestra. They are warming up."

There are moments when things take hold, and that was one of them. For the Orchestra went from a hodge-podge of flutes and brass and drums to a thing. The notes gelled and made music that built and became a thing all to itself. A thing that rose from a hole in front of the stage as if lifted to heaven. All those people and all those instruments lifted as if they floated. Impressive to the max. Then it dropped a bit but lived on as the curtain opened, and there were dancers and entertainers of all shapes and sizes. It was like Jackie Gleason and those June Taylor dancers, only it was right there on stage. They had these dancers called the Rockettes, and they put those June Taylor chicks to shame. They held each other and did human pinwheels and lines. They lined up and did what Mom told me later was their trademark kick. Those legs went way high, and all at the same time. It was beautiful.

Jersey Sure

There was some other stuff too but those Rockettes were the highlight. Mom and I talked about it as we left Radio City. Alright, I talked, she listened. That was so cool. Wait until the guys heard that I saw a stage show! Dancers and everything on a school day. I leaped side-to-side and hopped a bit as I told Mom how neat stage shows were. "Can we come again? To Radio City? Can we?" She smiled and said she would see. That was better than no.

I was awed. Gape jawed. Won over. It was my mother's and my day. She knew things. She liked me. We had fun. Missed school? Yes. But I learned a lot that day. More than any day in school. I had fun with a woman I sometimes under appreciated and often underestimated. She was young. She was beautiful. She was worldly. She held my hand in companionship as well as protection. Many never tasted this joy. I am glad I did.

The trip home was as usual. I watched for the Jersey marker inside the tunnel. Saw the skyline twilighting the evening. Watched as the big planes entered and exited the atmosphere around Newark Airport and spirited worldly travelers to and from their adventures. We talked. Just of things. Sometimes we just sat. We savored the moment. Prolonged it. I looked forward to being home since I was tired, but that bus ride was nice. She and I headed back from a joint adventure. It was peaceful. Special. At one point, just as the Turnpike became the Parkway and meant we were over halfway home, I caught my mother as she looked at me. She saw something that would and could be. Parents sometimes did that. Mom did it that day on that bus ride home. She looked at me with eyes on tomorrow. I sensed and liked that she was proud of who she saw there in the future. I looked back and smiled a smile of thanks. She gave me a gift that day. The gift was that day. Mine to savor. Mine forever. Mine to share.

Giving thanks for Christmas (RH Macy and Christmas Junkies)

Christmas was an addiction and I was hopelessly hooked. At ten years old, even at a just over a month away from turning eleven, the Yuletide high was measured in months. All year, the concept of Christmas and everything it entails nestled in my mind like a warm spot on a bitter cold day. It was always there. It promised solace. It offered joy. This volcano of excitement that erupted sporadically throughout the year. Mount Christmisisus was never truly dormant. It was merely contained from the inevitable cornucopia of delights that waited at the end of the calendar pages. By November, it spilt the banks, ready to flood every aspect of existence in a sea of red and green lava.

But even Father Christmas and his volcano of bliss were no match for my parents. For they expertly sandbagged each possible premature spill of joy. Their non-negotiable timetable for the season was tied directed to Macy's. A hang over from their youth in the City. For Macy's ended its Thanksgiving Day parade with a fat, jolly old man in a furry suit. If R.H. Macy, a master retailer, alive more

Jersey Sure

at Christmas than whoever Sears and Roebuck were, said Thanksgiving closed meant Christmas opened, my parents figured the idea had merit. There were indeed benefits to their approach. At least in their eyes.

Kids had a way at Christmas that simultaneously amazed and annoyed. Near the end of November and into December, kids went into overdrive and did not stop until sometime in early January. I was no exception and went into light speed before even knowing what light speed was. Christmas was not just in the air for children, it was the air. Kids lived it, breathed it, ate it, and slept it. Once that volcano erupted, nothing escaped the outpouring. Given the choice, children would celebrate Christmas every day. While this would foster an economic boom unparalleled in history, it would drive the adult population to suicide within a week. Sealing its own demise, for then who would wrap the gifts?

R.H. Macy saved my parents from the deluge of Christmas for eleven months. Their amazingly effective look or nasty word reinforced the threat of nothing under the tree if we "rushed the season". My sister and I felt guilty if we dared speak of the holiday of holidays too soon. Mom and Dad successfully sandbagged the dikes of our euphoria. We were silent while the calendar urged us forward to a dam burst of epic proportion.

Then came Thanksgiving. The sweet, enticing aroma of turkey eased through our nostrils and into our spirits. Thanksgiving morning was the dawn of the Christmas season and the first glimpse of the sun came in the form of Macy's Thanksgiving Day parade. On Television. In Black and White. We sat and enjoyed the show with little nagging about chores or time wasted, a small parental present we appreciated only years later. My father and mother watched the parade while they drifted in and out between cooking, phone calls, and holiday preparations.

Conversely, we were paralyzed with glee. Helpless to resist, the first annual fix of Christmas Crack filled our veins with euphoria unmatched by any drug known to man. Glued to the TV set, we watched the parade in all its uncolored glory. There was a wonderment to it. A magic. A promise of joy. It was a reward after a 11 month fast. The first sip of water after a long drought. Macy's Parade was our doorway to Christmas freedom. Ironically, we could have hopped on a bus in front of our very own home, exited the Port Authority toxic way station, walked two blocks, and watched it first hand each and every year. But we never did. Although they never said it directly, somehow my parents convinced us that would never happen. Forty miles away, it may as well have been on the moon. We watched its glow, without ever imaging being there. Just a few weeks ago, Mom and I were right on the parade route. But not today. Not any Thanksgiving. Brainwashing at its very best. TV worked though. It was how I knew the parade to be. Gray and small. Exciting as heck, too.

Balloons floated in a concrete sea. Bands played to fill the gaps between the good stuff. Festive floats ballooned with partiers and seasonal bliss. All preludes to one thing and one thing only. The man himself at the end of it all. For as soon as he eased into sight, the waiting was over. The season was here. Rockettes be damned, this was his show. Santa kick started Christmas with a wave and the first pitch of "Ho, Ho, Ho".

Each year it was the same. Each year it was magical. He eased into sight and the volcano erupted. My parents always managed to be in the room when Santa arrived. First generation Junkies passing the torch no doubt. My mother's half-hearted sigh as sure a signal as the lead reindeer, we moved to our feet. The drug of Christmas

Jersey Sure

kicked in. Bodies jumped involuntarily. We twitched with joy. We spoke in tongues. Garbled screams of joy. It was here! Christmas! We looked like a National Geographic special on pagan rituals. A riotous display of hysteria or drug induced glee.

Somewhere along the way, the parade ended. Somehow the television blinked to black. My sister and I missed those events from our stupor. We were in that other dimension. The reality of Christmas. It blurred time and space. We ate a great meal but thought little about it. Sure we gave thanks. The thanks of a junkie high from another fix. Sis and I exited the real world and joined the dimensional bliss of Christmas.

That high lasted over a month. Television specials. School Bulletin Boards touted reindeer and Magi. Previously drab houses were festooned with decorations. Streets were ablaze with electronic bliss. The season was everywhere. Already carefree hearts grew even lighter. I tasted the joy, and it sweetened each and every bite of the day.

I intuitively knew adults did not share more than a small fraction of this high. But I also knew something else as sure as I knew Frosty would be back again someday. My ten-year-old mind absorbed as my parents smiled at the twenty-second revision of our letter to Santa. The Sears wish book suddenly became shared reading, sometimes even during the educational shows like Bonanza and Gunsmoke, previously sacrosanct time when I ceased to exist. I observed sour-pussed teachers, with little everyday love for anything other than neat notebooks and ass-kissing students, suddenly sing of Rudolph with gusto. They even knew about the light bulb and the echoed lines. I pulled and tugged Mom and even Dad as we stood in line to see Santa. They merely smiled and accepted it. Behavior that merited a swift boot in the butt in July made them smile in December.

Adults not only tolerated me and almost any kids at Christmas, they actually understood us. It was a bit of Christmas magic in and of itself. For adults saw the shadows of their own childhood addiction to the magic of December. As hard it was to imagine them as children, they once lived a month long high of Christmas. The drug of Christmas lost its intensity, but it never lost its grip. Teenagers measured it in days, young adults in the occasional hours. The passing of time reduced the euphoria each year. But adults still sought it, just like any addict. They wrote checks hoping for even a second or two of the high. They watched each new Christmas movie, fully expecting disappointment but helpless to resist, in quest for the effect Jimmy Stewart had on them effortlessly decades earlier. It seldom worked, but they continued their search. Passionate, displaced pilgrims on an odyssey for euphoria.

They often settled for the secondhand high achieved by watching children enjoy anything and everything associated with Christmas. These stalwart, serious breadwinners and responsible, mature adults suddenly saw beyond the smiling youth and peered into yesterday. Like Romper Room's magic mirror, they saw themselves as they once were. Every so often, perhaps only for a second or two, they felt the lightheartedness and purity that once lasted a month. It was enough. They would be back next year, looking for more. Willing to pay virtually any price for it. For Christmas was much more than presents, songs, and memories. It was bigger than trees and decorations. It was not measured in time or money. Christmas was joy. Once you tasted it, you never lost the hunger to feast on it again.

BLUE CHRISTMAS
(The tin foil tree and a hazard to navigation)

My mother had a somewhat bizarre idea of class. Class was blue. Why blue? We never really unraveled her thought process, or lack thereof, on this unique perspective. Largely because we were afraid to ask. All part of our survival instinct. But to this frustrated Contessa, class had a color and she wanted it. She tolerated her lack of public recognition for eleven months but decided this Christmas was the opportunity to show the entire world how dignified she truly was. In a universe of middle class and lower, she placed her nose firmly in the air and proceeded to infuse our lowly existence with haute de culture.

Her mania completely disrupted our sense of Christmas. For although we did not understand how class could have a color and why that color was blue, we knew Christmas did have a color. In fact, it had two colors. Red and green. Along with multi-color lights and tacky decorations. This was a season with a look of distinction. One my mother decided to alter. My sister and I sensed impending doom. We looked to our father to intervene. He knew Katie longer than we did. He was our only hope to slow her assault. But, he knew Katie longer that we did. He saw the impending doom for what it was. A force of nature beyond his control. Wordlessly, he shrugged his shoulders and watched as Katie recreated Christmas in her warped idea of upper crust. The other members of the house mere victims along for the ride on a holiday highjack.

She headed for ground zero in her Yuletide Blitzkrieg. The tree itself. Our tin bells were ready to grace the room with angel's wings. The brass Santas nestled in a box, actually crammed, but that image seemed unfit for such a hero, laid in wait for another year with a hook through their heads in hope to once again dangle in glee. Our tree top angel waited patiently to be volted to life. All in vain. For Katie targeted the tree and all its trimmings for replacement. The new dictator of the season decided to go artificial.

The science of artificial tree making was not quite perfected. Perhaps someday it would be. Someday, the fake pines and fur may become things of beauty, accepted by people as safer, easier, and equally pretty. Although there would most likely always be purists who claimed fake seedlings of any shape or size defiled the very concept of the Holiday, artificial trees may someday evolve to an acceptable substitute for the real things. Perhaps. But not yet. We committed to putting a man on the moon by the end of the decade. Maybe artificial trees would someday be beautiful. Not yet though. Technology did not equal that challenge. The moon shot thing looked a lot more likely than a nice, fake, Christmas tree.

Artificial trees looked, well, artificial. And that put it kindly. These bastardizations were basically a bunch of green pipe cleaners stuck in the corner. Most people waited to see if science could do something nice as time moved on,

Jersey Sure

Christmas tree wise. Not Mom. During what was clearly the Stone Age of artificial trees, my mother decided to jump on board. We squealed like stuck pigs when she announced her edict. Even my father gingerly voiced protest. This woman on a mission assured us the tree would not be a bunch of pipe cleaners but a thing of rare beauty. Besides she wanted it. What else did she ask for it life? Everyday she went to work, and finally she asked for one thing…….. Somewhere, as this verbal guilt trip headed into eternity, we lost all sense of time. Her verbal erosion ate away our dam of resistance. We surrendered. We do not know who caved in first. Probably my father, for a winter of nights on the couch loomed with his resistance. It may have been my sister, and it could have even been me. The pain blurred the exact sequence. One by one, we each cried Uncle and resigned ourselves to the tyranny of an artificial tree.

But my mother was not heartless. At least not completely and totally heartless. For she kept her word that the tree would not be a mere collection of pipe cleaners. She selected what qualified as a thing of beauty in her eyes.

It came in a box. Roughly 4 foot long, and two feet wide and deep. My sister and I gaped in wonder at it. Perhaps there was wonder in this technology. For how did they stuff an entire tree in that small box? Did it expand? Was it inflatable? My mother smiled at our naiveté about this state of the art invention. She explained it to us like a science teacher describing space travel to a retard. The box held a six-foot tree unlike anything we have even seen, she spoke slowly so we could grasp our luck at being selected as part of this adventure. It had to be assembled. She waited for our oohs and aahs. She never got them. We were a lot closer to boos and hisses.

I was picked as the one to open it. Slowly, I folded back the lid but cleverly bent my torso to avoid the inevitable branch in the eye when the tree sprang forth from the box like a gag snake. But it did not spring forth. With great trepidation, I peered inside the container and saw a cardboard honeycomb. There was no tree. Only some metal spikes stuffed into each opening in the honeycomb.

Helpless to resist the magnetism of the box, all four of us gathered around it like witnesses at the first alien encounter. A strange visitor from another dimension had invaded our Christmas. Our small corner of the universe was forever changed. Three of us looked at the traitor who invited this intergalactic intruder. She was there, with the eyes of a little girl who'd gotten exactly what she wanted for Christmas. It was actually quite cute. This woman, who refused to miss a day of work except for an all too rare bus ride to the City and who accepted far less monetary wealth in life than she deserved, was transformed. She had the face of a youth and a smile of satisfaction seldom seen. Her awe was a thing of beauty. It was the only thing that kept the three of us from ripping her eyes out. That and the prospect of jail time. Unless, of course, we knew prison had real Christmas trees.

The tree building began as the first branch was removed from the honeycomb. Christmas destruction began as well. For the branch was silver. We were stunned. Katie was ecstatic. Ironically, our diverse reactions were for exactly the same reason. No one had a silver tree. No one even had heard of a silver tree. This was the first of its kind anywhere in existence until that very moment. It was unprecedented. It was unparalleled. People would talk. They would spread the word of it throughout the neighborhood. This silver tree would be the major focus of discussion all across our social circle. Katie saw it immediately. So did we. She basked in glory. We looked for ways to slash our wrists, contemplated putting ourselves up for adoption, and simultaneously considered life as hobos.

Jersey Sure

The afternoon became an odyssey of the unexpected. We never before knew the importance of twirling branches as they were removed from the honeycomb. Katie somehow did. Some instinct that only she possessed, dormant until this year of transformation. But she reinforced the art of twirling countless times as we eased the branches from the hive. We learned the concept of color-coded branches as the holey stick in the corner filled with tinsel like appendages. The object took shape. Perfectly even on each level as the length of the branches shortened to the top. The designers cleverly left the trunk of their creation in two pieces for ease of assembly. It prevented reaching over the bottom branches to place the upper ones in their predetermined holes. The result was half a tree in the stand, seemingly aborted at mid truck, and a smaller tree on the floor, listing helplessly on it side. My father and I gently placed the two together to complete the job and stood back to see the creation.

My mother was true to her word. It did not look like pipe cleaners in the corner. Instead, we owned the first ever tree made from aluminum foil. This was not a Christmas tree. It was the off-spring from an ill-conceived romance between a TV antenna and a lightening rod. My father, sister, and I starred at it, wondering what could be worse. My mother showed us with more surprises from her Christmas mutation.

It was time to decorate this festive folly. But aluminum did not lend itself to lights. While that streamlined the decorating process, a Christmas tree without lights was, well, not quite a Christmas tree. Our innocent pleading for strands of bright bulbs met righteous indignation. My mother knew it was inherently unsafe. It said so on the directions. It would kill us all. Three of us seriously considered doing it anyway.

She cast aside our request for lights and told us to get the decorations. At last, we saw a glimmer of hope. We could hang onto our past glories with balls and trinkets of yore. But Katie ended that prospect quickly. For a new tree deserved new decorations. She placed bundles in front of us. Bundles that held boxes of brand new decorations. We opened them with intentions of salvaging some seasonal glee.

But there must have been some mistake. Surely, the folks at Sears made some mistake. For all the decorations were exactly the same. Blue Balls. Same size. Same color. Not a variation in the lot. We looked to her. We knew again without words. It was not a mistake. Not by her standards at least. Our aluminum foil tree would be festooned with class. The class of color. Blue balls. With faces more in shock than celebration, we hung our heads as we hung the ornaments. Each year, during the tree decorating, my heart had music in it. This year was no exception. But this year it was a dirge. We finished the job. A scene more Hitchcock than Capra. Helpless victims, we eyed the thing in the corner. Sought the appeal. Missed it.

My sister looked at me. Me at her. Both at our father. Was this a nightmare? Was this really happening? My mother felt the joy as if an out of body experience. We equated it more to out of her mind. But she was not done.

For the silver tree needed color. She introduced us to another innovation. The reflector. We eyed this plastic globe with fear and question. It was red. It held a light bulb. It had a plastic wheel that rotated with three colors on it, red, green, and sort of a putrid orange. The artificial tree designers devised a concept that turned a silver tree into different colors with the wonder of light alone. At least, that was their plan.

The reflector moved through its limited color spectrum and cast light on the silver embarrassment that occupied the corner of our living room. The silver tree first hosted a green hue. The motor of the reflector filled the awkward

Jersey Sure

silence, and the tree transformed to silver with hints of a yellow-orange not common to anything in nature. We watched as technology gone amok changed the tree to something reddish. My mother was amazed. So were my sister, father, and I. Amazed that one single tree could be ugly in three different colors.

Our only hope of reducing public humiliation laid in keeping this tree from view. It would be difficult. It was placed in the corner of the room facing Main Street. The windows on each side highlighted its existence to any passers-by. This was intentional in years passed. But in years passed, we never had a tree that was better unseen. It was beyond comprehension prior to this dark day as this tinseled nightmare gleamed before us. But the harsh reality was here and now, and it held us helplessly. Like Prisoners of War linked by the experience of this not-even-close-to-looking-anything-but-fake tree, the three of us in the room who had not lost their minds evaluated an entirely new concept simultaneously, minimizing collateral damage. If not seen, the metal menace would not be discussed. If no one knew of our shame, we would not have to explain it away. There was a faint glint of hope in our agony of defeat.

But Maniacal Mom on her Christmas Campaign evaluated the visibility of her newborn glee and found it sadly lacking. The world must know. Each and every one who saw the house on Maple Avenue must know first hand the caliber of people it contained. She instituted Plan B. As diabolical a move as I had ever witnessed in all my ten years.

Our house was strategically placed. People saw it a quarter mile away after a bend on Main Street. It was known for years as a beacon of Christmas joy as drivers and passengers turned the bend and witnessed a gaily-colored structure ablaze in seasonal glory. This year they would turn and see a place that screamed with class. At least, that was my mother's plan. She replaced every light that decorated our house with bulbs of one color. The color of class. Blue. All of them. This removed any chance of our hiding the transformation. Like Frankenstein's monster, it looked a hell of a lot better on the drawing board than cascading into the night.

Multi-color lights worked in tandem. Bright reds eased into the hue of the orange ones. White lights blazed forth but were tinged with the subtlety of the greens. The effect was peaceful. Tranquil. Pretty. A house decorated with all blue lights was something else. More abomination than attraction. The blues combined like a synergistic scream from hell. The house was a laser blow to the retina, more frightening than festive. But the demise of anything glorious about our decorations did not end there. For in her warped world where blue equated to class, twinkling lights were something only Ralph Kramden enjoyed. Mom forbad such indignity. Instead, she tied her sense of class again to technology. Another innovation from the people linked to artificial trees and reflectors. The FLASHER.

The FLASHER, a high tech solution to crass twinkling lights, made twinkling lights a thing of the past, The FLASHER gave high-class folks the entertainment value of twinkling lights without the grittiness of such an obviously low classed spectacle. The FLASHER was distinctive. The FLASHER was new. The FLASHER was something few had. The FLASHER cost less than two dollars. In essence, The FLASHER was marketed directly to my mother.

For The FLASHER allowed all the lights to go off and on together. It achieved a far more spectacular effect than mere twinkling. It lived up to its promise fully that eventful year.

For the house of blue lights did not merely ease into view as drivers turned that bend on Main Street. Thanks

Jersey Sure

to The FLASHER, every light on the house went out. The FLASHER did not just entertain the drivers. It ambushed them. They turned the bend, perhaps even singing carols, blissfully unaware of what lay in the darkness before them. When suddenly - WHAM! Where there had been nothing, a house appeared. Trimmed entirely in blue lights. Blue lights that did more than eek with class. Blue lights that penetrated their corneas like bullets. Blue lights that removed any semblance of night vision and replaced it with blindness mixed with stark terror.

We heard new sounds that year. Ones normally not associated with Christmas. The squeal of tires. The grinding metal of locked brakes as helplessly blind drivers scrambled frantically to save themselves and their passengers. Screams of panic sliced the night air as a house appeared from nowhere and emotionally scarred holiday travelers. A house that then, thanks to the wonders of THE FLASHER, disappeared from site and left drivers blind and disoriented.

My mother did not hear any of it. She reveled in glory as the reflector turned her tree of silver to shades of beauty beyond comprehension. With her occasional glance outside, she saw firsthand the joy of the bugged-eyed people who locked their brakes to share her marvel. This Christmas Queen accepted their waves of recognition as her due as they eased their cars back off the sidewalks and out of neighbor's yards. The dramatic effect of The FLASHER caused her to squint though. She missed that not all their fingers were extended in greeting. She basked in class and saw things from another place. A place three people in the big house on Maple Avenue vowed would not be inflicted on Christmas again. Three people who prayed the designers of artificial trees, reflectors, and the FLASHER had nothing to do with the space program.

Christmas Magic
(Santa and Sears)

It began as a rumor. Mere words. But they became a rite of passage. No Santa? I dismissed it in the third grade as lies from an unreliable source. What did Margaret O'Malley know anyway? She was the first to blaspheme thus. Luckily, she had the credibility of a politician in an election year. A contested one at that. This bizarre girl was in more trouble than any two boys combined. This would normally endear her to us, but she was pure snot. She rarely ever made it through a week of school without feeling the sting of the yardstick. On numerous body parts. All clearly not intended for such use. But this was Catholic School and that made torture good for the soul. Margaret must have had a wonderful soul. The quality of her soul aside, her denial about Santa was easy to ignore.

However, each year, this cancer spread. To even kids who were not yardstick beaten low-lifes. A few more kids every time. In fourth grade, my buddies and I discussed it as an actual possibility. With great reservation, knowing that speaking of it fueled the infection. It tainted our euphoria. This year, the conversation was back. With fifth grade fervor. It worried me. It was tough not to talk about it, it seemed.

"But why do we tell our parents what we want if Santa really brings the gifts?" Greg's question was a good one but easy to answer. I fielded it like Mantle on a good day.

"Santa doesn't bring all the gifts, Stupid. Our parents buy some of them. He brings the big ones." My answer eeked with smugness.

Our dialogue continued amidst a chill wind and even cooler enthusiasm. It generated more questions than answers. We searched for something we already had but feared losing. The beach was deserted this brisk winter day. The emptiness invaded rather than comforted as it normally did. The wind chilled a cold more of the spirit than the body. Two kids. We skipped rocks while we faced one of life's crossroads.

"I guess." But his words rang false. "It sure makes me wonder though." His next throw made the rock skip six times. Pretty good with the size of the waves on the bay.

My attempt yielded three, but my mind focused on building doubts. With Greg and I, almost everything was a contest, but there was no competition today. Just didn't feel like it. Neither of us. The pebble sank along with my spirits. "Did you ever see him?"

"Who, Santa?"

"Yeah, Santa. I never really saw him. On TV and stuff but not at the house. With gifts and stuff. Did you?" Part of me wanted him to say yes. Badly.

Greg paused. It made me wonder. "No. I think I heard him once though."

I left the beach but the questions stayed with me. All through dinner and then even later, doubts nagged. That night, my young worries tested even my parents. My father was first. When sober, he was the path of least resistance. This night qualified.

"Hey, Dad. If we don't have a fireplace, how does Santa come down the chimney? He would end up in the furnace." A daring question based on some juvenile detective work earlier in the week. I tracked our chimney and ended up in our cellar. Part crawl space, part cave. Not the best first impression for the man in red.

He smiled. "Don't worry, Fat Boy. Santa doesn't need a fireplace. He got into my apartment when I was a kid, and we didn't have no fireplace. But he always made it." He rubbed my head and smiled. A sure sign the conversation was over. He returned to his television show. A box of unshared Thin Mints at his side. A sleuthing stall, so I moved on.

Mom handled my direct question easily. "Of course, there is a Santa. Don't believe everything those kids say. If they jumped off the Brooklyn Bridge, would you?" The connection eluded me, but it was as sure as conversation stopper as any rub on the head. Parents-2, Kids-0. The sky over my Christmas parade darkened.

Each day found another challenge to my beliefs. More kids scoffed at it. Questions answered with smiles and less than precise answers. Virginia helped with her long ago letter but the ember of disbelief warmed. It chilled me in a way nothing had previously. The days moved by but not with the normal joy. Each day found another chink in the armor of Christmas. My beliefs slowly and surely eroded, lapped by the growing tide of evidence counter to Saint Nick's very being. The dreaded "wink and nod" by neighbors when they asked if I still believed in Santa. The very question more challenge than inquiry. Friend after friend scoffed at the very legend they embraced so dearly just a year ago. This was the year of transition.

It was also the year of the bicycle. A few kids at school already had them. Actually most of them. At least in the fifth grade. I tried not to notice though. But almost everyone in my class had bikes. Big ones. Not hand-me-down 20 inchers like mine but full sized bikes. It was my turn. Granted this was a self-imposed edict, but I learned early to declare with assurity and hope like hell. But this was a stretch for even someone with my gift of incredibility. For bicycles qualified as mega-purchases in a town where a nickel candy bar occurred quarterly. My only hope for something this big was Christmas. It began, as did most wish lists, with the Sears Catalog.

Massive. Bigger than the phone book. Loaded with everything from toys to adult stuff, it was our passport to shopping. Local stores had nothing like the offerings in this book. Keansburg stores offered yesterday's crap at tomorrow's prices. Sears came into our house with promises of every good imaginable. Sears and his buddy Roebuck had pages of bikes for my review. There were short ones. Tall ones. The bikes, not the pages. The pages were all the same size. Bikes for the young and the not so young. Tricycles. Unicycles. Old Lady basket bikes. It was a treasure trove of transportation. All varieties. All prices. Some even in the range of fiscal reality.

With a net worth somewhere between nothing and 35 cents, depending on the day, I learned money was indeed an object. Not just because my pockets were usually empty. It was environmental conditioning at its finest. Sort of an economic osmosis. A by-product of life in a town of used cars and wishful thinking. Chicken as the meat of choice, when there was a choice. Potatoes in every shape and size to fill hunger. Patched pants and second-generation everythings. Subtle but consistent reminders not to let your reach exceed your grasp, especially monetarily. Financially, folks in Keansburg led lives of quiet desperation. We were children, but we clearly sensed the harsh reality of our parents' financial limitations.

Gilbert Van Wagner

Just as my Dad knew his new Buick was decades away, if ever, my eyes dismissed the Sears English Racers as toys for other kids. Pretty to look at but not a possibility. My Father taught us the concept of not-so-great expectations, by example. We saw it each time he eyed the new GM line. Dad never even dared ask for his new Buick. He knew what would happen. I did the same with English Racers. For we both feared the Mercenary of Menace. His wife. My Mom. Katie with the oh-so-tight purse strings.

My Mother's thrift was legendary. More Beowulf than Camelot. She lived with fiscal fanaticism. Bills paid in advance in even blizzard conditions. A good credit rating the Holy Grail of life. She squeezed a nickel so hard the buffalo squealed. Her reign of penny-pinching terror reeked fear in the hearts of all within her domain. This bastion of budgeting was impervious to begging, pleading, tantrums, and hissy fits. Even my Father's. As kids, lower forms on her food chain, we were helpless in her spendless spell.

Without a word, my mother eliminated any impractical and over-priced selection. She sucked at dishes, but she washed brains like few in recorded history. She even made my wishes practical. Her children price-compared their joy. Parenting at its best. Like a salmon headed instinctively to who knows where, I headed for Sears, middle class offering of transportation.

My quest was a low priced, sturdy but reliable bicycle. Sears had it. If the Sherman Tank Company ventured into the bicycle market, this would be their entry. An industrial strength, fire engine red, beauty of a bike. A full quarter panel picture of my dream machine. Drool eased from my open mouth as my mind raced down streets with lightening speed on this two-wheeled wonder. It mattered little that it was basically cast iron and as aerodynamic as an anvil; in my imagination, it was a burst of speed. As a side benefit, it

Jersey Sure

could survive all but a direct hit by a nuclear weapon. Mom would be proud.

Each day found me in that catalog. I knew the page by heart and sat in awe with the book opened to it. Agape in wonder and glee. Fixated beyond belief. My parents heard of it. My friends heard of it. My siblings heard of it. This became more than a bicycle. It became a quest. In this year of seasonal doubt, it also became a test. My desire for the bike was so strong, I reached for Mr. Kringle's help as well.

Part of me felt a letter to Santa was a waste. Everyone knew what I wanted. Letters to Santa seemed a bit silly for someone my age. Last year's felt funny, and that was a whole year ago. But still, secretly, almost as if embarrassed, I took pen to paper and wrote. Feverently. Alone. My script to this fading superstar outlined more than my desire for a bicycle. It spoke of my need to believe. To hold onto something very special.

Christmas Eve came. The best day on the kid calendar. The same excitement. The same butterflies the size of Mothra as I headed to sleep. A night when even Margaret O'Malley was good. The world was awash with freshly bathed brats in clean pajamas. Sleep was rushed that night. Bedtime at 4 in the afternoon was more than a possibility on this Bizarro night of parents telling children it was too early to go to bed. But with glacial speed, bedtime finally came. Sleep, awhile later. My slumber was bittersweet this particular Christmas Eve. I headed to dreamland fearing the morning would bring a harsh reality. The cold and distasteful death of magic.

It was not the sun that woke me, for the room was dark. But something stirred me from a dreamless sleep as surely as a bright light in the night. A noise. Close to my ear. More echo than real. A sound nowhere to be heard once I was awake, but it had been there. I knew without a doubt. Cobwebs eased from my mind and the reality it was Christmas Morning, albeit just a few hours after midnight, spurred me from the bed on shaky with sleep feet. The idea of that noise still quivered in my heart. A warm twinge in the still night air.

I eased down the stairs, avoided the creak spots and in turn the inevitable "get back to sleep" cry. The pause at the end of the stairs before opening the door was deliberate. As if planned years in advance. For beyond that door laid a crossroads. A fork in the road. One path led to a lifetime of belief in Christmas magic. The other----the road of the cynic. I opened the door and peered cautiously. Sensed something. A noisemaker, silenced and waiting in ambush. Much more friend than foe.

Presents surrounded the tree like a colorful barricade. But I saw what was not there. There was no bike. No red machine. My major wish unfilled. It seemed beyond belief but my dream machine was not there.

But there was something there. A presence. Something, paused and poised, as surely as I was at the foot of the stairs. I rubbed my eyes, barely suppressing tears of rejection at the missing bike.

When I re-opened them, fate stepped in and forever shaped my belief in the spirit of Christmas. For there, between myself and the boxes around the tree, something faded into view. Where there was nothing a second earlier, an object appeared. It materialized in a way I had not seen before nor since. It shifted from one dimension to my own. An answer to a prayer. Tangible proof of things beyond the senses. It gleamed with chrome on the handlebars. The red iron frame of a Sears bike eased into existence.

The presence in the room intensified with each molecule of the bicycle. There was a smile in the room even broader

Jersey Sure

than mine. For as the bike took on substance, the task at hand was complete. A doubter was converted. Almost in a daze, I moved to the bike, to touch it, confirm it was really there. It was.

Surely my mother purchased it, right from the catalog pages in answer to my pleas. Just as surely, wrenches were flung as my father put it together in a valiant effort to please his budding offspring, with directions as only a last resort. But the one who delivered it? Right before my very eyes that Christmas Eve? Santa. Relegated to but a few stops each year, he chose the big, white house on Maple Avenue that distant winter. He deliberately reached into his magic bag and had a Sears industrial strength bike appear before eyes on the precipice of disbelief. He pulled me from the abyss of reality and embraced me forever with Christmas Magic.

The bicycle was awesome but I instinctively knew it would succumb to age. Someday it would be victim to the intensity of my own youth and the ravages of time. But for the moment it was mine and it represented more than quick runs to CBS. It was the answer to a prayer. It was belief. It was hope. I knew right then I would look skyward each December 24th for as long as my eyes could see. With a squint. With a smile.

Birthdays
(Corsages and Anti-gum Nuns)

At eleven, birthdays were real important. Another year alive. Wooo hooo. It only happened once a year and January 12th was my turn. Mind alive and ready by the time Dad yelled up the stairs to get me out of bed, I did not want to waste a minute of my special day. Some days made it easier to get up than other days. Vacation days. Snow days. Going on a trip days. Actually ready for the exam days. Lots of money in the pocket days. Birthdays were at the top of the list of easy to get up days. I popped from the bed like an over wound jack-in-the-box and bounded to the bathroom, a year older. Time to put on my birthday clothes and head downstairs for a birthday breakfast followed by a birthday walk to school, a birthday lunch, a birthday dinner, a birthday cake after the birthday dinner, and then some birthday television. On your birthday, everything was birthday related. Yahoo!

Birthday or not, breakfast on a school day for Keansburg kids was a bit different. It was a fend for yourself affair. No flapjacks and sausage. Hazel did not greet us with a smile

Jersey Sure

and pounds of bacon. Mr. French was nowhere to be found. Mom was at work via the carpool, and Dad ensured I was up and in motion. I dressed quickly and headed downstairs in a pattern that mirrored the day before and templated the days to come. It was beyond routine. It was carbon copy. But today it had a birthday tint and that made it different. Exciting.

Dad at the table, cross-legged, drank his coffee. Harry Harrison eased in the day via the radio on the sideboard tuned to WABC, 77 of NYC. Seems Harry loved the song "Sugar Shack", since it greeted my morning almost everyday. Even on my birthday, although Harry Harrison seemed not to know of this very significant celebration. Dad said good morning and added "Happy Birthday, Fat Boy." I beamed. It was my birthday! I headed for the kitchen to make an egg sandwich. A process that began with the small frying pan. Not a small frying pan. The small frying pan. We had three. Small, medium, and large. The Goldilocks line of cookware.

The frying pan was battered and bruised, but well cast meant long life, without hope of reprieve. Rumor had it that the frying pan was really not jet black. It most likely was not actually lumpy by design either. Seems it morphed in shape and color thanks to less than stringent cleaning. Washed by less than enthusiastic, underage laborers, it was well on the other side of clean as I lit the burner and flamed its bottom. A quick slab of butter greased it further. The popcornish smell of melting butter told me it was time to crack the eggs. Crack. Drip. Sizzle. A calliope for the senses. Morning sounds. Sizzling filled the nose and the ears. The warming eggs heated up my taste buds as I moved to the toaster.

The small kitchen made for highly efficient movement since everything was within arms reach. The kitchen at One Maple Avenue was compact to the extreme. Worked

Gilbert Van Wagner

great for kids but adults felt strangely claustrophobic nestled between the sink, the stove, and the refrigerator. To move from the stove to the counter top for the toaster required a grand total of zero steps. More of a pivot. So I pivoted. Time for toast.

It was old. It was marred. It leaned a bit to the right. It has a sad, discarded look. It was all the bread we had so I used it. A flick of my birthday wrist, and it was sandwiched between the coils. The bread tanned while I ended sunny side up with a youthful but adept flip of the eggs. One yolk did the tilt a whirl and remained intact. The other oozed to another state. A quick jiggle of the pan and the eggs were set. Toast to plate. Butter to toast. Plate to stove. Eggs to bread. Viola! Breakfast. I headed to the dining room table to join the heretofore quiet father figure as he listened to the radio he didn't really hear.

"Sugar Shack" must be the longest song in recorded history or WABC was now the all "Sugar Shack" all the time station. Dad sat in his chair. The only one at the dining room with arms. Chairs that is. Both he and I had arms. Hopefully always would. His chair was the chair of power. The chair of supremacy. The chair more throne than mere sitting spot. I was surprised Mom let him have it. He enjoyed it though. Made him feel like he was in charge while we all knew it was really Katie's roost. But Dad had his armed chair, so he pretended he had power. Much easier to do with Mom at work. With the Matriarch carpooled away, Dad seemed a bit imperial and sat in a unique style.

His posture amazed. Bones with the consistency of putty, he curled his one leg under him to form a bony pillow of sorts. As a consequence, he listed a bit as if to escape the very leg wedged under his all too skinny butt. His yoga like ability was not appreciated outside of carnivals in the US. But there he sat. Curled almost. Pensive. Content with the moment. Quiet. Part of all yet somehow above it all. As

Jersey Sure

peaceful as I ever saw him. He set a tone of reserve as he charged up for the day ahead. We began the day together. We did that every school day. Today we began my birthday together. Besides, he had something to do with making today my birthday. At least, I certainly hoped he did.

An egg sandwich for me. A cup of coffee for him. Both of us still a bit groggy from sleep. The day ahead. The night behind. It was dawn. We eased into it. We sat. Few words from either of us. Sometimes we talked. Sometimes we didn't. A grunt and groan conversation of little substance but infinite consequence. This was as close to father-son time as we ever had. It lasted little more than 10 minutes. Five days a week except for holidays. I chewed. He sipped. We said a few things to each other but mostly just were.

He finished his coffee and rose slowly. As if he did not want to leave. As if just staying home would be much better. We exchanged an all too short hug and kiss that sweetened breakfast for the rest of my life. He wished me well on my birthday and left for a job he hated but needed. A place he dreaded yet spent most of his waking hours. With people not worth, in his words, "the powder to blow to hell" that would not give you "the sweat off their balls." But at that moment, it was a world of two. A good world. For ten minutes, we had each other. No one else. Just the father and the son who loved egg sandwiches. Breakfast was indeed the most important meal of the day. Not just on Birthdays although that made the day important as well.

I headed for school and, just like anyone in my class with a birthday, fully expected to be the center of attention. Fate and pretty weak attempts at planned parenthood made it kinda difficult for me since, in a class of less that 30, three shared January 12th as our birthday. That was crappy. Steve and Michelle both had the same birthday as me? Sharing was tough enough. Sharing a birthday was really tough. Michelle had an advantage as well. The dreaded birthday corsage.

Girls got birthday corsages to enhance their special day. A careful selected arrangement of flowers, the size of a Volkswagen, festooned with ribbons, one for each year of life, dangling some candy or sweet somehow linked to the significance of the number of years. Not sure who determined what goodie related to what year. It was all very secretive and must have been in the girls' handbook, because it sure as heck wasn't in the boys.

Sugar cubes hung from their sixteen year old chests of the budding ladies on their birthday. Sweet sixteen theme it seemed. As if sixteen-year-old boys needed another excuse to look at the chests of the females of their age, or almost any age. Luckily, there were no sixteen year olds in my class. No one was that stupid. You would have to be left back every year and start a year after everyone else to be sixteen in the fifth grade. This was not the hills of Kentucky. But sweet sixteen was not the only age that girls got to celebrate with the birthday corsage.

I was not sure why bazooka bubble gum signified one year on the corsage key to birthday bliss, but bubbles waiting to be chewed to life were just another of the signs of age on corsages. There were lollipops for another and red-hot dollars for another. Whatever number of things dangled from whatever gaudy flower on whatever female's bosom, the effect was the same. Birthday corsages screamed, "Look at me! It is my birthday!" Sharing birthdays sucked. Sharing birthdays with a girl with the corsage advertisement was brutal. Like all boys, I hoped someone remembered my birthday or had to determine another way to ensure people knew. As a last resort, I would use Michelle's birthday corsage by association. But that would be a very last resort. Dang birthday corsages.

Jersey Sure

There were only a few kids in the playground when I arrived. Mornings in the playground were different. It was really more of a place to assemble than to frolic in the A.M. Not much playing. More talking. Joking. But not the screaming at lunch and recess kind. Quiet time. Quiet by our standards at least. Nuns stilled routinely shushed us. Only one Nun there, Sister Constance, or as we called her, Sister Constipated, the sixth grade nun mingled without actually talking to the few of us there. The Nuns had morning play ground time down pat. A ratio of sorts. One nun for every twenty-five kids. As the playground filled, the nuns sent in more players to control the rabble. I think the convent had a dugout and the nuns sat there. They waited for someone to tap them on the habit and say, "you're in" and then felt each nun pat their butt as they ran to the playground for action. For now, Sister Constipated ran the place. She didn't take any crap from anyone. I steered clear of her and stood by the auditorium.

No sign of Michelle and the magic birthday corsage yet. No excuse to mention it was my birthday to the guys there. I mentioned it anyway. Attention was a good thing.

Guys were weird about birthdays. Weird but predicable. First thing they mentioned was birthday whacks. Two chased me to inflict the celebratory spanking. I bobbed and weaved to the fence but one cut me off and the other caught me when I turned to avoid him. With some half-hearted resistance, I pulled away, but they proceeded to swat the now eleven-year tush.

Sister Constipated was there in a flash. Nuns did not like a fight, at least without a referee. When she saw it was playful and they explained it was birthday whacks, she smiled and left. I was relieved she did not join in.

The half-hearted, more grab ass than spanking, whacks through winter clothes were weak and ended quickly but were almost as effective as a birthday corsage. We lined up loosely for class, and other kids asked what was that all about. The conversation about my birthday began. It continued as other kids drifted in and asked what we were talking about. When Michelle walked up with her puffed out, already slightly swelling, chest all adorned with a birthday corsage, someone turned to her and said, "Hey, it's your birthday, too?" Florists and flower plots be damned, it was my birthday and I took the whacks to ensure folks knew.

The day was all birthday. Each thought centered around birthday. We had a Mass that day, not sure why, but the Catholic Church did not really need much of a reason to make Catholic School kids attend Mass. It was not one of the Holy days; we were safe from them until Ash Wednesday. It must have been one of the obscure saint days, saints like Bartholomew or Ignatius, the patron Saints for what the hell were you thinking with that name, or a pop-up mass for some cause like Pagan Babies. Whatever the reason, we had a Mass that morning, so it was line up and parade over to the Church.

It was overcast and cold, but that really didn't matter. It was my Birthday. So I walked happily to the Church, whatever the reason. We entered the church, headed for our pew, genuflected prior to entering the pew, kneeled on the leather covered wooden kneeler designed to make our subjection easier, and prayed. Good little automatons. We said Hi to Jesus and thanked Him for letting us in His place. I prayed Birthday prayers and then sat while we all waited for the rest of the audience to sit so the show could begin. There we sat, evenly spaced, hands on the knees as trained. Devoted and hopeful servants of the Lord. Three of which had a birthday that day.

A few of the kids violated the hush level, so Sister moved to their pew and shushed them. She reminded them that we were here to celebrate with God. That one confused

Jersey Sure

me. Celebrations should be noisy and fun so why mention the celebration of God and salvation when Sister basically said shut the hell up? Regardless, it was another birthday moment since Sister smiled and acknowledged the three birthday children in the class and how they would most likely celebrate with a party this evening.

My face blushed as I swallowed hard and hoped no one saw my embarrassment. That was a bittersweet moment. There were not birthday parties at the Van Wagner house. Other kids had parties. I did not.

I enjoyed parties. Gifts. Games. A center of attention. Cupcakes. Your own little personalized-sized cake eaten without a fork. Way cool. Candy. Goodies. Everyone all dressed up. Laughter. All of it there to be shared and enjoyed. People took pictures. Same pictures. Different kids. Pin the tail on the donkey was the same. One kid peeked. One kid did the wrong wall. One kid felt the wall and then pinned the tail. Laughter and yelling as the game progressed and tiny competitive beings fought to win the big prize, which secretly matched all the other prizes. But it was better to win than merely get. Then the center of attention opened gift after gift after gift. Quite the spectacle of decadence.

Birthday candles lit the spirit of the crowd. Eyes glowed at presents opened and enjoyed. Tales told of tails pinned on Jackass by kids who chuckled at jackass just as they did at cocks crowing. Silly snickers from little nuts in the making. Birthday parties had all of that and more. Birthday parties tempted and tormented with that when the parties were always someone else's. Then I took my goodies and went home. Slightly different. Not sure why.

No parties for Sis and me. We did get cake. We did get presents. We did get out of doing the dishes. We did get love. We just did not get parties. That was the way it was. I enjoyed parties. I just envied them a bit. Balloons were festive but that air popped in glory or sizzled to death. Balloons never filled were listless and sad. Birthday unparties were like that. I watched with growing envy but understood my parents just did not host birthday parties. Mom worked. Dad worked. We got cake. We did not have to do the dishes on our birthday. Mom and Dad gave us a gift or two and loved us. Just no parties. Parties were something other kids had. Something to be envied. So I did. When Sister mention birthday celebrations, it was bittersweet.

The eleven-year old mind rebounds quickly. The twinge of longing and envy quickly subsided when birthday thoughts filled my head. Mass moved on but I already tasted the joy of cake that waited after dinner tonight and the bliss of walking from the dining room table without clearing my plate or drying and then putting away the dishes. Not that the folks did it for me. Sis inherited all the dish duties on my birthday just as I did on hers in March. I was a boy of leisure on my birthday.

The birthday was mentioned several times throughout the day. Even while on the candy line at lunch. Saint Anne's school was not the most progressive institution in the country, but it had one of the best candy lines anywhere. A school that sold its own candy was state of the art in my little world.

How they sold that candy never really made sense to me. Money did not change hands. Not at the point of sale at least. Not like normal candy stores where you went in, picked your candy, paid your money, and went away. Saint Anne's had a line where you gave your money to a nun who in turn gave you little pieces of carefully cut poster board

Jersey Sure

labeled 1 cent, 5 cents, or 10 cents. You gave the nun your real money, and she gave you the different size pieces of poster board, and then you got in the line for candy and exchanged the little pieces of poster board for the sweetness of your choice. Not sure why they went through this process. Rumor was it was due to some abstract ruling of the gaming commission. Whatever it was, the little poster board pieces were coin of the Saint Anne's realm.

The candy selection was superb. Everything but gum. Nuns were anti-gum. They were militantly anti-gum. Were Wrigley and Bazooka Joe the antichrist's cousins? Did gum money fund the crucifixion? Was Dubble-Bubble a front for the devil? Whatever it was, gum was not to be anywhere around or near anything associated with Catholics. Nuns hated anything to do with gum. Bubble. Chewing. It did not matter. It was bad. They did not sell it. They did not like to see it. Chew gum, and Nuns saw it a hundred yards away. It was more than sight though. They heard it and erased the sound. Chew gum in class, and they stuck it on your nose for the rest of the day. Chew gum in church, and they levitated you by the earlobe as they dragged you screaming from the congregation. Nuns hated gum.

I brought my gum elsewhere and chewed very carefully while in school. In the candy line, the aspect of a gumless selection was of little consequence. This day I had a 5-cent and a ten-cent piece of poster board to spend. As I exchanged the tokens for candy, Sister behind the counter quietly handed me the tokens back and smiled. A smiling Nun unnerves, and I looked at her to see if it was a smile of death or a smile of life. It was a smile of life accompanied with a "Happy Birthday". I smiled back at her. Cool. Way, way cool. That little exchange buoyed me for the rest of the school day.

Gilbert Van Wagner

The surprises continued at home that afternoon in the form of the Red Bank Register's birthday club. Each day, the Register, the closest thing Keansburg had to a daily paper although it was published way over in the town where I was born, listed the birthday boys and girls for the people of Monmouth County to see. One special boy or girl was selected each day for a free birthday cake from a bakery in Red Bank. Part of my birthday tradition was to rush home to see my name in the paper and see if I won the free birthday cake. My name was usually there. Grouped with the names of other little girls and boys from Monmouth County of the same age. Each year I looked. Each year, I was not the one lucky boy or girl named for a free cake. Not until today that is. I was a winner! There it was in bold print! A free cake! From a bakery in Red Bank. Woooo hoooo. Life was not just good. It was fantastic. Fifteen cents in free candy from a nun and now a free cake from the wonderful people of the Red Bank Register. Who needed a damn birthday corsage?!

Mom was not quite in the door when I told her of my winning. She smiled and kissed me a Happy Birthday. I said we had to get to Red Bank right away because the cake waited and I did not want to disappoint the people from the paper.

Mom did not drive. Ever. She carpooled. She walked. She rode with Dad. My mother never got a license. She was raised in New York, and ladies from New York did not drive. She stopped being a lady of New York well before I was born, but she never adopted the ladies driving concept just because she now was from Keansburg. She could not take me to Red Bank since she did not drive and did not have a car. Dad had the car and would arrive about 5 o'clock and then we could get the gift. That was my plan. Mom said we would see if, and this was my first warning, "Dad was up to it when he got home."

Jersey Sure

Up to it? How you could not be "up to" a free birthday cake? Who, in their right mind would not want a free birthday cake? Surely, not Dad. Surely, he would want to drive to Red Bank as soon as he got home. Right?

Wrong. Dad was home from work and stated nicely that he was home from work and would not be going back out. I looked at him, stunned. But, Daaaaaaaaaaaaaad. He stated all the reasons we would not be going to Red Bank for the free cake. It was too late. It was dark. It was too far. It was probably some little bitty cake anyway. The paper most likely was closed at this time of night. Nothing worked to make sense of why we would not go get a free birthday cake. I finally won the birthday cake lottery, and we were not going to collect the prize? That sucked worse than a room full of birthday corsages.

I was in a funk. Life was cruel. Dad and Mom prepared dinner while I sulked. It was quiet, and I pondered what would happen to the cake I won. What would they do with it? Would they eat it themselves? I hope those people at the Red Bank Register were not waiting for me. Would they understand I tried to get it? Would they forgive me? Would they give me another chance to win? In a few years, when I was old enough to drive, I would go get the cake myself.

The funk overwhelmed and tainted a special day. Then I heard singing. The birthday song. Before dinner? I turned and saw a parade. A three-person parade with Mom in the lead. She carried the birthday cake, ablaze with a dozen minus one candles. Dad and Sis followed and sang the song people butchered on days honoring beginnings. I smiled as they brought the cake right into the living room and brightened the funk away.

Birthday cakes are special. Birthday cakes eaten before dinner in the living room while opening cards and presents from family are extra special. We had chicken that night. I wore the pin that said "11!" from the card Nana sent

Gilbert Van Wagner

while we did. None of us ate much. Chicken after birthday cake tasted a whole lot different than birthday cake after Chicken.

I did not do the dishes that night. I did not miss the ride to Red Bank either. I also had another piece of birthday cake after dinner. Mom and Dad let me. After all, it was my birthday.

Play hard, sleep hard (Extra Chores and Burning buildings)

School kept us busy, but if we found time to do homework during school, and I usually did, we were free from the job of school once the bell rang. We put our books away, and lined up for the walk out the door to freedom. Two lines. Beach and Church. I was a Beach line kid since home was that way. The few times I took the Church line it was like attending a different church. A strange feeling. Not quite connected with the others who belonged in this line each day. Today I was a Beach Line kid on the Beach line. A place for everything and everything in its place.

Like a bunch of people from the town of Bedrock, as the bell rang, we yabba-dabba-did our way to the streets and other aspects of life. Run and play. Those were the priorities. Sure, there were chores, but they were not priorities. They were chores. Do 'em and stay out of trouble. Don't and get into trouble. Run and play and sometimes you got into trouble anyway, so why do the chores and still get in trouble? So I headed out to play. The chores could wait.

Gilbert Van Wagner

That was the premise, and it held really well until I got home to an angry mother. Mom worked all day and returned home at 3:30 every afternoon. It did not matter that we were in school all day. It only mattered that she expected our chores done. Chores like picking up not just our clothes but also any clothes lying around. Chores like making not just our bed but her bed as well. Chores like vacuuming the house and doing the dishes. Seemed like a lot of chores to us, but she thought it was just right. So home I went after running and playing after school and, wham!, I ran smack dab into a mother not playing at being mad.

Sometime around dinnertime, she calmed down. I ate quietly since it was not wise to test the simmering adult. I ate quickly because I was hungry. An appetite enhanced via lots of chores completed under lots of pressure did that. After dinner, I got to wash the dishes for Sis, as well as do my portion of the dish cycle of drying and putting away the now cleaned dishes. I also got to go to bed early that night. Perhaps running and playing instead of chores was not the best idea, but it seemed it that afternoon and would most likely seem it next time as well. My mind worked that way. I was eleven years old. I headed for my room with full knowledge a friend waited as he always did.

At eleven, the idea a stuffed animal was a bit much, so I kept Monkey to myself. He lived in my bedroom and was with me through some very hard times. When I was grounded, Monk kept me company. I was grounded a lot. I spent more time with Monk than anyone else on the face of the planet. I was eleven.

We wrestled. We wrestled hard. So hard I tore off one of his arms once. Luckily, my mother sewed it back on. Monk used to be as big as me but now he was much smaller. Black mostly but he had a chest of yellow. I guess it was

Jersey Sure

actually his torso that was yellow since his upper arms were the same color as his chest. Not common in nature, for sure, but I did not question. Monk was mine for years. So long that I was not even sure where he came from. I think he was from my brother Jack. Even if that wasn't right, I liked thinking it. Jack was important to me. Perhaps Monk came from one of my brother's boardwalk adventures. Wherever Monk came from, I loved him. Even if Jack did not give him to me. Even more if he did. I think he did. Monk felt like a Jack thing to me. I loved him.

It was easier to love a stuffed animal when I was younger, but time did not change my love, it just made it feel sorta silly. Still, it was love, so Monk went from best buddy to best kept secret.

He was a cuddler. He liked to be held. Especially when I was mad or lonely. He was not easy to cuddle to either. He had a hard plastic face that was always happy to see me. His hands were plastic too. Monk had human hands. That seemed strange to me. National Geographic said monkeys and men were different because men had thumbs. National Geographic did not know Monk. I was not about to tell them either. He was mine. All mine. When I needed him, he was there. Anytime I needed him. He sat and waited for me. He wrestled when I wanted. Always willing to wrestle. He listened. He absorbed tears. He warmed. He comforted. He was totally mine. Monk was a great friend. Thanks to him, I was never alone in my room. He listened when I griped that night. Then we wrestled a bit. I won. Then it was time to sleep. He slept with his painted eyes open, just in case I needed him in the middle of the night. Good buddy.

Sleep just came. I laid down. Closed my eyes. Slept. Mom and Dad had that, too. Sleep. Wake up, and then live a day and sleep again. The neighbors mentioned they did not sleep well. Seemed strange to me. Didn't they get tired? If they did, why didn't they just sleep? Go figure.

I slept really well. Perhaps a little too well. We had a fire whistle across the street. It blew at noon every day. It also touted fires and emergencies in town. That was cool sometimes because I could run to the corner and watch the volunteers speed from their homes to the firehouse. I think the ability to drive like Batman and not get a ticket was the main reason they volunteered. So the whistle blew and the show began. The whistle kept us in the loop.

Fires at night were still fires, and the whistle did not care that I slept across the street. A middle of the night fire whistle, cars speeding, and all could ruin a night's sleep. My body knew that so learned to sleep through the whistle. Mind over matter. It worked real nice.

Real well, too. One morning in March, I woke up and stretched. It was sorta spring, so I looked out the window to savor the already dawned day. Across the street, there was a burned hulk where the Police Athletic League building used to be. It had been there. Last night. When it was time to go to sleep. Now it was gone. Charred. Damp. It smoked slightly. Surely something strange transpired, so I headed downstairs to see what.

"Hey, Mom. Where did the PAL building go? It was there last night."

They were quite surprised that I missed the three-alarm fire. The fire burned through the night right outside my window. The window right above where neighbors stood and firemen ran hither and yon. They even used the phone in our living room a few times to call other fire stations. Quite the show.

Sleep was good. But sometimes you missed a show. If Monk saw it while I slept, he kept it to himself.

The Cellar
(Part theme park, part food storage)

The cellar in the house on the corner of Maple and Main had a personality all its own. It was a crawl space on steroids. Too small for most people to stand erect. Too large to go unused for at least something. Dante on uppers. Disney in his dark period. It was a strangely appealing mix of dungeon and storage shed that became my space. A bit by choice and a bit by functionality. I was the shortest and, therefore, the king of the cellar. No one ever tried to dethrone me. Despite numerous requests.

The entrance to this not so cavernous cove was hidden from view. This dubious distinction should have told me something about the cellar. What kind of place requires someone to conceal even its entrance? What sort of monstrosity do you build and then hide and bury under a house? Why would you have something and do everything in your power to keep it from view? Secrecy? Embarrassment? Both? One Maple Avenue had its own bat cave, without all the gadgets and cool stuff. The Van Wagners' version of Bruce Wayne's lair did not include bat poles or a butler to hold your hats while you slid down the pole and into your tights. Those daring enough to enter the cellar, usually it was just me, did so via a walk-in broom closet in the kitchen that doubled for storage. The broom closet, not the kitchen, that is.

There was little rhyme or reason for the contents of this broom closet. There was a broom, to keep with the name, along with its cousins, mop, bucket, dustpan, and dust broom. A virtual family reunion of floor care implements. The sweeps were not alone. Proximity to the kitchen meant a strange array of kitchen utensils called the closet home. There were flippers, the same things rich folks call spatulas. There were knives of various shapes and sizes; none ever sharp enough for my father, so none worth the power to blow to hell. One of my favorite things in the broom closet was the cast iron meat grinder. It was one of those hand crank things, and Dad looked liked he was cranking one of the cars in a Laurel and Hardy movie when he turned it. The grinder itself was so heavy that when my father mounted it to the table to grind up ham for his patented, to-be-avoided-at-all-costs hash, my sister and I weighed down the opposite end of the table. Mom said the grinder was made from the same steel used to make the Bismarck. We had no reason to doubt her. The broom closet held even more. There were pots and pans, a pencil sharpener and knife sharpener mounted in tandem on one wall, bags of onions and potatoes on the floor, some tools waiting to be found, and miscellaneous odds and ends. All spirited there in the concept of "putting things away". In the Van Wagner household, away equaled out of sight. I knew. I was usually the one told to "put that away". So away things went. The broom closer was a great away place. This hiding method did have a down side. This hodge-podge of randomness served as the gauntlet and barred the faint of heart from the small door at the back of the unlit and littered broom closet.

I was the cellar king and was not allowed to be faint of heart when it came to going downstairs. It was my job.

Untrained eyes would not even see the door. Doors had tradition. Doors had shapes. Doors had some standards of construction. Doors had knobs. This three foot high ensemble of packing crate wood had none of those. It was more a patchwork of shoddy repair. It was Dad's creation and unique because that was what Dad created. Ask for a door and Handy Andy made, well, whatever the heck this thing was. It did not look like a door at all. It looked like, well, the back wall of a broom closet. Where there should have been a doorknob, there was a tarnished latch of sorts that blended into the dark with nocturnal naturalness. Doors beckoned just by being. Doors advertised the existence of something behind the very opening they close. The back wall of the broom closet held a few pots and pans on nails-turned-hooks, just as its brethren walls did. The overall effect was that you had to know there was a door there to see it. Once you found the door, the rest of the cellar experience was not any easier.

The munchkin size opening inhibited evolved adults. Even my small frame assumed the simian position when I ventured into the chasm. The stairs, actually a mismatched collection of wobbly wood assembled by dear old Dad, were as narrow as any staircase in existence. I discovered the trick to descending them. I had to, since no one else would do it. I merely bent like a heavily burdened chimpanzee, leaned to the right, used the left wall to guide my arched back, placed my feet as if each stair was about to fall away if any excess weigh touched them, and prayed. A lot. It was quite an art. I became the cellar virtuoso.

Past the gauntlet, through the secret passage, and down the stairs of death, I was five foot nearer to hell. It seemed a lot closer though. One light bulb fought ineffectively against the dark. Cement feebly smoothed part of the earth while the coldness of the atmosphere forever tempered the floor. The weight of the house pressed downward, mere inches above my head. It was cold here regardless of the season. Smells entered the cellar and stayed, unchallenged by fresh air or gentle winds. A coal chute, long abandoned and decades away from its last chuck of anthracite, held a musk that told of its history and its decay. The furnace fire sulfured. The hot water heater gassed a bit. Previous rains stagnated pungently. Dog hairs and dust snuck here to ferment. All things destined for the nose of any cellar caller. All part of the experience, these aromas mixed to create something not common in nature. Something that had me looking over my bent shoulder during my visits south of home. Each visit to the cellar made me stronger, for I conquered the beast of the place. The visits were always better in hindsight though. I was quite uncomfortable while actually in the nether regions.

The unfinished half of the cellar, ground level, so waist high for my eleven-year-old frame, oozed fragrances of dirt, dust, and something scary. Less than 2 feet below the floorboards of the house, this darker and dirtier part of the cellar was too small for even me, except in games of extreme hide and seek. Real extreme. The boogey man was coming extreme. This dark side underbelly of Maple Avenue was reserved for night crawlers and nightmares. The other part was for canned goods.

My mother was a hoarder. Katie hoarded things just in case. The usable portion of the cellar was her storage spot for things we needed, may need, or may never need but should have just in case. Her obsession with extras was her defense against eventualities. She answered life's question of "what if" with canned goods. She saw safety in cans. Canned everything. Corn. Tomatoes. Peas.

Jersey Sure

Carrots. Peas and carrots. Baby Carrots. Baby peas and carrots. The entire bean catalog. Green. String. Baked. Lima. Even a bean that did not occur naturally, waxed. Succotash, the vegetable choice for the indecisive, the same people whose favorite color is plaid. Yams. White potatoes, peeled and devoid of any flavor. Apple Sauce. Fruits of all kinds. Peaches. Pears. Pineapple. (When in season, which defeated the entire concept of canned). The ever-popular Fruit Cocktail, a hastily assembled melody of chucks of all the left over fruit with one, on a very good day two, cherries thrown in to add ambiance. Sweetened condensed milk, later relocated to an undisclosed location for safety reasons. The impressive Campbell's Soup collection. Chicken everything--noodle, rice, broth, gumbo, and stars. Vegetable. Tomato. Soup that is. Pea. God, please let it be soup. Lipton never had a chance with my mother. Soup in a box? Never! This from the same woman who stocked up on Franco-American spaghetti while surrounded with neighbors who made pasta from scratch and never called gravy, sauce. Put it in a can and my mother brought it. After all, she had a cellar for just that purpose.

She hoarded. I inventoried, hauled, stacked, and organized her hoard. The cans were hers. I decided how they were stored. I chose rows, and not just because Mom said to do it that way. Rows made sense. Labels forward. Each row a particular selection. Corn first since it was the most preferred and saw the most turnover. Campbell's merited a few rows with the popular soups, i.e., anything chicken in one row and the others distributed based on my mother's cravings at the time. In the Van Wagner house, Mom decided what we ate, and we ate what she liked. Occasionally, I tried to sway her choice of vegetable. It did not work, but I still tried. Sent to the basement to fetch her selection for dinner that evening, the King of the cellar would yell with a pleadful, "Hey, Mom. Can we have (fill in the blank) instead?" Her "No" was quick and consistent. Demigods always eased decision-making. My mother cooked what she desired. She purchased what she desired. We were along for the ride. She was the one who decided what we stocked, how much we stocked, and when we stocked it.

My mother's shopping ritual began with me in the basement as she yelled down the inventory. She had "The List". Her paper with the names of the vegetables, soups, fruits, etc, and how many cans of each were in the basement when last we inventoried. She called off "Corn". I counted the cans and let her know how many we had. She updated her list and then, speaking aloud but not to communicate, said how many cans she needed to get at the store. We inventoried all the items and "The List" was ready for its trip to the store and the re-supply process. It was my first lesson in supply and demand. The nuns never taught supply and demand. Mom headed for Shop Rite, way up in Hazlet, since their prices beat CBS all to hell and were better than Safeway, too. Mom rode. Dad drove. I went along. Laborer.

When we returned from the store, I sorted the items, hauled bags of canned goods down the stairs of death, and placed them on the cement shelf. Carefully to ensure the valuables were off the ground and away from the dark side of the house's underbelly. I stacked and lined the cans. Even out of her sight. Testimony to my mother's power. Mom did not go into the cellar. She did once to bail water after Hurricane Donna way back when I was just six, but she had not since. Still, I placed the cans as if ready for her daily inspection rather than risk her wrath. Granted, I rebelled occasionally and placed corn last or at least in the middle, but it was rare. It felt good when I did it though. Be a man! This was my cellar! It was my choice of sequence! It was my empire and I arranged it as I desired! Besides,

Jersey Sure

she hardly ever visited the cellar and would most likely not even notice that one slight discretion.

Dad visited the cellar more than Mom did. The odds of him even commenting on the cans were very slim indeed. As long as the cans did not have the magic word on them, "Budweiser", Bud was none the wiser. My father went down to the cellar only when left no other choice. He descended those rickety stairs and entered that dankness only when absolutely necessary. Water leaks did not merit his attention unless they qualified as pours. After all, a mere drip took months, if not years, to generate enough water to lap forth from below. Gas leaks had to hiss as well as smell. Wisely though, he restricted the use of matches or any lit flame to the upper regions of the house. In case of fires in the basement, he was the second alarm. I was the first line of defense. As the default master of the basement universe, I was relieved that my father limited his forays. For Handy Andy, as we called him, was the clown prince of home repair.

My father started each job reluctantly and ended each with disaster, either immediate or concealed as a job well done for months or even years. He believed preventative maintenance was for wussys. He operated on the "wait until it is broken" premise. Consequently each repair effort was both urgent and inconvenient. A volatile combination for any endeavor. Home maintenance in the Van Wagner household was out and out dangerous on many levels. It began with the denizen of disaster himself, Little Will, the ticking time bomb of fixer-uppers.

My father was an unskilled know-it-all armed with Craftsman tools and an unwillingness to ask for help. He began each home repair debacle with some grumbling. A low, almost simmering sound dripped with frustration and tinged with anger. His strangely religious murmur damned fate, suspects, and all points between. This creature of habit accessed the damage and headed for the shed. Here, the true ritual began. For my father lived with the false hope of tools in their place. He forgot he had children—natural foes of things in their places.

He saw tools. We saw toys. We played with them. We forgot about them. We left them where they lay. It was our investment in entertainment at his expense. Sure, tools were neat toys but the real fun was later. Sometimes days. Perhaps even weeks or months. We were never really sure when this jack-in-box of laughter would spring forth, but we knew it would. Usually on a Saturday. Usually when he was stressed over a broken something or other. Sooner or later it happened. The planets aligned and the pay off began.

Our ever-wishful father gamely looked in the least likely place he would ever find his tools - his toolbox. Hopefully, God never honored his pleas to damn us and all like us. He fussed, stomped, stormed, cussed, yelled, pounded, threw, and blustered as the game of "Where the hell are my tools" started in earnest It was quite a demanding game since there was little to no logic in the locations for the tools nor much repetition in our pattern of usage. The only consistency was our answer to my father's futile plea as to the whereabouts of the errant hand tools. We didn't know.

The scavenger hunt was underway. A hammer in with the dolls in Sis's room. Three screwdrivers under my bed. Chisels nestled with the butter knives, most of which were down the drain. The razor knife safely stored on the ground where we repaired flat tires on our bikes, the blade dulled with layers of burned airplane glue. He searched with an urgency that amused and entertained us for days afterwards. Part two of the ritual involved us swearing to never do it again and him headed to weave his magic of handiness. My mother liked when the repair work was in the cellar. She slept better when she did not actually see what he did.

Jersey Sure

My father "fixed" things in ways only he understood. His handiwork was everywhere, just below the floorboards of what was always a second or two away from becoming ground zero. Mad Ludwig had his castle. My father had the cellar. Pipes elbowed around and under and through in random patterns of inefficiency. His selection of angles and juts defied any form of logic. He drilled through brick and then U'ed piping around 2 x 4 studs. He worked with pipes and wrenches with abstract imprecision. Electrical tape marked the leaks, tied wires to pipes, and mummified trouble spots on surfaces ranging from concrete to air.

The effect on the cellar was bizarrely beautiful. My father's maze of repair bobbed and weaved everywhere the eye could see, and a few places it couldn't, with variety and even amazement. Just overhead dangled an amusement park of repair incompetence unmatched in recorded time. Part roller coaster. Part fun house. Part obstacle course. It turned. It bent. It doubled back. It circled. It looped. It defied logic and safety. It was masterful. It was impressive. It was scary as all get out. We could have charged admission to see it. With the purchase of three or more tickets, you got a free can of succotash!

Classes and Special Effects
(A day that will live in Infamy)

In 1965, school did not have a lot of special effects. Textbooks. Rulers, in the form of Nuns as well as measuring devices. Pens, but not ballpoint, for Nuns did not like ballpoint pens. Nuns insisted their loyal minions used fountain pens. Fountain pens which made for those lovely ink blowouts in shirt pockets. Were Nuns anti-ballpoints or pro dry cleaning? Hmmmm. Made me wonder. Chalk. Chalk to write on blackboards. Blackboards that were really green. That always made me wonder, too. We learned our colors early in life from people who wrote on blackboards that are really green. Did they know their colors as they taught us ours? The Crayola people would not sell us black crayons that were really green. At least I hope they would not.

Saint Anne's School had the green-blackboards, chalk, fountain pens, textbooks, and Nuns to guide us daily in the art of learning. Occasionally we had a "guest speaker". A guest speaker in the form of a Nun. Not an outside Nun. Just one of the locals. A rotary speakers bureau from within. Our Nun went to another room and somebody else's nightmare turned flesh incarnate "guest" spoke in

Jersey Sure

our room. It was different. Nice to see other kids had Nuns worse that our own. I guess they thought the same thing when they heard our nun.

The highest point of technology in Saint Anne's was the PA system. It was one step above a bunch of paper cups connected via strings. Barely. Depended upon the weather and wind. Sister Mary Bernadette sounded like she was on board the Nautilus during heavy seas when she reported daily events and threatened to find out exactly who soaped the convent windows with "Men Wanted" last Friday evening. Although she never mentioned the "Men Wanted" part. She just mentioned the soaped windows part. We all knew about the "Men Wanted" part. Some kids did not know about the "Now!" or "Badly" parts. I did. I did not divulge the source of my knowledge. The entire incident was even good for a chuckle at the dinner table. Nuns were fair prey for humor from all age groups.

In this relatively archaic atmosphere, a portable TV in a classroom to watch America inch to the moon via a missile launch ended up as a family story as well as a Saint Anne's legend. As with most adventures, and misadventures, it began as a relatively normal day. A typical school day.

I was in my Danny Sheehan period in that Danny and I walked to and from school together. Danny straddled the line between everyday friend and someday friend and for a few weeks as of late, he was on the everyday side of the line. We got to school early. His mom worked, as did both of my parents. His dad, well, we were never really sure what the story there was. I heard everything from his dad having died to his father being of unknown origin. Not that they did not know if the father was human but that he was one of several suspects. Not sure where the truth laid but Danny was an okay kid and an everyday friend for a few weeks, and this was one of the days in one of those weeks.

We arrived at school early, about an hour early, and hung around. Not many kids came to school early, but we did. The teacher showed up, and we helped her with some books from her car to get into the warmth of the building. She saw us as courteous. We saw her as a way into the school.

She settled in and prepared for the day. We putzed around. Teachers settled in for a day in a manner almost cookie cutter in nature. Put the book bag down. The same book bag they had for a few years. Worn leather. Nicely though. Beaten but not broken. Impressive, since it was almost always jam-packed with papers to grade, books to read, books to lug around, supplies of all shapes and sizes, and a baloney sandwich of questionable age. There was a smell to this book bag and all like it. Something between locker room and old icebox. Not fermented. Not appealing. The smell generated the quick crinkle of the nose for all who caught a whiff. Mrs. Talbot was no exception. It was her book bag, and even her baloney sandwich, but she crinkled her nose while she took stacks of papers and things out of her magic bag of tricks. She was our teacher and replaced the nun who was in the nun hospital with an illness that, according to the other Nuns, was none of our business. Mrs. Talbot was an alright teacher for a permanent substitute. I liked her.

She ensured the blackboard was clean and arranged the chalk like a gunfighter arranged ammo for a shoot out. She opened drawers, dropped some things in, and took others out. A ritual of sorts for her, since she chatted aimlessly while doing it or at least did it aimlessly while she chatted. It was hard to see if the ebb flowed or the flow ebbed.

Jersey Sure

I pictured her planning the day in her head as she arranged her tools of the trade. Perhaps we would have Jersey history today. We had some last week and even yesterday, but seemed there was more history each and every day. Mrs. Talbot liked history. I sorta liked it when she talked of local things as well as those over the ocean things. New Jersey had some cool history, it turned out. It also had some not so cool history. Teachers sometimes failed to see the difference.

New Jersey had Indians. Lenapi. Lenapi? I resented them. You never saw them on Gunsmoke or Bonanza. John Wayne never fought them. I did not even know if they had arrows, since there were not arrowheads lying around in evidence. At least not in my neck of the urban woods. We studied the Lenapi and heard of villages and co-existence. Seems they were farmers and hunters but with ne'er a mention of warriors and the like. The boy in me wondered if we lived on a land formerly owned by the geeks of Indianworld. All the cool Indians, Apache, Sioux, Comanche, Navaho, all those ones from the movies and TV, were out west somewhere. There was never a Lenapi uprising. Nothing. New Jersey was not noted for the Indians. Drats. Wigwams were okay but warpaint was better. Mocassins and handicrafts only did so much for me, a would-be cowboy and all American hero. Battle reports and carnage did much more. Thank God for movies and TV where Indians were a force to be reckoned with. At eleven years old, peaceful bored.

We had the Lenapi, who were not cool, but we had lots of colonial history that was really sorta cool. Jersey history was big on the Revolution, since we were pretty much knee deep in it. Even though the books talked more about that home of the Red Sox up north. According to the history books, Boston was the center of it all. Bunker Hill. That Tea party. Lexington. Concord. Jersey was hardy even mentioned. Philly got some press since they had the Liberty Bell and Independence Hall but seemed it all centered around Boston. Most of the big names called Massachusetts home. Hamilton and his continental sized ego. Adams with brothers and cousins everywhere. Had to like old Ben Franklin though. Kites. Lightening. Inventing stuff all the time. Heck, he even wanted the turkey as our national bird. A national bird you can stuff and eat. Ben was one cool dude. Paul Revere and his ride to glory as he called to arms. I am glad they had two arms; at least I think they all had two arms, and that they took a minute to fight. Minutemen fought for years so the name always confused me. I pictured Minutemen being from Massachusetts and imagined all the other guys a bunch of rabble with attitudes. But it was not just the Minutemen who fought the Revolution. No matter what the folks up there in Massachusetts claimed, they did not do it alone. There were soldiers with guns, knives, and hatchets from the good old Garden State. Jersey was in the thick of it.

Washington used Jersey as the area to attack those nasty Hessians. He planted himself in the Garden State and then headed to fight paid assassins and really bad guys. Jersey was the right place for that. Jersey folks always liked a good fight. The seventeen hundreds were no exception. I pictured the Garden State militia as the one off to the side with the attitude. Prissy little folks from Boston carefully arranged their tri-cornered hats, and the soldiers from New Jersey snuck up and knocked them off. Just because. Good old George probably resented the Jersey troops since they caused so much trouble but liked that they kicked ass. That's how I always pictured it.

We did History to death in class and also did Geography. Places that were names on the map filled our reports. I did the standard thing. Picked a country, got the basic facts, population, location, neighbors, etc, etc, and jazzed it up

Jersey Sure

a bit. I headed south of the border and picked Brazil this year. Some Ann Page coffee and Planters nuts served as the visual for Brazil's major exports. An encyclopedia, a piece of poster board, and a pair of maracas later and, quicker than you can walk the sands of Ipanema, you had one each report. Carefully researched. Well presented. Quickly forgotten.

There was not a report due today. There was not anything out of the ordinary due today as Mrs. Talbot settled in for the day. Danny and I just hung around and figured we had about a half hour before the rest of the kids showed up. It was then Mrs. Talbot mentioned a thing that began a sequence of events that shaped not just my today but many days to come. "Isn't there a rocket launch today?"

Danny and I looked at each other and confirmed there was indeed a launch. It was Gemini 3 and would lift Gus Grissom and Alan Young into space. This third flight in Gemini was the first one since the Mercury flights that held people. Space flights all part of the effort to take human beings from terra firma herea to terra firma therea in the form of the moon someday as announced by the now deceased President John F. Kennedy. A man so important his picture hung in our classroom right alongside of the living Pope. Despite him being dead and all. Mrs. Talbot said she hoped that someone remembered and brang, yes, she used brang all the time, in a transistor radio so the class could share in this modern day adventure of exploration. That was when the innovation in my mind kicked in. For in the house I called home on Maple Avenue was something far better than an transistor radio. For a transistor radio was small and sounded, well, it sounded small. In my home were two televisions sets. The console set in the living room and the portable one in my parents' bedroom.

Television sets were called sets because that is what they did. They set. They were too damn big to do anything

Gilbert Van Wagner

else. It took two men and a boy, and a strong boy at that, to even budge them. These television sets were so big the makers just built consoles around them, added stereos, lamps, and other things and turned the set into something that did not just bring in shows. It filled the room and was only slightly smaller than the couch the viewers sat on to view it. Television sets were massive.

There were portable models. Portable meant they could actually be lifted without forklifts and hoisting equipment. The screen was 24 inches big and the tubes and magic stuff that powered it filled out a case about 2 feet thick, 2 feet wide, and just under three feet high. Portable? Sure. Just not often and just not easily. But I only knew it was called portable and offered to bring it to school so we could watch the launch. Somewhat to my surprise, Mrs. Talbot accepted the offer, after I ensured her, quite confidently and with a cosmopolitan air, that my parents would be okay with it. I was sure. Since they were both at work and I would take the TV to school and have it back home before they ever, or would ever, know. A perfect plan, so Danny and I headed to my house for an errand of scientific education.

We headed back home from school when everyone else headed in. That was quite heady. Kids looked. I merely smiled that smile of superiority since this was kinda an approved hooky, albeit a short one. Danny and I let the others wonder what the heck we were doing and walked Carr Avenue back to Maple and Maple to the house.

We got to the house and had to be quiet. My sister attended afternoon sessions in the crowded Middletown Township High School. Hence, she was asleep and I did not want to disturb her. Truth be told, it was not for her sake, but for my own well-being. She may well not understand the importance of bringing a TV to school for a space launch.

We entered with stealth, which at 11 meant we snuck. I unplugged it and pushed the rabbit ears back into their

Jersey Sure

hidey-holes. I carefully, as well as quietly, wrapped the cord around the plastics things on the back of the set. Safety first! Then we lifted. Oomph. The TV was heavy. Two hands to lift it from the stand and put it on the floor heavy. We looked at each other wordlessly. We questioned. In a glance. We were going to get this to the school with just the two of us? I shushed him with a look, and we went to work.

The side porch was tough. We made it down the rickety, handy Andy did it his way stairs, in tandem, and I took the first turn lugging the so-called portable set. With two hands on the plastic handle, I bent back and sidestepped down the lawn. Twenty steps turned out to be the record. Twenty steps before we had to switch and let the other lug it a while. I did my turn and Danny did his. We even tried to lift it jointly but that promised to result in a dropped TV. Not a good outcome by any definition. We lugged in turn.

It took quite a while to make it to school and we were winded by the time we got to the stairwell to the second floor. Other years, my classes were on the first floor. The floor without a stairwell rising to it. Years when I did not bring a portable TV that weighed about as much as a small washing machine. And was about as small as a washing machine. We looked at the stairs with a sigh in our hearts and took the now dreaded electronic monstrosity up one stair at a time.

Classes were in session and we had the stairwell all to ourselves. We paused at the top. Somewhat to plan our entrance. Partly to savor the victory of having lugged the TV all the way from the house to the school all by ourselves. Mostly to catch our breath.

We entered the hallway and felt the second wind kick in. Classroom straight ahead. Grand entrance to be made. So we did. It was glorious.

Gilbert Van Wagner

The class looked to the door in wonder at who entered in the middle of the first class. When they saw Danny and me, most looked quizzically. When they saw they TV, they gasped. They actually gasped. A TV! In school! Whatever the lesson was, we upstaged it as we, with all the strength we had left, put the portable TV on the center of Mrs. Talbot's desk. I, with great technical ability and aplomb, plugged the set in and pulled the rabbit ears from the safety of their hidey-holes. The class watched, and Mrs. Talbot used the moment to explain the situation to the class.

Being called Mister Van Wagner in a classroom was normally not good but it was grand this day. She talked of Mister Van Wagner and how he, and Danny almost as an afterthought, arranged to bring a TV to school so we could watch the space launch.

It was a black and white portable TV with reception no one envied, but it was a first. The first time the teacher and the students even considered the idea of TV in school. It was a quantum leap in education and I was the source. Mrs. Talbot could have announced I found the cure for cancer. I was the Jonas Salk of TV in the classroom. My moment in the sun, and I was just eleven years old. What a glorious moment.

The picture cleared and we were about 2 hours from launch. Walter Cronkite bantered of things past and things future as we watched the impressive Saturn 5 idle on the pad. Students looked at the set and then at me. In awe. With reverence. It was heroic, and I lapped it up as my due.

Somewhere amidst the T-minuses, the PA broke the moment. It was not tinny as usual. It was crystal clear. Sister Marie Bernadette called very slowly with an enunciation that eliminated any doubt of her message.

"Gilbert Van Wagner, report to the Principals Office. NOW!"

Jersey Sure

The gulp was physical as well as mental, psychological, spiritual and any other level of gulp possible as I eased from my revelry and headed for the Principal's Office.

She greeted me before I even got to the office. She stood in the hallway. A stance that spoke loudly. Arms crossed. Foot tapping. A scowl on her face. Again this day, I was called Mister Van Wagner. This one felt a helluva lot different.

"Mister Van Wagner. Do you, by chance, have a TV in school today?"

I saw the trap but had nowhere to run. The film clips of my life ran in front of my eyes. Gulp. She did not ask this in the heroic, set the precedent for education, tone that was my due. She asked like having a TV in school was a bad thing. A very bad thing. Something was definitely amiss. If I had a robot buddy, he would be screaming "Danger, Danger!" right about now.

With the very best innocent face I could muster, I answered, "Why, yes, Sister. I do."

Her eyes looked knowingly as she leaned to me and hissed, she really actually hissed the words like a character from Riki-Tikki-Tavi, "Get into that office, and get on that phone. Your sister almost called the police because she thought the television was stolen. Get on that phone. NOW!"

I gulped again. This could indeed be trouble. The phone was on the desk. The head thingy laid in wait. She stood over me as I picked up the instrument and let the music of trouble begin.

"Hello?" Softly. Tentatively. Calmly. Although I was far, far from calm. An angry Nun stared at me, the principal nun no less. I had a television in school that was here without permission. Things were pretty bad. Calm was not part of me. Things were bad. Things then got worse.

My sister spewed forth her story at a pace that amazed me. I had never heard her speak that fast. It ran together. I listened. I watched Sister Marie Bernadette watch me.

"Gil, was the TV here when you went to school this morning? It is gone now. Someone broke into the house and took it while I was asleep upstairs. They were right in the house when I was upstairs. Who knows what they could have done? The TV is gone. I was about to call the police but called Dad at work. He said to call you before I called the police. So I called, and now I am going to call the police. Someone came into the house and stole the TV while I was upstairs in bed. I gotta call the police and report this......"

I think she said some other things as well. Her mind had rapists and burglars in the house while she lay upstairs asleep and vulnerable. She spoke of calling the police. She asked questions about if I knew anything but blasted onto the next thing without a pause for an answer. There was panic in her voice. There was violation, or the threat of violation in her voice. Sister Mary Bernadette stood over me like a hungry vulture over a warm carcass. All that and I heard only one thing.

Sis called Dad at work? My sister called my father at work? That was absolutely, positively a very, very bad thing. No one called my father at work. It just was not done. He worked in a factory and on smoke stacks and never, ever got called at work. Not until today when his panic stricken, idiot of a daughter decided to call him at work. I never even knew we could call him at work. The concept never crossed my mind. This was a bad, bad, bad, bad thing.

Somewhere along the way, my sister stopped talking. In that moment of silence, while Sister Mary Bernadette watched, I explained that I might just have some knowledge as to the whereabouts of the errant TV set. It went downhill from there. Sis sounded adult as she screamed ever so loudly about the situation. It did not matter. I did not hear

Jersey Sure

her. Dad was on my mind. Because he would soon be on my case. Life over. Game done. The call ended, who knew how and who cared. I was toast. The Principal told me to get that television home now.

Fame is a fleeting thing. One minute a hero. The next a heel. The rocket was about to lose its second stage as I returned to the room and shut off the TV. Crowds turn quickly. This one did. Lauded now loathed. They hissed. Actually hissed as I lugged the TV from the room and headed home in the middle of a school day. With the Principal's direction. Danny helped me again. He was quiet as he did. Dead man walking silence.

Sis was leaving for school as we arrived. She did not have to mention that Dad was mad. She did not have to mention how much trouble I was in. She did not have to mention that "this one tops it." She did not have to mention any of that. She did not, but she mentioned it all nonetheless. Salted a festering wound.

Class that afternoon was long and very awkward. Kids looked at me with disappointment and anger. They did not care how much trouble I was in. They almost got to see a lift off in school and only remembered that they did not see it all. They shunned me. It was stunning.

Dad came home and ate dinner with that looking over his glasses at the amazingly stupid fruit of his loins thing he saved for special occasions. Special occasions that lived on for quite a while.

Gus Grissom and Alan Young were back to earth before my chores were done for my then seemingly valiant attempt to forward classroom education. In fact, they were back and the next crew was up before the chores diminished. We did not see any other launches that year. Not in school that is. Seemed that people cooled to the concept of TV in school. Too much trouble. I agreed.

HOSPITAL VISITS
(Secrets and Faded Bricks)

Something was wrong with Mom and they would not say what. There were hushed conversations and worried glances. Adults thought kids did not see that stuff. We saw it. It screamed at us the quieter they got. Sis and I spoke about it. That was when I realized she was older and just a bit different. Because Sis, for quite possibly the first time other than secrets about Christmas presents, kept something from me. I was not sure what, but she was a lousy liar so I knew it was something. I was odd man out, and it bothered me. Not all the time. But everyday. In spurts.

When you did not know things, you sometimes pretended those things that you did not know were not things at all. So I did what any eleven year old would do. I forgot about it. At least, I tried. It did not work.

Life and school and homework and TV and friends distracted me, but the thing was there. Undeniable. Hidden and unknown. Enhanced by its very mystery. A mystery pieced together from bits of overheard conversations. Gaps filled in sometimes do not really fill in at all. They changed the picture you could not see. But the picture was there. Nobody would tell me so I had to figure it out on my own. I

Jersey Sure

got some of it right some of the time. Some of it wrong, too, but could not tell which was which and that made it tough. Something was up and I deserved to know what, even if I guessed wrong.

Mom was different, and she would not tell me why. Asking over and over was not a good thing. So I did not ask. Dad was different, too. He looked at Mom in a special way. A sad way. A something is wrong way. A do not ask me about it Fat Boy way. Sis was suddenly older and in the loop. Dad did not tell me what it was, but I could it tell by his actions that it was not about him. It was about Mom.

It took me a while to find out it was Breast Cancer, but I found out. I did not let them know I knew. They never mentioned Breast Cancer so I could hear. It was secret. It was adult. It was the thing they could not and would not say to someone so young as me. So they did everything to ensure I did not hear. I heard nonetheless. Kids were not supposed to know those things. Cobalt. Chemo. Mastectomies. Too grown up for young minds to handle. Screw them. I could handle it. Besides, Mom was going to be around for a long time, so it would all work out just fine. She was Mom. Mom would be here for a long time. Parents did not die before kids. Dick and Jane taught me that. Dick and Jane were not spotted in any hospital in any book I remembered.

Mom went to the hospital. They told me about a week or so earlier, in that brain dead, you are just a kid voice that made me feel retarded. At least emotionally. I played along. What the heck were they talking about? "Mommy is going away for a few days. She has to go to the Hospital. Mommy has an illness, and they are going to make her all better." For crying out loud, I knew the difference between a boo-boo and an operation. Dad spoke to me like I could not handle it. He seemed like it would crush me. Not the case. But he did not know that. He was busy trying to make sure it did not crush him.

So I did not worry, and I did not bother Dad since he worried enough for both of us and a few more just like us. Sis pranced around all somber and grown up. I let her be. She helped Mom with stuff around the house and that kept me from doing some chores. All because Mom was going in the hospital.

Hospitals were not happy places. They could sell toys and flowers and cards and snacks, but they did not fool me. Bad things happened in hospitals. Hospitals did not make me feel safe and healthy. But if we had to go to a hospital, I liked going to Riverview Hospital. It was named right because it had a river view. I was born there. It was way over in Red Bank. Red Bank was a neat place. It had a really old inn, the Olde Union House, so old it had the e at the end of Olde. I pictured folks in tri-cornered hats drinking ale there. Red Bank had more shops than Keansburg and a hospital we called our own. Plus, it was on the River. The Navesink River. Whenever we went to Red Bank, which was not too much until Mom got a lump in her breast and had to have surgery to make it go away, I got to go down to the river and walk on the boards by the boats. It was neat, but I could not show it. A trip to Red Bank meant someone had to go to the hospital.

That was a shame. Sort of a waste of good town. Like a garden in a graveyard. Pretty to look at, but do not enjoy it, please. I was in Red Bank because Mom went in for tests to get ready for her visit, not to enjoy the ice cream Dad brought me while he smoked cigarettes and went somewhere in his head where things were alright. I was there because Mom went in for surgery, not to enjoy the beauty of the river or the walkways and the docks. Those trips were about Riverview Hospital, not Broad Street and the things in store windows. It was time to remember someone was in the hospital for tests or worse, not time to look at homes with their very own docks and staircases to the water and think how cool that was. Hospital visits were all about hospitals.

Hospitals are things of beginnings and ends. I started there. My grandparents ended there. At least, I think that was where they died. Mom would point to a particular window and say that was where Grandma stayed when she was here. I looked but the windows up there all looked the same, and Grandma no longer had a room with a view. She was dead, and I saw that clearer than any window Mom pointed out to me. Hospitals were the last thing many people saw, and I saw that each time I saw Riverview. River views were always good, even if seen from the last window you ever got to use.

I saw too much of Riverview that year. Mom went for tests that she would not tell me about, and I got to go. Mom went more and more and then she went there for a few days at a time and I got to go. Not to the hospital actually. They did not let kids my age upstairs. Creeps. So I got to go and did not get to go at the same time. Strange. It was alright though. Right up until the day Mom waved.

We rode to Red Bank for another visit when I did not get to see my own Mother. Same route. Dad, Sis, and me. Two to see Mom. One to hang outside. Sis went up first, and I hung out with Dad. Sis was gone for a while, and Dad went up. A few minutes later, it happened. Sis smiled and pointed up to a window. Mom and Dad were at the window, and Mom leaned out to wave. At her son. The one who did not go to the see her up there. She waved to reassure. She waved to comfort. It did not work. The wave hurt.

I saw the window and saw a little woman in hospital pajamas waving. They had my mother in there, and I could not go there to see her. All the other visits, I knew she was there on all the other visits, but I did not see her on those visits. Now she was there and waved. That wave made me miss her all the more. I wondered why the heck they kept her there and did not let me see her. That made it hurt. That made me doubt. Why did they let her wave and not let me up there? For a second, I forgot everything was going to be alright. It passed. But it was not easy on that visit. Not the visit when Mom waved.

Riverview Hospital never looked the same again. That window was small and lonely. I knew right away that it would be a small and lonely window forever. I vowed never to point it out to my kids if I ever had any. What the hell good would that do? Look what you cannot have. Look at what they keep from you. Do not worry, everything is alright. See Mom? See Mom wave. Mom could not wave unless everything was alright. Wave, Mom, Wave.

Sis headed back upstairs to tag-team with Dad so he could come down and mind me. I sat on the fender of the Buick and sulked. Just looked at the Hospital. To the window of the room I could not see and hated all the more. Then I discovered the brick balance for the first time. About half the bricks on Riverview Hospital were faded. Not overly so, but faded. I looked closer. It was something other than faded. It was lifeless. A color of spent.

Bricks on Riverview Hospital were dying one by one. I spied the rest and they were colored correctly. Not faded.

Jersey Sure

My mind realized the significant secret I just unmasked. Faded bricks were zapped of life. Others were not. Yet. The balance was still in their favor.

Riverview Bricks were hospital bricks and hospital bricks were balanced in that the hospital had to save more lives than they lost. Hospitals saved lives with operations, births, therapy, etc, but they lost lives as well. The balance should be to the good or else they lost the use of one brick. If not, death absorbed the bricks one by the one. The souls exited and took pigment with them. The bricks lost their power.

In time, hospitals changed colors as deaths sucked away the colors of life. When hospitals came close to out of balance, they expanded, with brick additions to stem the tide of discolorations. Hospitals never got smaller. They expanded to get closer to balance or they just went away. Bricks were magical, but their magic was limited.

This theory was mine alone, but it held. It held up with Riverview and any other hospitals, even General. Hospital brick balance was there for all to see but only I noticed. On a day of a wave from a missed mother. A discovery born from the fender of a Buick by a boy that hoped his Mom's brick was the recovery kind.

Mom stayed in the room I could not go a few more days after that. Each day, another brick or two faded. Each day, Dad and Sis took turns and walked to the river with me while the other one was in the room I could not see with the Mom I could not see. Dad and Sis walked to the river with me but left their minds back in the room with Mom. Even when they could not see her.

Rivers healed. Running water cleansed thoughts. Even sad ones. Even really sad ones. Go to the bank. Deposit your sadness. The River listened and carried away a bit of the sadness. Not all of it. Just enough to make you stronger until you next came to the river. Dad walked but did not talk on those visits. I let him. All the way from the Hospital to the river. The winding road from Riverview to the River it viewed was not all that long. Less than half a mile. But it seemed longer on those walks.

Dad walked without purpose. He moved to the river as if the molasses of life stuck him hard. The sad walk of people with problems. He did not skip. He did not smile, except that fake, smile for the kid smile that did not fool me. Perhaps it fooled him. I could not tell.

We walked the docks of boats we would never own. We saw the freedom they showed. We sensed the man over elements tune they hummed with each bob of the waves. For a few minutes, those boats cleared our decks. Dad's deck awash with worry as his ship sought refuge from the storms of life. Mine cluttered with things I supposedly did not know. Those walks helped us both. Rivers are like that. Even ones with hospitals of fading bricks on the banks.

Dad walked up the hill a little lighter. I let him. On one of the last walks, a voice without words inside of me spoke that all would be well. The deed was done. The light at the end of the tunnel was more than a rumor. Dad's facade of hope took foundation and it showed. His hope was less false and more truth to me as well as him. We usually walked side by side from the river. Man with boy to comfort and boy with man to comfort. Lighter yes but somber still. Except once. When things felt the warmth of hope. That day, I ran. I ran to the park nestled in the crook of the land just below the Olde Union House.

Swings and slides were not right for most trips but this was towards the end. The time Mom's breast went from mammary to memory. I just ran. I did not ask Dad if I could. I just ran. From something. To something. The

Jersey Sure

grass pressed beneath my feet crushed something into place.

I ran. I slid on the slide. I swung on the swings. Not just for me. For him. For her. For them. There was purpose in my play. To live and let live. To help the man over by the wall that watched the next generation. Somehow I knew no bricks faded while I played, so I played hard and long. With hope. With vengeance.

My father stood, propped against the stone wall in a leg over leg casualness. He watched. I let him. He saw a child play as if all was right with the world. His child. Her child. It took a few minutes, but it worked. He smiled. An everything was going to be alright smile. That he believed. I let him. I knew it all along. Faded bricks and sad windows did not change that. Things would be alright. Adults sometimes took a while to get that feeling back.

Snack Wasteland and Corner Bars
(Raw Potatoes and the Deposit Bottle)

Lower middle class life for a kid sucked sometimes. Sure adults romanticized their youth, but I instinctively knew they gleaned over some of the darker spots. Life in Jersey embedded experiences that nothing could shake. Images forged by pangs of hunger and longing that scarred souls. A different universe. A snack wasteland.

Some kids outside the Burg lived this as well. A childhood more Dickens than Dick and Jane. They knew. But this is about life in the Burg and things I knew because of it. I knew in my heart that Ward Cleaver did not live in New Jersey. The Beaver would not have lasted ten minutes in the Garden State. The little putz never stood a chance. If June and Ward even drove through New Jersey, she would have quietly eased the pearls from her neck and hid them in the glove compartment while Ward had Wally and his pesky sibling lock the doors and look straight ahead. I liked the Cleavers, but they were not real to me. Families on TV

Jersey Sure

were not real to me or kids in the Burg. We looked at the TV Andersons as unbelievable fiction. Hazel and Mr. French were as much science fiction as tribbles and Vulcans. We lived a much different reality.

Some kids in town did not know of these things. Twinkie eaters. Twinkie eaters never tasted the dark side of lower middle-class. They were ignorant of "the other kids". The ones who toiled while they tickled the ivories with wussy indignation in piano practice. They thought stories about the urchins who scavenged for goodies, or even sad imitations of goodies that they found waiting on a tray with a nice, cold glass of milk after your hard day at school, were fiction. Urban legend. They took the goodies for granted, blissfully unaware of kids that envied them silently.

For kids like me, it began with food. Or lack thereof, actually. Kid food. Junk food. In my New Jersey universe of middle class, snacks were not. It was that simple. That direct. No snacks. Waste of money. Stomach be damned, my parents and their peers did not bring in chips, pretzels, candy, snack cakes, or anything appealing to sweet teeth or snack cravings. Instead, they fed us gruel, also known as the all-American, arteries-be-damned, it was good enough for me it is good enough for you, shut up and eat, meat and potatoes diet. These parents-turned-despots were raised by a generation who survived the war and depression. It forever warped them. Second generation cheap and mean. Now that they ruled their fiefdoms, they ensured we knew war and depression, even if history said the war and depression were over. They left us kids on our own resources for other sustenance. They underestimated our creativity.

Potatoes, when washed, were eaten raw as a snack. Hunger, especially in large amounts, enhanced the poor spud's appeal, but a raw potato as a treat falls under the "any port in a storm" defense. According to the Nuns and that guy on Mutual Of Omaha's Wild Kingdom, this was the survival instinct. We simply called it the "there has got to be something good to eat in this house" plea. In a model of child rationalization, the taste of victory over our parents sweetened the taste of a raw potato. For our naïve parents thought they did not buy snacks and then unwittingly purchased some by the ten-pound bag. We washed them thoroughly, removed their eyes, and ate them raw, skin and all. All these actions refer to the potatoes, not our parents. Although….. Admittedly, this was not a daily routine and, in fact, was quite an act of snack desperation. But it worked. In a pinch. A very tight pinch.

Conversely, sugar on bread was a sweet but gritty treat on most any occasion. This mutation had its roots with the more socially acceptable habit of sprinkling powered sugar on French toast. With our perception that French toast, along with the wonder of modern times, French Fries, actually came from France, we warmly embraced this cosmopolitan treat. Sugar-bread was easy to make and was sweet. While fresh bread, with its soft and inviting texture, enhanced the overall sensation, fruit of the cane on even day old bread, admittedly short of divine, definitely tasted above acceptable. In fact, I wondered why this treat never went mainstream instead of much blander things like fruit and nuts.

Ever since Kellogg first stuck flakes in a box, kids knew that handfuls of cereal filled a hunger void quite nicely in a pinch. Shredded wheat, the most noticeable violation of this rule. Cheerios and Corn Flakes amazed our taste buds by tasting good right from the box without the word Sugar in front of the name. But frost those little anythings and, viola, we were home free with a snack disguised as breakfast. We learned quickly what an adjective could do, especially when that adjective was sugar. Sugar as the first

Jersey Sure

word on any cereal box made the second word merely filler. Crisps, Pops, Smacks, Chex, Crunch, Oats, Bits, Bites, Floats, Boats, O's, A's, Z's, Turds. It all worked. A snack in a box and we didn't even have to beg.

Sugar cereal. Plain cereal. Sugar bread. Raw potatoes. They filled a void in my snack-less household, but there was something even better that became my substitute of choice. This tasty target began a war of epic proportions in the big white house on the corner. The battlefront? The refrigerator. The warriors? Two.

In the Van Wagner household, the main players in the snack war were my Mother, a formidable foe with a dangerously cavalier disregard for our pleas for goodies, and myself, armed with a sweet tooth and desperation. We skirmished over other substitute sugary treats, but our main battlefield was far sweeter. Condensed Milk. Milk so sweet and laden with cream it could be sliced. This can of nectar was my mother's secret ingredient in her coffee. She valued it. She guarded it. She relished it. It was my target of choice in a war for sweetness that raged for years.

Katie was formidable and did not make things easy on my sweet tooth. A infallible memory and a ironclad belief that what was hers was clearly, undisputedly, and irrevocably hers, she laid down the law the first time my condensed milk laden fingers moved from the container to my drooling mouth. I was drawn to it like a thirsty bee to honey, and it did not matter to her. Condensed Milk was hers and hers alone. Her righteous indignation was real when my grubby fingers, from places she dared not even think of, violated the inner sanctum of her stash. She lashed out and clearly outlined the boundaries. In my innocence, I awoke a guardian of treasure. In retaliation, she birthed a creativity in me that I know she secretly grew to admire over the years.

Gilbert Van Wagner

The war was on. Katie and her can (of condensed milk) versus her hungry, eleven-year-old. The battle waged for years. As with most conflicts, it began small but spiraled out of control. First, my fingers in the goo and her threats. Once I realized she would not really cut off my appendages, although for a while it seemed a very real possibility, I escalated. Dips turned to sips. Sips to spoonfuls. Spoonfuls to "what the hell happened to all my condensed milk!" sessions. I ran amok, and she, for the first and perhaps only time in her life, felt helpless to control the situation. She threatened. She grounded me. She asked my father to intervene, but his halfhearted attempts at "leave your mother's condensed milk alone" failed miserably. His roll of the eyes upon delivery a sure give away for his apathy. If he actually liked the stuff, this tale would have been entirely different. But he did not care for it, so reserved his involvement. My mother was a weaponless soldier against a formable and hungry foe.

At one point, she futilely penciled a line inside the can to show me she knew how much condensed milk was in the can. This act of desperation only heightened her frustration as I discovered erasers worked even on surfaces coated in condensed milk. Rather that admit defeat, she risked lead poisoning and drew the lines in ink. Pride can be a powerful motivator, even in the face of overwhelming odds. It did not work. I knew of the other cans of condensed milk on the storage shelf in the basement and found the can opener was mighty than the pen. With great pride, I drank the marked can empty, opened a new can, and then refilled the original can to the mark. Although finishing the reminder of the condensed milk in the replacement can challenged even the sweetest of teeth, I rose to the occasion. This action perplexed her for some time. The evidence said she had won but her gut knew there was a catch. She never said it directly, but I knew she sensed the catch. She did

Jersey Sure

not brag when the evidence indicated her victory. Her quiet contemplation screamed suspicion. A few weeks later, she figured out my ploy and raised the roof. She resorted to a war of attrition. She waited me out, knowing some day I would have to leave the house. She began the slow painful wait for me to leave so she can reclaim her fiefdom. It was basically victory for me.

I was not alone in this battle for sugar. Other kids in the Burg suffered similar droughts in goodies. Keansburg was the panacea of snack wasteland. We found occasional chinks in the armor, though, and exploited them. Soda bottles and the wonderful concept of refunds helped. Not with my mother, for she understood the monetary value of everything. Besides, she was spending more money on condensed milk than planned. She was not a source for extra cash. To her, money for candy and goodies would be aid to the enemy. My father was a different story. Ask him for a quarter, and he would say no as a matter of habit. It was heredity. He was a blue-collar parent. His denial of any request for money was instinctive. Not malicious, just habit. You did not give what you did not have. However, ask him if you could return the coke bottles for the refund, and he would normally acquiesce. Asked. Answered. Gone in a flash. I bagged those puppies quickly and headed for the Main Street Bar. I struck while the iron was hot or Dad may have me trade them in for another bottle of soda. That would turn me from quarteraire to mere errand boy, lugging five or six empties for one full. Refund money strait ahead!

The entire concept of refunds for soda bottles was quite sinister. Born years before, the idea of deposit bottles had

Gilbert Van Wagner

dark and dirty roots, masked in a charade of concern for the environment. Recycling initiative? Not even. Just part of the cover story. In truth, the deposit bottle was the first and only joint effort between the forces of Pepsi and Coke. It was post World War but mid cola war. A monumental point in consumer history.

The day was dark and overcast, befitting events that generated this clandestine meeting. The exact year was not specified, and in fact not clearly documented, for this was beyond secret. The people were as depressed as the economy. Jobless people everywhere said Hoover sucked more than the vacuums that later bore his boring name. They drowned their sorrows in newsreels, cartoons, and slapstick escapades and washed down popcorn with colas that jolted them from their dreary reality.

Meanwhile, deep in the corporate offices of Coca-Cola, warring factions from Coke and Pepsi-Co joined to counter a new foe. One so huge, it threatened both the cola giants. A danger so large that these bitter rivals cooperated, albeit for this one moment in time only, to counter a looming, common enemy. Coke and Pepsi faced a crisis of epic proportions. A crisis in the form of a heartless and ill-conceived government edict. Those bureaucratic bastards in Washington directed that cola companies stop using addictive drugs in their mixtures. How dare they ban cocaine from soft drinks?

Damn it all! How could Pepsi and Coke, along with those bush league buffoons over at Royal Crown, the American Motors of cola, keep their customers hooked without the sweet repetitive nature of drug addiction? It had worked so well. What a masterful marketing concept. Let your customers taste of narcotics in their youth and have them hooked on a feeling for life. Consumers so passionately loyal that it took interventions for them to stop using your product. Such a sweet cycle of sales. All due to a simple white powder fresh from the wonderful poppy flower. Slip a little in the syrup and Presto! Zing equaled cha-chings at the register. Cocaine was good for the soda business. The soda business was good for America. America needed Cocaine. Still, the law now made Cocaine a controlled substance and the end was near. Consequently, senior soda executives, bitter in their hatred for each other, met to counter this threat.

They were the best in the business. The Cola Cartel. This was not about the jonesing customers in their future. Perhaps there would be someday be clinics or some pharmaceutical based solution for those helpless beings. This day they met to find tomorrow's addiction. This was about continuing the cycle of repetitive business that made them millions. These bastions of consumerism devised a scheme so daring that it awed even them. They could go public with a concern about waste, the good earth, and all that tree hugging crap, that really was targeted to keep consumers in a buying loop. Under the heretofore classified, "Operation Lemming", the Cola Cartel created the deposit bottle.

"Operation Lemming" was brilliant. The U.S. government touted the deposit bottle as a major step in corporate good citizenship. Politicians became Pepsi's patsies, Coke's clowns. Talk about irony. The government banned Cocaine and then endorsed its replacement. For cola drinkers now left money (2 cents for the small bottles and a nickel for the large) with storeowners, a.k.a., dealers, their cola connection. Money to ensure they would return. A twisted soda spiral of demand and demand. Buy. Leave money. Consume. Return to get money. Buy. Leave money.... It was brilliant. Legal addiction that was good for the environment. The Cola Cartel headed home happy that fateful day. Not knowing that years later, kids like myself would do all in their power to break the cycle, actually refund the bottles, and turn the cash into Hershey Bars and Ring Dings. Coke and Pepsi had many challenges. RC Cola hoped they would someday be more than something to have with a Moon Pie. I headed to the Main Street Bar with a bag of six empty bottles and eyes full of hope, blissfully unaware of plots of global magnitude.

The Main Street Bar was about as far from global as anything in existence. In fact, what transpired inside that building was virtually divorced from the rest of the planet. Basically, it was a typical corner bar. In the one square mile town of Keansburg, there were 36 of these Black Holes. This dubious distinction made the town itself a spacial anomaly worthy of full shields and phasers permanently set to stun. The Burg was the Milky Way of taverns.

Keansburg was a virtual quagmire of corner bars. Bars in all shapes and sizes. Bars named for streets, Center, Main, Park, etc. Bars named for the owner and person most likely dispensing the libations like Ted, Pete, Kay and Ted, a different Ted, I think, but who knew what the hell that particular Kay was up to. In the spirit of creativity, owners like Crawley, Keelen, Kinlin, Balbach, and others opted for their last name in neon lights over their establishments. Being a beach town, some of the bars had nautical names like Marina, Club Miami, odd, being we were not even close to anything named Miami, and the Clipper J. Keansburg was home to the Wagonwheel, the Flamingo, The Willow Wood, and many others. No Dew Drop Inn though. Sounded too made up for the Burg.

Bars were real things owned by real people in Keansburg. We knew Crawley. He knew our family. Bars were a part of the fiber of the town. My father did his part to support the fiber. It was a big part. When it came to taverns, our town was on a high fiber diet. Do the math.

Jersey Sure

Thirty-six bars in one square mile. Take the population and subtract those of us under age. Alright, only subtract those of us underage who did not drink. Then minus the folks who owned the bars as well as the others who worked at the bars and you have a few less people than there were actual bars. A dry spell for my father signaled economic recession in Keansburg. Bars were the town's economic base. There was no such thing as too many of them in this blue-collar oasis.

The Main Street Bar was our tavern choice since it was the one that hosted my father most often and it had a package store alongside that, among other things, refunded deposit bottles. Just as a first kiss becomes the comparison for all to follow, the Main Street Bar stuck in my mind as the typical bar as sure as the memory of that first tongue visitor in a virgin mouth set the stage for all thereafter.

The Main Street Bar, located as one would suspect, on Main Street, was a good representation of all corner bars. It was a simple cement building with an unassuming neon sign beaconing travelers. Innocent. Inviting. Once inside however, travelers entered a substance-based Twilight Zone. Things that entered the gravity of corner bar ceased to exist in the outside universe.

Many locals were stuck in the orbit of such places, more so than they would even admit. They were linked by the seemingly colorful camaraderie of kindred spirits. Kindred spirits, more ghoulish than Casperish, gathered around the cauldron of kegs and bottles. The circular bar their altar of hope in a bottle and answers from a glass. The congregation was friendly, deceivingly so. Everyone knew your name. They also knew your weakness. The delighted denizens of the dank and dour welcomed you to wallow with them. All those lovely faces in the dark.

For the Main Street Bar was dark regardless of the time of day. Visitors greeted the place with squinty eyes that never fully unsquinted while there and, in extreme cases, never returned to full unsquityness. A souvenir of your visit as sure as a T-shirt claiming "I went to the Main Street Bar and all I got was squinty eyes." I knew that look well since folks from the darker half of the place had to ease over to the lighter, but still darker than normal, segment of the bar known far and wide as the Package Store. The jangling bell over the door advised them of a visitor from the outside world. Reluctantly, they shielded their eyes and inched from their ground level underground to sell joy by the six-pack and bottle. This time a kid with a bag full of empty bottles greeted them.

The crew of the package store portion of the establishment did not exactly welcome me with open arms. Once their eyes semi-adjusted to the light, they realized their visitor was merely a kid with empty bottles to return. They hoped against hope that I was there to exchange the empty bottles for another bottle of soda. They prayed to omnipotent gods of the cola cartel that I would keep the cycle of demand and demand alive. I saw it in the slits they called eyes and placed the bottles on the counter and spoke. My words cut like a knife. "Deposit, please." Their already lukewarm welcome cooled noticeably. Luckily, there were some advantages to Buddy's binges. I was offspring of one of their best customers, so they did not refuse the request. Nor did they relish it. Change changed hands with silent indignation on one side of the counter and only slightly repressed glee on the other. They headed back to their cave of choice. I headed to the candy store.

My candy-buying skills were among the best there was. I knew the terrain, the odds, and my own tastes. A few years, or even months earlier, and I had not experienced enough longing to hone the art. Older, and the concept of

Jersey Sure

self-sufficiency would taint my efforts as it had Sis and, even more so, Jack. I was in the zone. At the zenith of candy buying ability. I was one of the best.

While most stores in the 'Burg carried candy, only a few qualified as true candy stores. I knew them all but frequented the store closest to my house, an obvious choice for my budding shopping needs. It was right across the street from the Main Street Bar. The stereotypical corner store across from the stereotypical corner bar. My own crossroads of comparisons. Buddy mastered one corner, me the other.

Joe's Corner Store, actually Louise's but affectionately called the Guinea's, qualified as a candy store. Barely. The items stocked there ranged from foodstuffs to household items, normally one of each and all overpriced. The owners lived above the store. Shop for some bread at dinnertime and the sweet smell of spaghetti greeted you, along with a grumpy owner who complained while you struggled not to notice the errant strands that dangled precariously from his chin. Joe was an older gentleman renowned for his goiter. It was big and grew out of his neck like a small head. Complete with whiskers and occasional pus, Joe's goiter was quite the marvel. It was what you remembered about Joe. The guy with the beard? The man with the straw hat? The gentleman with the walking stick. Joe? With the goiter? It was his mark of distinction. Not in malice, just in fact.

Joe was a quiet man. Not mean, but not friendly either. More store equipment than real person, Joe just was. He was rarely seen alone. First generation Italian immigrant, Joe spoke but a few words of English but knew enough to fill a few orders and made change if required. But except in the rarest of cases, he was not required to do so alone. Someone else ruled Joe's universe. A four-foot tall and equally wide force to be reckoned with in that particular corner store in the form of Joe's dominant spouse, Louise.

Largely due to Louise's sheer determination, this first generation American- Italian duo adapted quickly to American capitalism. They knew where the money was. Big stores had better prices. Big stores had better selection. Big stores were clean. Corner stores took the "we have only one, you need only one, you are gonna pay" approach to the shopping experience. They stocked for desperation. Owners like Joe and Louise loved selling toilet paper, the ultimate supply and demand product. They enjoyed desperation in their clientele. They thrived on stressed and captive customers paying top dollar for a roll of dried and crunchy toilet paper caked in dust from the shelf on high. The urgent customer asked and Joe slowly grabbed the picker thing and fetched the item from on high. They charged whatever the market would bear plus ten percent and smiled as they rang it up on the cash register that was older than both of them combined. Although they could not say the word monopoly, they became one and used it to their full advantage. These two Italian-American entrepreneurs stocked one of most items and laid in wait. USA sono bono.

Candy was a different story. The selection of sugar-based items was vast and very, very sweet. Joe and Louise even had a case solely for confectionary delights. They went for the traditional approach. Display cases were the norm. Louise opted for that. Not the stand alone case but a case on the shelf, between the rack of bread and another of soda bottles, glass ones, with just enough room for two, four in a pinch. Kids, not soda bottles.

Kids nestled in that snug space, with bread and soda bookends, and reviewed an impressive collection of possibilities while Joe and/or Louise shuffled from the back of the store to service their prey. The drug of choice? Candy! The penny stuff was stocked on the bottom shelf,

Jersey Sure

eye level since it was the most common purchase. The more expensive nickel items on the second shelf, tiptoe for us most. Louise reserved the top shelf for the Almond Joys and Mounds, a childhood rarity at ten cents each, along with gum and lifesavers, a strange hybrid of sweet and habit.

To eleven-year-old eyes, it ran for yards with shelves upon shelves of future dental work. We knew of the enamel erosion therein or the Novocain from hell that could lay ahead but risked it nonetheless. We saw only sweetness in all shapes and sizes.

Penny candy offered a broad array of choices. The gummy ones; red-hot dollars, Mexican hats, Mike and Ikes, etc. Licorice in the all shapes and sizes; red, black, and even brown. Whips, ties, even record shaped. Good old standby, Bazooka bubble gum, encased in Joe's, bazooka not goiter, adventures and the promise of wonderful and valuable gifts. Bazooka comics were Green Stamps for kids. I pictured one of us as a 60-year-old man hoping for another 2,365 comic points to redeem boxes and boxes of them for a ten-speed bike or several dozen pairs of X-ray specs. Jawbreakers lived up to their name in the form of chipped teeth and sore molars. Flying saucers, that tasted just like Holy Communion only with little beads of candy inside. Yum, yum. Wholesome and sacrilegious at the same time. Who could resist? Then there was the Tootsie product line. The rolls, in penny and nickel size. The Pop, which was a tougher choice since it cost 2 cents and thus equaled 4 red-hot dollars. A kid had to be committed to a Tootsie Pop for it was an expensive choice. We may not know how many licks it took but we knew how many cents it did. Caramels and all the varieties of caramels. The ones that were square and came in chocolate as well, ummmmmmmm, or the others with the caramel around white filling, white is a flavor when you are a kid, that made for fun as you oh-so-gently eased the white filling out of it little hole. Viola, caramel turned ring! A strangely exotic tongue exercise even for fifth graders. But the King of Candyland was born with the beloved cocoa bean and its many uses.

Chocolates of all shapes and sizes. Nonpareils with the strange name but awesome taste. Chocolate encased in foil to represent doubloons of decadence. Treasured coins of chocolate treasure. Eatable enigmas. Chocolate wrapped balls of stale malted milk. Cocoa was king! Licorice be damned. The company that ruled in Chocolate, controlled candy consumerism. Competition was tough in chocolate land. In the land of cars, Chevy and Ford vied for the public like Archie and Jughead after a ready to put-out Veronica. In Cola land, Pepsi and Coke duked it out like Superman and Batman to see who was really super. In the sugar-based battleground, the superpowers were Hershey and Nestlé's.

By far, Hershey had the better selection. Two for a penny kisses of sweetness. Plain bars with handy preformed squares that made sharing a science, as well as unavoidable unless you were alone. The almond bar that fostered hording since it broke so badly. The less-popular Krackle. Nestlé's Crunch kicked Krackle's ass while Hershey won in the almond selection. The plain bar was a toss up. Both Nestlé's and Hershey offered chocolate bars of equal joy. Nestlé's was a tad bit lighter in taste and my personal choice, although Hershey had a lot going for it. There were rumors of an entire town centered around chocolate and all things chocolate hidden somewhere in the hills of Pennsylvania. Hershey had a town of chocolate? Wow. Still, I was loyal to Nestlé's because they sponsored the Roy Rogers Show and had Quik, the chocolate powder that made milk a good thing. Got milk? Without Quik, who cared? Nestlé's also had Farfel, the dopiest puppet dog ever created. Farfel sang

Jersey Sure

the Nestlé's theme song. A theme song that was really Farfel spelling Nestlé's as if on Quaaludes. After all, who could argue with a puppet dog who affirmed that "N-E-S-T-L-E-S, Nestlé's makes the very best……..chooooooooooocolate" Farfel sounded a lot like Goliath on Davy and Goliath. That disturbed me a bit for reasons I did not understand.

Nestlé's and Hershey were not alone in the fight for market supremacy in things chocolate, however much they tried. Mars entered the fray with bars in the form of Milky Ways, Snickers, which were basically Milky Ways with nuts, and the more unique Three Musketeers Bar and its velvety nougat taste. Mars' main success did not come from bars. Mars lettered in chocolate with what became a staple for candyholics. M&Ms! Treats that melted in your mouth and not in your hand. We saw naked peanuts on TV dive into vats of candy coatings and emerge as things we wanted to hunt, capture, and eat slowly. M&M bagged them for us and created a rainbow of tantalizing treats. Delights that could be jammed by the handful into a watering mouth or be sorted by color and eaten methodically. A cornucopia of colors and flavors. Yellows and greens, were eaten first since they were my least favorite. Dark Brown were most plentiful but still good. Most kids ranked reds as the best but I was a sucker for tan. Tan M&Ms were rare and hence desired. Mars knew how to market candy. There was also the choice of plain or with peanuts. Plain M&Ms were smaller ovals while peanut M&Ms were, amazingly enough, peanut shaped. Plain you popped in your mouth and ate. The Peanut ones were often peeled meticulously so the peanut was eased from the casing and eaten closer to its original form. Quite the science. Mars took on Hershey and Nestlé's and expanded the offerings for the good of all and the future of dentists for decades to come. All this in a case for the asking, if you had the coin of the realm.

Gilbert Van Wagner

A sometimes overpowering array of options for a sugar-deprived youth with deposit bottle money burning a hole in his pocket. I scanned the selection and weighed the possibilities. Bags of penny candy? Five nickel bars? A daring splurge on the rare Mounds? A mix of all of the above? I evaluated. I considered. I pondered. I took way too much time according to Louise. "Come on, I haven't got all day.". She had a tone that tainted almost every encounter.

Although a kid dealing with an adult, I was a kid with money and that equated to power. My selection was slow and deliberate to ensure Louise earned my patronage. She fussed a bit but acquiesced nicely. Money bridged the age gap quickly as she filled the bag and converted cash to candy. The outcome was a Nestlé's bar, a Milky Way, a bag of M&Ms, plain, with five cents worth of red-hot dollars, two brown licorice, a red licorice, and four Mexican Hats. A bag full of wonder in hand, I headed home to dinner. Meat and Potatoes tasted so much better with a Mexican Hat hors d'ouvres.

Catholic Everything (Alter Boys and Diners)

My Catholic youth was not limited to experience at the hands and yardsticks of Nuns. As a good little boy, baptized into the faith of my parents, church activity in Saint Anne's Church on the corner of Carr Avenue and Churchway, open to all, call for times of Services, was far more than Mass on Sundays. Like it or not. In the category of shut up, it's good for you. Catholic was not just in the inner sanctum of the building, it was all around me. I attended Catholic School, taught by Catholic Nuns, with Catholic prayers to start the day, Catholic songs at breaks, and Catholic kids all around me. Basically, it was Catholicism by immersion. Baptists thought they had the full body thing going on, but unless they never left the local river, they had nothing on how immersed the Catholics were. Especially for us kids. As children in the Catholic Church, our immersion was deepened by service to the church community. We had two choices. Do it or die. Slow and painful death. The Nuns, Priests, and parents used Calvary as the template should we think we had options. There was selection though. Not in the Chinese restaurant range of possibilities but choice nonetheless.

For girls, community service to God and Keansburg was most often accomplished via choir practice. Although the annual May cat fight to determine who was sacred and pretty enough to crown Mary with lovely flowers was a sight to behold, it only filled the community service square for one pristine virgin.

They did not actually test to ensure the lucky selectee was a virgin. They played the odds that the flower girl not deflowered. A girl around 10 years old. One a year. In a town of many families. The adults did not wish public embarrassment should their honored guest be known in the biblical fashion. They aimed for the pre-begatting stage of life. Rumor had it the selected virgin and family signed some form of release.

One girl, gussied up for Mary and the Fruit of Her womb. Community service with an audience. The other would-be flower girls for Christ settled for choir and hoped little Miss Prissy would fall and break her halo. Catholic girls were quite spirited when it came to being named the Crowner of Mary. It was a moment of public holiness. This was even better than a birthday corsage. Any girl with a birthday could have bubble gum dangling from ribbons in a corsage, but only one girl each year was the flower child for Mary. The whole town watched as a beautiful ray of feminine sunshine blossomed like a tiny bride and placed a small ring of flowers on a concrete statue of the Mother of Jesus. Sometimes even the Bishop came by for the festivities. Spring. Flowers. Songs of the Queen of the Angels. It was a moment of glory. The choir sang, while wishing the primadonna of the moment great bodily harm. Choirs were sometimes more than they appeared.

I actually tried out for choir. It did not go well. Seems they wanted people who could sing. Although I made

Jersey Sure

up in quantity, i.e. volume, what I lacked in quality, they recommended another career choice, church service-wise. The route for most Catholic boys. Altar boy. Serving Mass with Priests in front of all those in our community. Cassocks and Smocks were the uniform of choice, Roman Catholic Church choice, not the boys. Some of it was fun since we got to play with fire in the form of candles and incense. Sometimes, on the High Masses when holidays drew the occasional Christians, we walked up the aisle with the Priest and that was sorta cool. Made an entrance. I liked that. We also worked from the Sacristy before Mass, which was a pre-game show in and of itself. Being back stage, behind the scenes, we saw outtakes first hand when Father stubbed his toe and called Jesus in a way he did not mean to. Once he stubbed it really hard and called the whole Holy Family, "Jesus, Mary, and Joseph!" He must have thought Mary was not listening as he hopped about for he called her again, "Sweet Mother Of Jesus!" Repeat until pain subsides seemed to be his prescription that day. Most days he just came in. Black Cassock and collar. Priestly in the Spencer Tracy model. But the Mass required more. Robes, colored to fit the season. Altar boys got to see the Priests prepare for the work that was their calling. It was part theatrics and part theology as they donned their robes, suited up, and awaited their cue. Each had a style all they own on the Altar as well as back stage.

Most peeked and did a headcount. Father Corrigan did and almost always smiled at the familiar faces in what he clearly felt was his flock. Others were not so jovial and kind. Some had X-ray vision. They saw beyond the faces and right into purses and wallets.

It was most likely my imagination but one of the Priests, one I called Father McGive-it-to-me, cha-chinged when he counted. If he smiled that is. If there was not a cha-ching, the lecture was sure to involve the importance of giving. Father McGive-it-to-me did not play around when it came to the collection plate. He related grace and cash flow. Indulgences! Get your Indulgences! Two for the price of one! Sins forgiven! Step right up! Indulgences! He was a Catholic Capitalist. Charity began at home. Your charity. His home. He amused me. Jesus kicked out the moneychangers. It didn't take. Altar boys saw the men behind the curtain and some of them were a sight to behold as well as beware.

Before we got to see behind the curtain, we earned our way to serve the Lord in the form of learned rituals and rote prayers. Prayers memorized in a deader than dead language of Latin. Usable in no other setting.

Those who studied French hoped for a trip to France someday to be insulted about how badly they spoke the language. Kids who mastered German hoped to spekizee in Rhineland should the opportunity arise. Some chose to learn Spanish so they could head for The City and curse with a select group of the natives. Latin? We would need a time machine to find someone who spoke it just because they spoke it. Scholars learned it to be snooty. Archeologists learned it so they could read those stones and stuff they dug up in places with faraway names. Teachers learned to teach something with little to no risk of being corrected by anyone anywhere. Priests learned it to talk to God via the Mass. Altar boys learned it but never really learned it.

We memorized prayers the priest kick-started and we finished. Human parrots. Polly want a cracker. We said things without any real idea of what they meant. We sincerely hoped what we said was somewhere close to what was required. There was a cheat sheet but it was tough to read something that was meaningless and then speak it as it meant something. Perhaps Altar Boys who could went into politics later. As for me, I mumbled it rather than botching it and hearing from Father Whoever about my sad use of a

Jersey Sure

language not even used in Latin America, a region named for it! I went extra loud on the Aduim Que Latificots, since there were several, and cranked it up on the Spiritous. Basically, I bluffed as I knelt on the Stairway to Heaven. It worked. It helped that the Priest was pretty busy with robes, candles, incense, genuflections, and the hocus-pocus only he understood. Most of the congregation was asleep and the few who stayed awake most likely did not know Latin anyway.

Catholic congregations got their best sleep while visiting the House of Lord. Communion with the nap made it the bed and breakfast approach to honoring God Almighty. I guess that was why they called it the Host. Catholics loved sleep in church. Peace of the Lord be with you, but please do not snore.

Over the centuries, The Catholic Church tried many things to counter this trend but had little success. Sackcloth was sacked. Ashes reduced from full body dustings with hot embers to the Brylcreem approach of a little dab 'il do ya. Whips and chains were kept well out of sight due to some very bad press during the Inquisition. Fire and Brimstone threats failed to heat the audience awake. The omnipotent church almost gave up, but some conclave in some century opted on a special arrangement rather that miss the basket passing opportunity should people stay home to sleep. The best Cardinals met. Bishops of note entered the fray. A few Priests of renown consulted. They pondered and probed. They asked and analyzed. They wondered and wished. They sought and solved. The best in the business. Cream of Catholic everything. The answer? Bells.

Altar Boys were actually human alarm clocks, in the form of bells they rang. Bells that chimed at special times. Bells that let folks know when the good part of the Mass, the Communion, arrived. After all, we did not want the men and women of the parish to miss their opportunity to partake of our Lord and Maker merely because the monotone of a garbled language they did not understand put them to sleep.

The sequence of events with the bells was crucial. First bell, wake up and get out your money for we are a'coming for it. Second bell, get ready to come to the railing and have communion. The second bell was my favorite since the congregation herded politely to the railing to partake in the Eucharist. Orderly. One row at a time. Like very well behaved cows headed for dinner at the trough. Moooooooo. Mooooooo. Ring a Ding. Moooooo. Moooooo. I rang the bells and thought of the triangle Cookie used on Rawhide to call in the drovers. This Gil favored that part of the Mass for I got to ring the dinner bells and then hold the plate under each of their chins, some had more than one, while they opened their mouth for the goodness of the Lord.

There was only one option, a plate to the Adam's apple, or place where it would be for those graced with bosoms versus that lovely lump in the throat, and the placement of the wafered holiness on the tongue. Only the Priest touched the Host and he washed his hands in front of everyone so the Board of Health allowed him to serve so many. We approached the railing and fed the multitude. Priest and Alter Boy side kick. The Batman and Robin of host distribution. Mass was a Holy thing and Altars boys were important members of the cast.

The pomp and ceremony impressed everyone there. So serious. So somber. So solemn. Of course, we altar boys occasionally injected some levity. The slapstick of bells rolling down the stairs at a moment of solemnity was a sure crowd pleaser. An extra nudge with the plate to the throat of a buddy was a great gag. Chuckling through the Sussperiate could be a laugh. It was a tough crowd, since

Jersey Sure

most were asleep and the ones that were awake were busy praying and stuff, but they usually remembered being in any of my Masses.

I spent several years as an Altar Boy but somehow remained unaltered. Fourth grade was a serious time for my service, serious in that humor was limited. Fifth grade was much looser. Looser in the form of knowing what I could get away with and what would result in penalties. I served Mass at nine, snuck some wine, and had a wonderful time. All in all, it was quite fine. Then they scheduled me for the dreaded morning Mass in the convent. The Convent is the place they hold the Nuns. Goddesses of the classroom. Rulers of our days. Nuns who were faces encased in habits and Wimples. Wimples. Those white things that hid their heads and made folks wonder if they had hair under there. Were all Nuns bald? Did they shave their heads? We all pondered. Conjecture was that all Nuns were indeed shaved. We hoped to find out when assigned the duty of Mass server for the morning convent mass. Actually we hoped to survive being in Nun-Dom. An empire that had it own set of rules and was ruled by Queens. Serving Mass in the convent was an exact science. We were told to do it exactly as the Nuns said. They did not leave much room for interpretation.

Enter through this door between 6 AM and 6:15. Do not be late. Bring your Altar Boy costume, AKA Cassock and Smock. You will be directed to small room where you can dress. Do not talk with the Sisters should you encounter them. This is their home and you are a visitor who should not intrude on their time. If they address you, answer politely and quickly and go about your duty. Rules on top of rules for an experience that made for nightmares now and therapy later. One Altar boy, one Priest, and the Nuns.

Gilbert Van Wagner

It was the epicenter for danger. I was alone and potentially way out gunned.

Some small hope in that Convent Mass was usually quicker since it is in a smaller chapel with a small attendance. It was a Common Mass, the church had High Mass and Common Mass, the abridged version but not called the Low Mass. Too Common I guess. Each day the Nuns had Common Mass. As if a room of Nuns ever qualified as common.

The day arrived. After the warm welcome of the page of special instructions, I was eager to be in such an inviting territory. Just me, the priest, and the Nuns. It ran through my head like "Lions and Tigers and Bears, Oh My!" No trio of heroes here. It was me versus them. I would rather face flying monkeys but that was not an option. It was Nuns. A dream come true for a would be class clown and smart-ass. Basically, I was scarred shitless but did want the Nuns to see because they spotted weakness and crushed it with vengeance. I arrived early and felt like a visitor to a maximum-security prison. With a grand bluff of nonchalance, my little feet exited the safety of the pre-dawn dark into the seemingly even dimmer light of the convent. It was a civilian lady that showed me in. Surprised me a bit. A civilian in the Convent? Passing through? Indentured servant? Nun in civilian drag? What secrets did she know? Was she part of the Master plot to break me? To alter me? She seemed harmless enough, but I was on full alert when in this strange new land of many Nuns.

It seemed forever but finally the priest arrived. It was Father Corrigan. It was always Father Corrigan at the Convent mass. For the Nuns had clout and mandated which Priest served the Mass. Of the two in the parish, the ladies habitually chose Father Corrigan. He met their stringent requirements. He was a Priest. He was the ranking Priest of the Parish, a Monsignor. His Masses were reverent but short. He was punctual. He was old. Old is good in a man when you are a celibate Nun. Very good.

He suited up quickly and was extra quiet. Sure, it was early, but something told me he was nervous too. We were two males in female territory. Potentially very hostile territory. The Mass started, and it intimidated in ways few things ever could. They were all there. Sister Cornelia. Sister Celeste. Sister Mary Bernadette. All of them. A sea of black and potential evil. Critical mass, nun wise. All there with me and a priest as scared as me. I fussed throughout. We both did. Brethren. Linked by the common enemy. I sensed it. He sensed it. He was chosen because he was old. I was chosen because, well, I never did figure out why I was chosen. But there I was. Under the most demanding of scenarios. Boy in Nun-land. Sure each step was evaluated. Each kneel had to be extra crisp. Each ring of the bell exact. The jokester in me stayed home this morning. I was as serious as ever. The touch of the saving dish firm and offering safety, but not risking decapitation, as tempting as it might be. It was excruciating. Thirty minutes of abject terror under the microscope of twelve sets of very critical eyes.

Later that day, Sister Mary Bernadette commented I did a good job. My step was bolstered for weeks afterwards. I did not really understand that the nuns merely noticed the priest, and perhaps the small nervous boy, but saw exactly who they needed to. They focused on the right Guy. The Guy who was there before any of us showed and would be long after we departed. They saw Him in their room last night and in the classroom later that day. Their eyes knew exactly where to look. Inside.

Serving a week worth of Masses in the convent was stressful but did have its reward. for an altar boy. Father

Gilbert Van Wagner

Corrigan was good since he took his designated dish helper to breakfast on Saturday morning after the service. Father Corrigan was a lovable old Irishman who did not drink. That I knew of at least. Old Irishmen who did not drink had a lot of time of their hands. Old Irishmen who did not drink and were not married had an abundance of time on their hands. Old Irishmen who did not drink, were not married, and had no intention of ever being married had time not just on their hands but coming out their wazoo. Father Corrigan liked to bond a bit with the Altar boy of the week with his famous, after the service, breakfast at a diner.

Diners were places unique. It sure wasn't the food. Filling, but only in the "you gotta eat, so eat" type way. The sounds defined a true diner experience. Diners were symphonies of sounds. Violins of voices and cellos of conversations blended into hums of fits and starts. Communications not fully heard but always in background determined the ebb and flow of the piece. Dishes banged and slammed from table to washer and back in an endless cycle of replenishment like instruments of intense percussion. Dishes built to withstand a life of abuse and neglect, each thump a testament to sturdiness. The brass of the silverware added to the calliope like cymbals to fill out the orchestra of the slightly edible. There was a randomness to it all that formed the experience. Sometimes soothing as you surrendered to the Opus and other times offensive as it encased unwilling, along with willing, customers. Like it or not, the sounds were the show, and peace and quiet were not in the repertoire.

We had two diners in town. Mac's and Martini's. Names so real to the stereotype that they sounded fake. Food basically the same at each. Breakfast, greasy and available all the time. Lunch, but steer clear of anything from the

Jersey Sure

hash family. Dinners of meat and potatoes in all variations there of with the same effect. A stomach full to bursting and a tremendous urge to loosen your belt and belch really loud. Anytime of the day or night, patrons ate to excess capacity at these mobile homes turned restaurants. However, true diner aficionados knew diners were truly there in all their silver trailer glory for the just after midnight, headed home drunk crowd.

I experienced both diners but with different outcomes. My father liked diners. They were gritty. Colorful. Human. On occasion, not often enough to my liking, he took us there. Breakfast. Anytime of the day, at a diner, it was breakfast time for my father. He did not ask me. He merely ordered.

"How ya doing, Mac?" A question he did not really want answered to a man who was not really named Mac. Mac was more than a name. It was a term of endearment. "Can I help you, Mac?" made a stranger a friend in need. "What's up, Mac?" was polite inquisition to a new acquaintance. Mac was also a threat to an otherwise unidentified Joe. "Whatta lookin' at, Mac?" "Ya got something to say to me, Mac?" Mac was quite a diverse word. I wondered how all the real Macs out there felt. I do not think my father knew any real Macs, but he sure knew a lotta of fake ones.

"Bacon and eggs for both of us. Eggs over easy. Coffee for me and soda for the boy". We sat and watched. My father smoked and become one with the crowd. Just another blue-collar guy having lunch with his kid. Somebody's Mac. Happy to be so, if it was friendly. Ready to kick some ass if not. Occasionally we talked. Not much. But we communicated. Diners are like that.

Father Corrigan had a whole different idea of diners. We hopped in his car that Saturday morning and headed

Gilbert Van Wagner

for the highway. That meant Macs Diner since Martini's was down by the Boardwalk. Or so I thought. Not about Martinis, that really was on the boardwalk. About us heading for Mac's. That is what I thought. I was wrong.

He drove his really nice Chrysler New Yorker right across Highway 36 and headed up Palmer Avenue. No left turn at Robert Hall's to stop at Mac's. For a moment, I thought all the excess energy and build up passion had effected his thoughts but settled in after he drove and chatted as sure as any sane old Irishman. We went all the way up Palmer to Highway 35 and made a left. Hmmm. Last time I was up this way was for a suit from Sears.

Mom liked Sears suits. Hence, I wore Sears suits. They did not suck. The price was right. Sears suits for boys my age were made of some industrial strength cloth good for the time of purchase until too big to worn unless you were Lil Abner or kin.

Father Corrigan drove right passed Sears as well and did not stop until he arrived at what I learned was his Saturday place, his version of a diner, Perkins' Pancake House.

Perkins' is not a diner. It had aspects of a diner but was modified. A counter and booths? Yes. But the booths had cloth-covered seats and were comfortable. The counter was clean and spacious. Noise? The calliope of sound that made a diner a diner? It had some noise but most of it was muffled in the back and escaped in spurts as the doors to the kitchen opened and closed. It changed the entire experience. I entered with Father Corrigan and was accepted by association. The regulars, both staff and customers, greeted him warmly. In this circle, the Monsignor was a celebrity. I was his flavor of the week, Altar boy wise. I smiled that lame smile kids used for people we do not nor will not ever know. My eyes looked at the gathering as we were escorted to our table, Father Corrigan did not like booths. I did not see a Mac in the bunch.

Jersey Sure

We ordered. I did Pancakes. After all, when with a Roman Catholic in a Pancake house………. The pancakes were good. Father and I talked a bit about things. Conversation more than casual but not real personal. School. Teachers and classes I liked as he asked me of them. Free time. It was not awkward but it was not comfortable either. We learned a bit of each other but knew we would not be everyday friends. Although I did not know it at the time, it was a template business dinner. Dine. Talk. Enjoy. Move on.

The ride back to Keansburg was nice also. My stomach was happy. A week of Convent Masses was completed. We drove home in the quiet but it was a quiet of connectedness and filled me as much as the pancakes even could. Father Corrigan dropped me off in front of my house. That made for good press in the neighborhood. A priest in front of my house. Sort of when worlds collide. I could imagine the busybodies as they pondered. "Isn't that Father Corrigan's car?" "Is that Gilbert he is dropping off? " "Hmmpfft. I am surprised it is not a cop's car!" "Maybe there is hope for the boy."

Convent mass was finished. I was still alive and had not been excommunicated. Perhaps there would be more Convent Masses in my future. God, I hoped not.

The Boardwalk
(Trigger and the Ghost Town)

Less than three weeks before Easter and it felt like December, weather wise. The windows whistled in the war of heat in and cold out. The floorboards chilled and made the rugs more inviting. Brisk was the word. Cold was the feeling. More echoes of the past season than hints of the next.

It was a day to hibernate for many. The people at Campbell's lived for times like this. Soup, reading, and napping day for the older folks. Soup, TV, comic books, and getting on parents' nerves for kids. An inside day. The solitary inside eleven year old me looked out the window and felt the calling. I headed out.

Hat and gloves on, jacket zipped all the way, and hood up. Barricaded outside while most were barricaded inside. A harsh, crisp wind nipped but found few to bite since most stayed indoors. Weather kept others somewhere else and made outside more mine in the process. There was strength in that, and it fueled me. It was the right time for a walk. Not a walk with friends but all alone. My time. I smiled and walked into the wind. Purposefully, as if on autopilot. Destination determined but unknown. Neat stuff at

Jersey Sure

any age. The type mood that made you skip. Just because. So I did. My skip turned, as it usually did, to a gallop as Trigger and I rode down deserted Main Street, the sight of my breath our only company.

Seeing your breath is cool. Good for pretend smoking. I dismounted and enjoyed a Camel. Smoke from inside your body was also great for being a steam engine that puffed down the street and chugged in time with the pace. So I ditched the Camel and rode the rails a while. Woooooo. Woooooo. Puff, puff, puff. Woooooo. Woooooo. Breath seen also entertained so I enjoyed the show, as Director, Star, and audience. A few fake cigarettes and a train ride or two later, I was on the beach.

The sky was crystal clear. If crystal was blue and surrounded everything in the cosmos as far as the eye could see. It seemed the clouds thought it too cold to come outside as well. Across the choppy bay, the New York Skyline was as clear as if seen through brand new glasses with the right prescription. The wind literally took my breath away so I tilted to the side a bit. Mariah plastered my hood to my head. My stance braced against the force of the cold and honored Mother Nature in the process for we were together. Just me and her. Cold is cool.

With my hand eye shield, I spied intently across the water. The bridge in work was neat to watch any time of the year. The towers were up, the ramp almost over. Pretty soon it would be a real bridge. Something Verrazano or the like. My father called it the Guinea Gangplank. Something told me that was not a good thing to call it in mixed company.

It was low tide. The shoreline was longer at low tide. At least it seemed so. At high tide, it went from beach to bay with little room to wander, walk, or otherwise occupy the time. High tide was better for swimming. It was much easier to swim when the water came up above your knees without a four-mile hike to get deep enough. High tide was also better for skipping rocks. You got a lot more skips when you did not have to avoid sandbars and the like.

Low tide was different. Crappy for swimming and skipping rocks, but much better for other things to do at the beach. There were little islands you could jump to and almost stay dry. I did. The dry part not as successful at some times as it was at others. I leaped from island to island to shore to island and back. Rock throwing was tougher at low tide but I tried it. It sucked. So I walked. Feet where water would be in a few hours. I stamped. Piss-clams fountained in reply. I stamped. They fountained. Jump. Fountain. Jump harder. Fountain more. Wooo woooo. Train on water. Wooo wooooo. I chugged away from the clams. They most likely did not mind. Piss on them if they did. Woooo wooooo. Somewhere the train turned to Trigger, and I rode with the wind to the my back. Heeyah! Giddiup!

The Boardwalk! That's where I would go. No one would be there. Everything would be boarded up. All the rides would be elsewhere. All the tourists home in Brooklyn Heights and the Bronx. All the locals, except one, hidden from Mother Nature this special day. It would be a Ghost Town. Giddiup! Let's go, Trigger. Let's get to the Ghost town. My hand flayed the reigns as my faithful steed and I headed for the sure to be abandoned Boardwalk. Giddiup!

The Boardwalk on Keansburg actually had very few boards. The boards lived on in name only with state of the art asphalt in their place. Asphaltwalk just did not have the draw so the Keansburg Boardwalk was once and would remain a Boardwalk. It, as should all true boardwalks, even asphalt ones, bordered the water. In this case, the majestic Raritan Bay, complete with a 17 mile removed view of the famous NYC skyline. The Boardwalk drew city folks to the Burg. A blue collar mix between Atlantic City in its heyday and Disneyland based on card tricks versus magic.

Jersey Sure

This collection of rides, gaming stands, food booths, and bars was the major source for summer revenue and made my hometown what it was more than any other feature. The Boardwalk was Keansburg Central.

Keansburg Central was empty this day as I rode up on Trigger. The seasons under my Cub Scout belt were enough to know this was a different place. It was not the same Boardwalk summer folks experienced when they added to the census roles of our hamlet on the bay. For those of us who lived in Keansburg all year round, there were actually two boardwalks. Two places as different as Patty and Cathy. One pair of matching bookends, as different as night and day.

We shared the summer one with the City dwellers that came to live in our home, their resort town. Fathers rented one of the many bungalows, planted the family there when the kids were out of school for the summer, and visited on weekends to escape the heat of the City. They "summered" as sure as the la-te-ta, hoity-toity folks did but never thought it as such. They also thought they knew the Boardwalk. But they only knew the summer one. The summer boardwalk gave laughter and joy to all. It was background for pictures of laughing and loved children. The Summer Boardwalk wore a suit. The winter one, sweats.

The Winter Boardwalk was not a destination. Outsiders just did not go there in the winter. If anyone ventured to that part of town at all, it was most likely a wrong turn and very likely to be just a drive by. Reset in the town, you had to be going there by design. Folks who called our home theirs only in the summer and others who drove by what they thought of as empty did not get to see the Boardwalk that was mine today. That was perfectly alright with me. For this was the Winter Boardwalk and we did not like to share it. People who called resort towns home knew things of Boardwalks that visitors never got to see.

Gilbert Van Wagner

The Boardwalk in the winter was personal. It was special. Boarded up stands could be seen as lonely but residents knew they rested and savored the quiet as sure as any one in town did. Time to recharge. The stands barricaded with boards to withstand seven months of wind, rain, and loneliness. This faithful friend loyally waited for the summer folks. It knew those seasonal users were not everyday friends but donned a new coat of paint and withstood the barrage each year.

I slowed the palomino as sand became asphalt and open space closed to the outer edge of the Winter Boardwalk, a much, different and somehow more special place. It even felt like a Ghost Town. No one in sight. I dismounted. Trigger followed should I need a quick escape. I approached slowly, honoring the quiet and rest of the place. Trigger stood quietly as I pondered the place ahead. The entrance to the Boardwalk. Not a transition. In or out. The open space closed as the opening formed, kiddie rides on one side and stands as well as other rides on the other. No beach in view. No city skyline.

There was so much in that emptiness. It was a brisk day, exactly right. Thoughtful. Exposed. The wind buffeted as if to emphasize shelter therein. A solo wanderer, the wind, and buildings that beckoned. Silence that spoke of yesterday sounds, screams of wins and losses. Sounds that would return soon and change the Boardwalk. The sound now was of the wind and little more. Wind that funneled the main walkway between the stands as if to fill the space. A sound reserved for us year round folks.

I eyed the empty stands, so full of stories. The silhouettes of the kiddie rides now tucked into the owners' garage for a long winters nap. Where there had been hundreds, now just one. The quiet spoke to me, intensified by memories of those summer sounds. Just me and Trigger. These times of isolation turned the boardwalk into mine.

Jersey Sure

Others came and went. I was here now and would be again in days ahead. Summer days but winter ones as well like this day. This was my time with the Boardwalk so I shared it and headed for the entrance. The same wind that nibbled the paint and wood every day bit my face with moisture from the bay.

The Boardwalk bracketed me as I walked cautiously into the Ghost Town of memories. The midway a vacuum for the wind. My personal Wind-Tunnel of Fun memories. The fragrance of the bay and the snow replaced the aromas of hot dogs and zeppolies. Some sensed sadness on empty winter boardwalks. Not me. I sensed the specialness. Part of me saw what was there only in memories.

Kiddie rides in storage, the train tracks minus the train. Spaces where boats, planes, and cars should be. I saw the images of them with a smile. The magical Kiddie rides. In Keansburg, the rides on the Boardwalk are not just rides. They were part of the continuum of a lifestyle. Same rides for generations. My older brother rode them as a youth and ran them as a teenager. To the youthful me, there was nothing better. My brother drove the train! He slipped us extra tickets when we rode. I had connections. Someday maybe I would drive it as well. Is there a better destiny? I walked the rails and imagined.

The train was my personal favorite. It had it own track, as do most trains when you think about it. But this track was exclusive. Special. One reason for its course and one reason only. A gleaming apparatus of blue and orange proudly labeled just like the big trains. This oval was the domain of the spectacular Keansburg Kiddie Park Express. Our own Atchison, Topeka, and Santa Fe. A Super Chief of not so epic proportions. One engine and three pull behind cars. Barely two feet high but much bigger to the passengers. It was not there as I walked its tracks alone, Trigger on call, but the rails told me of its trips in the past and hopefully the future, although at my age it was already the look around in case folks noticed how big you were stage. So I savored the many in the past but knew there were but a few in the future.

It was not just a ride on a Kiddie train. For kids lived it as sure as any train trip. They lived each trip with a joy commuters and adults seemed to forget along the way. We sat in the diminutive cars with most of our tiny torsos bravely above the fray but we rode the rails as sure as anyone on any trip at any time. Alone. Adults strapped us in and wished us well. We were a whistle blow away from independence. Lap belts in place, we headed waaaaaay down the track, over an eighth of a mile away. Never out of sight but we may as well have been invisible. It was much more than an oval that looped back to the start. The Keansburg Kiddie Park Express took us away. No hands to hold. No looking both ways. No staying in the yard. No playpens to contain our bodies and our spirits. No older brother and sister to watch you. Woooo-wooooo. Escape! Out there was not just out there. It was anyplace and everyplace we wanted. An engine fueled by gas took us to places fueled by imagination. Imagination normally fueled by TV, but what the hey.

My train rides, today when it was actually a train walk and on days when the now empty rails really held a train, were normally Western since that was the theme of most of my favorite shows. I was a TV kid. Even the trip in my mind's eye today on a train that was not there with no one to keep me company was straight from the land of Cowboys and Indians. Not just because Trigger waited either. I was a cowpoke at heart and my rides on the rail showed it. Real or otherwise..

The train barely eluded outlaws, largely due to my sharp shooting from the high-speed bullet express. Bullets from bullet. Poetry. Indians chased me and all the passengers

Jersey Sure

with battle cries right from movies and TV. They never caught us because I was armed and dangerous. The other passengers always thanked God I was there with my trusted six shooters, rifle, and endless supply of bullets. Saving the day was always so rewarding. The engine on the Keansburg Kiddie Park express burned gas but I swear I heard the puff-puff-puff of the steam engine as sure as Dale Robertson's Iron Horse. It sure sounded like the best locomotive man ever made.

I walked the tracks once today but the Summer train circled the track three times. One ticket meant one ride but one ride meant three times around the oval. These pull-throughs resulted in waves and greetings followed by escape and adventure. Sometimes we stopped because some whiny little urchin could not sustain the adventure. The greedy me fed on it and hoped the engineer would lose count and go an extra lap for the inconvenience. Sometimes it happened. More often not. Today it was not a problem since I walked the oval only once and there was not a pull through. These tracks held great memories but were shit to hike. I hoofed it over to where the Cars would have been.

It was an empty circle, but I walked it and saw them in my mind, planted to an oval merry go round type thing that was somewhere else today. Cars right from a Popeye cartoon. One of the real early ones now on reruns courtesy of folks like Officer Joe Bolton and Captain Jack McCarthy. Not much adventure, but it was only one ticket and they had a bell. They did not usually hold my attention for long. Today was no exception.

The Airplanes that were not there today either were from the same early animation. Basically cars with wings hung from strings. The aircraft, not the wings. I buzzed the pattern and moved on. The merry-go-round went somewhere for the season, but the discolored concrete marked its parking lot. The Rockets were not but I circled where they did and would, albeit about three foot lower than them in their glory. The Boat ride was a bit sad since the cement pond was empty and looked lonely. Rides that were not rides were only cool for a little while. Giddiup!

The stands called. Some labeled. Some not. All known. French Fries. Some of the best in the world. Kill the Kats but, if the Kitties were in there, they hid from death pretty well. Trigger galloped but responded to my turn commands well as our path zigzagged the midway. I was careful to zag over to the bay side of the midway when we passed the Spook House. Nothing really scary in there, but no use testing fate. I spied it, and it spied back. Giddiup! We whirled passed the big merry-go-round place and the Ferris Wheel spot. Only echoes of yesterdays rides there now. Heeyaa! I picked up the pace. Bent into the ride just like Roy did on the opening of his show. Fast. Really Fast. Fast passed the presently empty stands that waited for another season.

Just boarded up stands on the winter Boardwalk. No one checked. There was no need. No one opened and closed. Those were actions of that shorter, noisier, more intense season. The boards, latched on those summer eves, nailed shut. I spied them and sensed the security therein. Giddiup! Into the wind. The stands could not turn to and fro on whims as I did on Trigger. The stands just stood. The weather beat at them from the hollow midway. The paint bore marks of storms that had been. No money slid the selection boards.

Whoooooooooaaaaahhhh! Trigger had a hard time responding to this abrupt order to stop but managed. Such a damn good horse. We walked over to one of the stands, and I dismounted. There was a crack in the board. Investigation was warranted. My eye to the crack adjusted and peered in. It took a minute. Trigger waited patiently. I adjusted to super squint mode. One eye closed, the other looked into

Jersey Sure

the hole and pierced the gloom of a stand all alone. Ah, there we go. Super squint worked. I saw. The very board itself, where you "lays your money and takes your chances" in boardwalk and carny lingo, leaned against the wall. It hid in the dark of the empty inner sanctum. The same dark embraced the seemingly lifeless cube. No sunlight filtered in. No power sprang the bulb to luminance. It did not matter for there was not much to see. The shelves, summer homes for teddy bears and stuffed friends, now held rat droppings, paint chips, and a solitary, rusted penny waiting for a new home in someone's pocket. Cold, musty smells filled the emptiness. No cheers or boos since there were no spins. No one shouted, "Here's your winner. Rolling in". The wheel that "never lied" in the summer laid against the wall, Dad the winning square for months where no prizes were awarded. I saw it all. A secret shared with the stand and me. Cool. Giddiup!

Next stop the pier. What was left of it anyway. Hurricane Donna took most of it away. The Keansburg Boat was no longer. Seemed folks did not like the idea of swimming out to and from the boat to ride to NYC. Go figure.

The hulk of this pier, as did the hulk of any pier, intimidated. There used to be boards there. Boards we walked on. Boards that held that little train that was really cool and that sometimes we got to ride. Boards that let fishermen do what fishermen did, or at least to let them stand there and have a beer. Boards that we looked through and saw the water down there. Boards there were now somewhere in the Bay or points beyond because Mother Nature, in the form of Hurricane Donna, decided to beat the shit out of the Keansburg Pier.

Now there were pylons. Pylons pointed to the sky. Pylons that missed their primary purpose in life. To hold the boards and make a pier. Pylons askew, asunder, and a mess. Pylons now a tribute to Mother Nature. Pylons now reminders that all things men made were temporary things. Pylons turned grave markers in the Bay. Pylons that inspired me to mount up and go home. Giddiup!

I looked at the stands from the beach as we rode back to the ranch. I needed to look. The pier tainted things a bit. I was not sure why but was sure it was did not feel good. Like that time Mom took me to her old neighborhood in Brooklyn. She saw what was. She looked through the eyes of memory. I saw it as it was right then. She saw smiles and laughs and love and people and memories. I saw the run down neighborhood and felt sorry that she had to live there at one time. She apologized and explained it was really nice back then. She seemed sad as she apologized for what was not there. I understood how she felt that day when I saw those pylons. For they reminded me of the pier and what would not be again. The stands reminded me of what was and would be again. Sleep is easier on the mood than death is. Suddenly I wanted to see Mom and Dad. Even Sis. The pain in the ass. I smiled. Giddiup!

EASTER
(Jelly Beans and Pagan Babies)

Lent is the perfect Catholic season. It is all about suffering. Catholics are big on suffering. Sackcloth and ashes were never far from the minds of good little parochial people. Wallowing in anguish was the overarching theme for the forty plus day pageant of pain. Lent took us Catholics to our roots. Like it or not.

It began with dirt. Dirt from fire. Fire like the fires of hell. The hell we risked if we did not follow the tenets of the church. Tenets owned us. The Church said so. Lent helped the Church say so. The Easter celebration began as a bunch of Catholics ran around the town with dirty foreheads. Foreheads dotted with ashes. Ashes shouted "Game on!", Lent wise. Wednesday was Lenten kick off. Why Ash Wednesday? Sundays were taken, Catholics linked Fridays to sacrifice already with the fish on the plate and the One on the cross, the Jews cornered the market on Saturday, and Thursday was tied to Ascension Thursday. The options were limited. The council of muckidy mucks that picked Holy Days ruled out Monday almost immediately. The odds of getting Catholics back in Church one day after Sunday were slim to none, so that left Tuesday or Wednesday. Tuesday did not split the week evenly, so Wednesday was named as the cigarette remains on people's temples day. The other two days remained up for grabs, liturgically speaking.

Catholics with dirty foreheads began the cornucopia of ceremonies. Rosaries said alone. Said in groups. Prayed on buses, in churches, while walking, just before sleep, to begin and end each day. Beads abounded. There was no bad place for a rosary. Novenas as people guarded statues cloaked in purple. Statues hidden in plain sight. Stations of the Cross every Friday, another reason we did not have Ash Friday. Special Masses.

All things combined and ensured Lent overpowered Catholics. Lent was the main event of the Church Year. Advent was okay but was overshadowed a bit by Santa, reindeer, and all those pagan things we loved so much. Lent was longer than Advent, had better PR people than the Easter Bunny ever mustered, and became not just a time but a month and half long journey. Heck, Mardi Gras was nothing without Lent. Mardi Gras was basically the "let's party down because Lent is coming and we have to give stuff up" celebration.

Some non-Catholics did not get Lent. What was all the fuss? Was it about no meat on Fridays? That was not unique to Lent. Was it about the Stations of the Cross and remembering how passionate the events of Good Friday were? Surely that helped. Was it about giving up candy or something else you like? That was part of it. During Lent, good Catholics gave something up. Something they liked but would not have all the way from Ash Wednesday clear through to Easter Sunday. Most kids gave up candy and sweets. A few gave up television but they normally did not make it. Catholics greeted each other with "What did you give up for Lent?" I answered "homework" once to a

Jersey Sure

Nun and discovered first hand, her hand, that Nuns did not joke about Lenten sacrifices. Nuns also did not let others joke about the Easter build-up. Lent was serious business. The Catholic Church reminded us to suffer as we took our unworthy, sinful, and sorry souls to the joys of Easter.

The messages were powerful and repeated often. Come let us celebrate the Stations of the Cross. This was where they jammed a crown of thorns on Jesus. He let them *for you*. Crawl to the next station with me. This was where they beat Jesus with a whip. Thirty lashes. He let them *for you*. This was where they made Him drag a heavy cross and watched Him fall over and over under the weight. He let them *for you*. The Nuns made sure we heard the message. The priests made sure we heard the message. Our parents made sure we heard the message. Guilt distributed freely and frequently. Made giving up candy seem a lame tribute for what Jesus did for us.

Luckily, Jesus' message was more powerful than the slanted version. His suffering was real. His death was as vivid. His offering was much more though. The true Lent message bobbed and weaved through the landmines of disinformation. Give. It was the right thing to do. For Him. For you. For others. As you give, appreciate what you have. When you are grateful, you are happy. When you are happy, you are a better person. The Lenten message was one of giving. The Catholic Church wrapped it in suffering and tied it with a bow of guilt. Some folks never got past the wrapping. They avoided a gift, earned hard but free for the taking, because the box made them feel bad. Lent was good. Once we got by all the trappings.

Giving took many forms in Lent. As with most things Catholic, money was the coin of the realm. Not just one collection each Sunday but two. Fund drives. Bishop's relief fund. I always wanted to donate an old bottle of Kaopectate to that one. Cash for Christ seemed the message. For

Catholic School kids there was no higher measure of giving than to redeem a Pagan Baby.

Pagan Babies were five bucks a pop and you got to name them. They did not come home with you. They did not need to be changed, at least diaper wise. Pagan Babies were from some foreign land and needed to be baptized and saved from being pagan. According to the picture on the box, they came in all shapes and sizes. Little faces. Innocent faces. Longing faces. Not much younger than us, but they did not get to go to Catholic School. They did not understand Lent. They did not have what we had. So we put pennies, nickels, and dimes, rarely was there a dollar bill involved, in a box to rescue unfortunates from across the sea. I always envisioned an entire village of pagan babies in Africa just hoping my dime would complete the fund that would have missionaries roll into the village with Holy Water and hope.

I knew these good deeds of missed Nestlé's Bars and Mexican Hats would not go without reward. Some day, someone would walk up to me and ask if I was so and so and if I went to Saint Anne's school in 1964. When I confirmed my identity, the person would grab my hand eagerly, eyes all aglow, and let me know they were a former Pagan Baby. They would shout to all within earshot that they owed me a debt of thanks for saving them from a life of paganess. It was nice to make a difference in the world. Especially when you could do so for a few pennies, a nickel, and the occasional dime. Especially during Lent.

Easter culminated the Lenten season. Part of the joy of giving up candy during Lent was the great amount of candy in the Easter basket on the important Sunday morning. This Easter was no exception. I sprang from bed and immediately looked for jelly beans. Why jelly beans? Seems in the Van Wagner house, the Easter bunny chose to hide jellybeans instead of eggs. My friends spoke of the hunt for eggs in

Jersey Sure

the yard as part of their seasonal celebration. I woke to discover jelly beans in my shoes, beneath the very pillow I rested, under my underwear in the drawer, in the pockets of my new clothes, and at places that made the quest such a challenge. Even little kids could find eggs since their very size often gave them away. A jelly bean hunt was not for the faint of heart. Sometimes, months after Easter, a jelly bean that eluded the hunters would surface. Took a while to eat those.

Jelly beans found, I think, and Easter Basket opened, tested and rebuilt, I took a bath and got dressed for church. A new suit. A Sears suit. A sharkskin suit from Sears. I do not think it was real sharkskin but that is what the salesman called it. It was shiny. It was silver. It was new. I had new everything on Easter, that was part of the tradition. New underwear. New socks. New shoes. A new haircut. New suit. Styling. The tradition was a new suit for Easter that became the school suit next year. The cycle of clothing that held for my brother before me and me now.

I walked downstairs and prepared for the compliments. The my-my-my, don't you look nice compliments. Not from Sis. She usually stuck her finger in her mouth as if to puke when she saw me all clean and stuff. The comments came from my mother. She picked out the suit and felt responsible for how it made me look. Dad would comment as well. Something nice but not over the top, sappy like.

Sis and I headed for Church. Easter was the single most important day of the church year. The day we celebrated Jesus rising from the dead. The day that signified salvation. The event that meant all would be well thanks to events of long ago. It was the high point of being a Catholic and Saint Anne's Church would be packed. Each pew full. Each service full. The choir loft jammed packed. Every seat taken and people standing in the aisles. All in their finery. Everyone would be there.

Mom and Dad stayed home. They gave us a dollar for the collection though since this was such a special day. Mom taped the envelope shut and marked the amount on the outside. She would have made us get a receipt but knew the priest would be too busy to write it out. Sis and I got to the Church and sat with friends for the biggest Mass of the Year.

It was also the longest Mass of the year. God, would they ever shut up? Two gospels? Songs about everything from Rolling Stones to Rising Hope. Songs written years ago. Songs designed to bring peace and joy and to enhance the celebration of the moment. Songs hopelessly butchered by Catholics of Saint Anne's parish. Seems all the good singers were protestant. We sucked at singing, so we sang low to hide it. It did not work. It not only sounded bad, it sounded like no one actually opened their mouths to let the words out. The result was a muffled cry of Joy to the Lord. Thank God Jesus did not die just for people who could sing. Otherwise, Catholics faced eternal damnation rather than just torture by butchered music once a week.

Once a week was actually a bit of an overstatement. The weekly folks were few. Old folks went each week. They figured it was time to get to know Jesus since they would be crossing over soon. School kids went each week. They had to. It was the weekly envelope turn in to prove to the Nuns they were there and then take home the Church Bulletin to waiting parents to prove they dropped off the envelopes of cash. Those two groups comprised the weekly attendees. On Easter though, there was five times that many. I guess folks did not want to buy a new suit and then stay home. They came to Church on Easter. They would be back on Christmas. A few would even make the Holy Days of Obligation. Most would not. It might have been the music that inspired them to stay away.

Jersey Sure

The Mass ended and Sis and I walked home. Together even. Nicely. The weather was nice. The day began with gifts of candy. Lenten sacrifice was over and made the candy all the sweeter. I had on a brand new suit. All was right with the world. What could possible go wrong?

The events that answered that question began with something my parents did not say. They did not say, "Change your clothes before you go out to play." We had a nice Easter meal, ham was the tradition and I headed out to play. New suit on. Complete with new suit jacket. The one new suit for the year. On a glorious spring day. I called for Greg and he came out in his suit as well. We looked great. We walked tall. Two little executives. We headed for the Boardwalk and opening day of the season. We enjoyed some time on the beach. Somewhere along the way, we forgot we were in suits.

Sharkskin does not hold up well when playing. First it got a little dirty. Then it got a lot dirty. Then it got a little hole in one knee. Then a little hole in the other knee. Somehow both those holes got bigger and bigger. So big that both knees came fully out of the place that should have been suit.

We wrestled in the sand but stopped for a bit just to catch our breath. It was then I noticed the suit. Was sharkskin. Was new. Was beautiful. I saw it clearly. It was no longer beautiful. It was no longer new. It was hard to tell if it was even sharkskin anymore. This was not good. I knew this was not good at all. Oh Jesus, help me on this special day. Oh Jesus, whom I gave up that candy for in Lent, help me figure out a way to hide this. Oh Lord God Almighty, take pity on me and help me find a way to explain this away.

Panic took the place of playing. I was not alone. Greg's suit was pretty bad as well. We looked at each other, linked in tragedy. A joint funeral? Side by side graves? We headed home. To doom. No denying. No hiding. He said

Gilbert Van Wagner

good-bye at the corner of Seeley and Main. I halfheartedly said goodbye too. Both of us too inside our own gloom to really ponder the other's fate.

As I walked up the lawn, the door opened. My Mother looked in shock at the person coming towards her. She did not wait long to react. She let loose words of shame that made the Stations of the Cross look like a Sunday picnic. Between the "What the??" and "How the hell could you???'s, I made it into the house. She took me to the dining room so my father could see what "his son" had done. Easter Sunday and I was suddenly the son to see. Mom lambasted. Dad scowled. I cowered. They dispatched me upstairs to change. To change from the brand new, now completely destroyed suit into something else. Something I would not wreck. Something less valuable. I was sure more chastisement would follow when I returned. Was not sure if there would ever be an end to the consequences of an Easter suit ruined.

Halfway across the living room, I turned my bowed head back to see the two who surely questioned what they had done to deserve such a dismal son. I spied both parents with hands covering mouths that only barely suppressed laughter. In that moment, a ray of hope almost as sure as a empty grave shone. Easter is a time of miracles. A time of hope. A time of life after death. My suit was dead. I crucified it but knew not what I did. There would be life ever after though. After all, I sacrificed Hershey bars and Mexican hats to make it so. This Lent stuff really worked. Thank God for Easter miracles. Thanks for answering my prayers, Jesus, I owe you one.

Weekends
(Bike Rides and Junk Cars)

The weekend. Woo Hoo. No school. If I could avoid chores, the days were mine. Alright, not fully mine since the Pope said Peter said Jesus said come visit me on Sabbath or go to hell. Sunday had an hour or so spoken for. The rest of the weekend was mine. If I played my cards right. I intended to play my cards right.

Intentions were one thing. Reality was another. I fully intended to enjoy the time. I was not sure what activities would be done when, but the days would be mine from eyes first open on Saturday. After all, there was no school. It was a weekend! I may not have a plan but I planned to use the time wisely. For fun. For nothing. For hanging out. For TV. For movies. For whatever happened. Weekends were like that. Two day summer vacations regardless of the season. So I eased from bed just after the sun and headed into the day. My time. Unless, Dad had his way.

Dad ruined weekends. He did not think of it as ruining weekends, but his idea of what kids should do when not in school was a far cry from my idea or even Sis's. Dad was a weekend party pooper. It was like he forgot what it was like when he was a kid. Unless of course he was a slave laborer or a rower on a galley ship as a child. Whatever screwed him up in his youth, Mister Buddy fuddy-duddy did not grasp the importance of weekends for kids. He thought no school time was work time. That sucked. So weekends were avoid Dad time. I loved him but could do it without seeing him on those special days between "school's out" Fridays and "Is it time to go back already???" Mondays. Dad was a line of sight tasker. If he saw you, he tasked you. Consequently, we played a twisted version of hide and seek with no all-e-all-e-in-free. Once he caught you, it was game over, working boy. I planned to win. Getting up early was the strategy with the best chance of success. Sleep in and not only did he find you easy but he woke you up with the dreaded "Are you still in bed? Get up. We have things to do." I knew Dad and intended to exploit that knowledge to escape his web of work. First question after eyes open was the same each Saturday. Was Dad home?

It depended upon the moon. Sunny side up that segmenting satellite, and Dad ran amok with abandon and alcohol laced glee. Since it was a non full moon weekend, Dad had two places to be this potentially fine Saturday. Work or home. When not running with the wolves, Dad was a creature of limited habits. He either went to work or worked at home. Dad's job was as blue collared as blue collar gets. He felt strongly about his place of employment. He hated it. He dreaded it and all about it. Sometimes the very thought of his job made him ill. Nevertheless, he did it. Definitely not for himself. He did it for me, and Sis, and Jack when he still lived at home. He did not just father most of us. He was a Dad. He hated every minute of every day at National Lead.

Located at the base of the not so scenic Edison Bridge, National Lead, a division of Dutch Boy Paints, would have shocked Upton Sinclair. This smoking cesspool of toxic happenings of little consequence belched fumes and smut

Jersey Sure

into the ever-graying skies over Sayreville. My father labored in working conditions right out of the dangerous side of Gotham City for people who could give a shit less about him and whoever the hell his family was. I knew that to be a fact since on the worst of days he mentioned it with helplessness and disgust. But except for the boneless caretakers or some really big demand for titanium-laced goodies that generated weekend and holiday efforts for all the laborers, the draconian National Lead usually closed on Saturdays. Dad had two days to forget the working conditions. Forty-eight hours to detox. To purge pollution from his body and his soul. But he did not do that. He had a hard time not slaving even when away from the masters. He worked at home, and we all worked at home when he did. We all shared the fruits of his discontent. Provided he saw us, that is. So once I answered the first question as to his whereabouts, the second question of the weekend was how I got out of the house before he turned me into chore boy.

If I was lucky, he was still in bed. If not, I was screwed. The dad-was-home version of my Saturday routine began. Shhhhhh. Don't wake the big, bad man. He had plans, and they were not the same as yours. Shhhhhh. I eased from bed with stealth and hoped to escape before Dad woke with chores and errands and crap that turned the house into a work camp. Stalag One Maple Avenue.

I snuck downstairs for some cartoons but did not make it passed Ruff N' Ready. Tough to enjoy television when two inches from the screen with no volume, but it was either that or risk waking the overseer. A hushed bowl of Cheerios later, the TV went dark as well as silent, and I eased upstairs for a quiet bath, a quiet get dressed, followed by a quiet sneak out the front door.

At the front door, my thoughts turned to Sis. Should I wake her? Help her escape before taskmaster rose? Risk waking the freedom sucker in the process? Screw her. She was on her own. It was every kid for themselves. Good luck, Sis. Shoulda got up early like me. So long, Pops. Work hard.

Not sure where to go or what to do, Maple Avenue became my path to whatever awaited. I walked. Without purpose except to avoid chores. Alone time. Just me. The virgin street was mine for the taking. I took it and penetrated the day. The street had that early morning Saturday feeling. Not much traffic. Actually none. Foot or otherwise. The go-cart sound of a power mower snaked across the terrain with that distinctive ebb and flow as someone rowed their yard a street or so over.

Crickets silent. Lightening bugs dark as the dawn doused their lights. Cars as cool as they would be as the warmth of the day eased upward. I savored the solitude, as temporary as it would be. My street was my street. It had one life form. Me. I was the man with the top hat and cane in the Maple Avenue monopoly. Awake, alive, and in charge as most of my world slumbered. Fleeting power though since the slumberers slumbered less and less each passing minute. Yawn here. Yawn there. I could almost hear them escape the sand man as I walked. Soon, the man in the top hat would be the boy in the crowd. Soon people would wake and turn me to we.

The town woke up differently on weekends. Especially on Saturdays. The world was a better place on Saturdays. A day of hope in lives of quiet desperation. Five days a week belonged to the man. Sunday was God's day. Saturday was everybody else's. Folks woke up happier. Waking lips spread in do-not-have-to-go-work, do-not-have-to-go-to-school, and do-not-have-to-go-to-church smiles. Hope made people happy. I liked that. Needed more of it than

Jersey Sure

walking would give me, so I snuck back to the house for my bike.

Fearing my footfalls would travel Maple Avenue, cross my yard, shake the house, and wake my father, I tippy-toed to the shed. It was not locked. It never was. The door creaked. The dank and dour dark held the morning light at bay, but the bike was the last thing in, so it was right there for the taking. I stepped into the cool carefully to free my bike and ride to freedom. The musty shed would be Dad central once he woke up. He loved to putz and that meant work now and repair later for him, or someone that really knew how to repair. The clock was ticking, so I moved from the shed to the street with transport at hand. The bike grooved the dew as I walked it to the sidewalk and mounted. Bikes got you where you were going faster, even when you were not sure where that was.

I did not know the destination but the terrain was well mapped. Mapped with experience. A hometown bike ride was exploration of the known. Cracks in the sidewalk did not surprise. Potholes were committed to memory. I rode down Maple and then up Carr towards but not to the school. Just in that direction. The way looked different on bike. Shorter. Not as personal. I planned to ride right passed Saint Anne's. Planned not to stop at the school on a day when there was no need. But I slowed.

The bike wobbled a bit as I reviewed the building that was my weekday existence. The school had that Saturday look. Empty, but resting versus abandoned. I slowed and stood on the pedals to balance the now unstable Sears industrial strength red bicycle. My Sears & Robuck bobbed and weaved. The statue of Saint Anne captured my eye. She seemed pure and smart. Inviting. Mother of Mary. Connected to the Man himself. The statue was not quite life-sized but looked as real as concrete people could. She was in my mind as the earth moved in directions not of my choosing. The concrete edge of the sidewalk embraced my bike's tire, and I headed over the handlebars as gravity took me for a ride

Saint Anne must have liked me that day for the grass greeted my head as I went from rider to person on the lawn. The bike veered towards the street but the front tire stayed put in the deeper than expected rut between sidewalk and lawn. Sears bikes could indeed somersault if the conditions were right. The conditions were right this morning. I tucked, rolled, and ended up the feet of Saint Anne. In one piece, both of us. I looked up at the sky in surprise and laughed. I was akimbo! Alive but akimbo. An ass over teakettle fall at the feet of Saint Anne made the word mine. For akimbo was a Wednesday word.

Each week, on Prince Spaghetti day, the teacher gave us a new word to learn. At least each Wednesday the teacher remembered. She usually remembered. She was big on learning new words. She planned to build our vocabulary, one Wednesday at a time. Her basic premise was if we used the word three times it was ours forever. She was right, and she had some really cool words.

Her first mid-week selection was cosmopolitan. There were not many words as cool as cosmopolitan. It sounded intelligent. Studious and all. I felt like I should smoke a pipe in my patched elbow tweed jacket whenever I used it. "I say, you are looking quite cosmopolitan, old chap. Pip, pip. Tally-ho."

Another Wednesday word was pensive. That became one of my favorites since it impressed my mom. One Thursday evening, Mom sat and read the paper. That was not something Mom did a lot, the reading part, not

Jersey Sure

the sitting part. Mom sat more than she read but tonight she read as she sat. There was something very interesting in the Red Bank Register that night for she was deep in thought. Opportunity presented, opportunity used. I said, with quite a cosmopolitan air, "You look pensive, Mom." She eased her head from behind the paper as if peeking from a shell. Her eyes smiled as she asked where I learned that word. We discussed the Wednesday word of the week, and Mom thought it was a cracker jack idea. I tried to make each Wednesday word my own. All of them became mine. Babble. Risqué. Yacht. Haberdasher. Melancholy. Ambience. Rabble. Right up until two weeks ago when the teacher introduced akimbo.

Akimbo presented a dilemma. Things were not akimbo much each day, never mind three times to capture and claim the word. I began a quest for things akimbo. Not much in the classroom nor on the way home. The word just did not present itself well in everyday life. Despite my efforts. It went from a curiosity to an annoyance.

At dinner, I pondered if the chicken with legs in the air qualified as akimbo. It did not. I forwent Quick Draw McGraw one night and watched the news. A big sacrifice since Bobalouie was more applicable in my daily life than Walter Cronkite. Walter helped the Wednesday word of the week program as he narrated some footage of the war in Vietnam. People in those shots were indeed akimbo. I did not speak it aloud in respect to those who were alive just before those filmed shots but knew akimbo applied. Akimbo worked once in the classroom when Sister Celone, aka Sister Sea Lion, dropped her chorus books as she headed back to her room after a lesson on Ave Maria. But two seemed the limit at opportunities to use akimbo. Until Saint Anne drew my attention and gravity brought the word to life. So I lay akimbo and laughed. Then righted the akimbo bicycle and got my previously akimbo butt out of there.

Not far from the statue of Saint Anne was the Church where we went to see her Grandson. It was church mouse quiet this morning. Saturday was not a big Church day for Saint Anne's. Confessions this afternoon. The early morning Mass over hours ago. It was silent time in the vestibule as I vehicled passed.

Church Street, named for the Methodist Church versus the Catholic one, was busy. Saturday on Church Street was quite a busy time. People hokey pokeyed into the Keansburg-Middletown National Bank, cash wise. Put in a little in. Take a little out. Then spread it all around. That's what its all about.

I stopped and rested the bike against the bank. The nearby bench had a much bigger seat so I used it and watched the world at the corner of Church and Carr. Starkey's was opened for business and business it saw. Seemed someone warmed each stool at Starkey's counter. Even without going inside, I knew it was the regulars. They looked comfortable there. As if in their spot. The coffee and paper bunch. Older folks. With money for coffee and time for talk. Although on the outside looking in, I liked the view. It was a club. Some smiled. Some drank. Others read the paper. The owner knew his turf. He wiped the counter after every visit. Coffee refill. Wipe. Pick up the cash left. Wipe. Take an order. Wipe. Chat a bit. Wipe. A shame he never bothered to clean the cloth. His coffee clients did not seem to care so he did not either. I did not hear his laugh but felt it as his head bent back at some clever, and most likely risqué, remark from one of the stool specimens.

The sounds on the corner played a chorus of life. The metal box that controlled the traffic light clicked each time it let cars go or let them idle. The gas station's I am here bell dinged as cars stopped for breakfast. Hither and yon sounds. Doors opened or closed as errands started or completed. Cars turned from Church Street and headed up

Jersey Sure

Carr towards the church. This junction in town was awake. Dad most likely was by now as well. That made me smile. Victory tasted happy.

I rode from Church Street to Main Street and passed Morrison and Sons insurance. Main Street was fully alive with people as well as cars and busses. So much so that I walked the bike rather than risk bodily harm, giving or taking. Kumizaki's was opened so I went in.

If there were other Japanese people in Keansburg, they never saw the light of day. In fact, Mister and Mrs. Kumizaki were the entire Oriental population of my world. They owned and operated a store that Mom said was a dry goods store. I guess that made sense since everything in the place was dry. I just knew there was a lot of stuff in Kumizaki's. Their store was crammed with crap. Cheap crap. Crap I could afford. Most of the time. Plus, they let kids just look around if they knew them and they knew me, so I looked around. The bell above the door let them know I was there. Mister Kumizaki waved and I returned it. Not sure if he knew much English but was sure he knew more English that I did Japanese.

All their stuff was made in Japan. Made in Japan meant it was cheap and would break easy. The break easy part was kinda bad, but the cheap part was right up my alley. All sorts of toys. Plastic cars of all shapes and sizes. Cowboy guns. Army helmets. Bags of soldiers with tanks in there along with cannons. Things in every shape and size. Plastic anything seemed the theme. Japan had more plastic mines that anyplace on earth, and the Kumizaki's were connected, plastic wise.

The Kumizaki's lived above the store. I never saw them out side of the store. They did not show up at CBS for bread and the paper. They were never in line at the bank

Gilbert Van Wagner

depositing money or paying their Christmas Club. They never walked the boardwalk on a summer day. They were not at Church asleep when they should have been listening. There were no little Kumizakis in class with us little Van Wagners. It was Mr. and Mrs., and they existed entirely in the building next to Dan's Music Shop and across from Safeway. They ate, worked, slept, and lived in the store. I liked them. Hoped they were happy. I waved and headed across the street to Safeway. Sayonara, Mr. And Mrs., Kumizaki.

The Safeway was crowded. Guess a lot of folks shopped on Saturday. Safeway was an in between store. In between CBS and Shop Rite. Not physically. CBS was a few blocks away while Shop Rite was clear over in Hazlet, a long ride away. Safeway was in between in that they had a lot more than CBS but less than the much bigger Shop Rite. We did our daily things at CBS and saved Safeway for fresher meats and produce. Today I just wanted a few grapes. They had good grapes. The store was three times the size of CBS and much cleaner. They had Lay's Potato Chips, too and that was special since they were new and much different than Wise. Lay's even advertised on TV with the whole betcha can't eat just one thing. Cool. Today, I did not have money for Lay's so had a few free grapes and headed up Main Street.

The Post Office was crowded, as well the pharmacy. Keansburg had three drug stores in town. We went to Marquet. They were all basically the same, but Marquet was closer to the house so they won our business. I stayed on the drug store side of the street, away from the thugs and drunks on the Flamingo Bar wall. These wanna be Bowery Boys were usually drunk and almost always pains to any kids. They were there almost all the time. I always

Jersey Sure

wondered what they did when not at the wall of the bar. Not much, since they rarely were somewhere else.

After the traffic light, I crossed Main Street and went over to the billboards. There were two in town. Both in the field between Crawley's and the Flamingo. I parked the bike and climbed up the back of one, using the crossbeams like the ladder they were not intended to be. The platform in front of the billboard made a great perch, even better than my tree in the front yard since I could see all of Main Street from here. Unfortunately, all of Main Street could see me as well so I did not sit there long. Adults were strange about things like kids sitting on billboards. Sooner or later, one of the them would say something that would ruin the whole thing. Safety and all that crap. But it was nice just to sit and watch as people went on errands and for walks. Time was nice to use when you used it to watch things. But time was still time and it was almost time to head home.

There was no more postponing the inevitable. I had to go home to face the music. To pay the piper. To take my comeuppance. All those things that came with escaping. It was time to pay for freedom. It would not be too bad. Dad would not kill me. Just make me rake or clean or tote or bale or something like that. The sun was an ally since it's day was almost half over and Dad usually did not work us in the dark, unless we really pissed him off. Mom would be home, too and that helped as well. Not that she was soft or anything when to came to warden-like pulling the switch things. Heck, she was brutal compared to Dad, but she was content as long as the house was clean and she was not the one who cleaned it. Also, she did not see the need to redo the rotting plywood in the cellar window wells with pieces of weathered wood not much better than the termite eaten shells that covered the only hopes for sunlight to the air pocket below the floor of the house. Plus, it was a nice day so Dad may well find the neighbors in the yard as all commiserated about life, love, and monthly bills. All in all, it seemed safe to head home now. I was also hungry. Home sounded good right about now.

Sis was in the yard and scowled at me. I smiled. She smiled a bit, too because she knew I won. Her half-hearted "You're in trouble" did not fool either of us. She appreciated cunning and guile as much as any kid. I looked for Dad so I could corner him before he cornered me. If he came a'lookin, my butt would be a'cookin. If I found him, he may be busy enough to just give me a look and send me to get something. Hopefully, he would not have time for a lecture. God, I hated his lectures. Dad was a first class travel agent for guilt trips. Smack me and get it over with, but lay off the lectures. Make me paint the house, rearrange the furniture, or clean out the oven, but do not hit me with any conversation that started with, "I am very disappointed with you...." Sheesh. Hated those damn lectures. Hoped Dad did not have time to talk. Yell, alright, but do not talk.

The twisty sound of a ratchet wench told of his whereabouts. Dad was having a car moment. He was a big car guy. Albeit used cars but big, used cars. The driveway showed it. No rinky-dink Ramblers or Mopar monstrosities for this man. No, Sir-re de. Dad was a body by Fischer man. A cushy ride man. American iron in massive quantity man. Only the best for Dad. More tanks than cars. Buicks and Cadillac's.

Three cars in one driveway. A Caddy and two Buicks. One worked. Partially. For now. He said the other two would. I think he knew he was lying as sure as we did. He was delusional about his mechanical ability. He thought he

Jersey Sure

had some. He did not. Put a hood up and Dad was there. Clueless that he was clueless. But his LeSabre worked, and he loved it. Dad had a thing for cars. Cars did not return the love.

The driveway showed it. Three cars resided in the grooved grass. It was easy to tell the one that worked. Air in the tires was the first giveaway. Mother Nature added her own clues. Grass and weeds encased much of the immobile pair. Two of Dad's fleet would have to be weed whacked as well as jump started, if the batteries were still there. If the engines were as well. Another clue about the one that worked was to look for the one that actually had all the panels and doors and parts and things that made cars look like cars. Only one of Dad's car looked like a car. The others looked like what they were, junk.

The two junkers looked comfortable, even if not complete. One car listed and the other squatted. Rust embraced wheels snuggled well inside their wells. Settled. Deep. Tire air long hissed elsewhere. The duo had not seen action as long as I could remember. Dad shared his fleet, one piece at time, to other shade tree mechanics with less understanding wives and smaller yards. Dad was a man of means when it came to auto parts.

They were parts bins to my Dad, rust heaps to my Mom, and playgrounds to me. His junkers were my get away vehicles. We did not have swings but we had a windshield slide, at least on the Caddy since it had a hood. Off the window and onto the crankshaft was not a good thing, so we did not butt wipe the windshield of the broken Buick. The Buick was the better hulk for pretend driving, though, since four flat tires made it nice and level. It also had a back seat so we could have passengers not crammed into the front as with the rear seat-less Caddy. The cars may have been eyesores but they were fun to have at hand. This day was Dad's day to work on the one vehicle that worked though.

The hood of the Buick was up. The hood was like the car. Big. Heavy. It blocked out the sun. It also blocked Dad's view. I dismounted, kickstood the freedom mobile, and headed for Doctor Dad, the mechanics' friend. His work on the car could mean several things. Ten minutes of tinkering and pretend knowledge or hours of flying wenches and bruised knuckles to go with his bruised ego. Dad was proud and did not like reminders that he was a bozo, car repair wise. I moved around the hood to be in view and see what he had in store for me.

I almost stepped on his feet. He was not just under the hood, he was under the engine. Feet out, tools at the ready. I squatted and asked, "What's up, Dad?'

He bent sideways a bit to peek at the upside down head peeking at him and asked, "Where the heck ya been, boy?

"Went for a ride, Dad." Then I shifted to offense. "Need some help?"

The rest was easy. Hand a tool or two. Ask a question and know that the answer was mostly mechanical term laced bullshit. It kept me outta trouble, though and made him feel good.

His work on the car was short-lived, lucky for the car. The neighbors came over and soon the yard smelled of cigarettes and beer. Lunch came and went. Burgers on the grill made for a nice dinner. Once the sun headed elsewhere, we headed inside for warmth. It may be spring but it sure the heck wasn't summer.

Dad watched the Big Preview that night. Neat movie with Susan Hayworth in prison for something she didn't do while she tried not to do things people in there wanted her to try. Dad wanted a treat so I popped the popcorn. In the pot. The old fashioned way. No Jiffy Pop for Dad the Purest. Oil. Seeds. Salt. Cooked with the loving hands of his child

Jersey Sure

while he watched the movie. At least with popcorn, I got a small bowl of it since I popped it and all. Dad and Mom got the big bowl. Sis and I got small ones. But it was good.

Headed for bed once Susan Hayworth was free, her dignity in tact. Took a bath first though. Had to be clean. Tomorrow was Sunday and Jesus waited to see me.

Sunday mornings meant Church. So off we went. Sis and me. We were dispatched to church together. It was overcast and cold for a spring day. It did not matter. We walked. Kids in Keansburg did not ride to Church or school. Come rain or come shine. Bodies by Fischer were not for us.

The 9 o'clock mass was the kids' mass, so that was the mass we attended. Off we went. Siblings. One simmered. The other smiled. The smile was on my face. Sis did not smile. She simmered and sulked. Seems she did not want to be with me today even if we did not have time together yesterday. She had an attitude from yesterday when I ran free and she helped Dad all morning and part of the afternoon. Especially since I did not get into any trouble thanks to my creative offense of helping Dad with the car work. Seems Sis was a bit put out. No big problem. She would get over it. Someday. So, I smiled. Just to piss her off. She walked without words. I let her and smiled even more.

Sister and Brother headed for time with Jesus as a family. Mom and Dad had other priorities. They were center aisle Catholics. My parents attended Mass when someone they knew walked down the center aisle, as in Weddings, First Communions, or Confirmations, or were laid out in a box in that very same center aisle. However, these same selective practitioners righteously required that we, their offspring and hope for the future, attended church each and every Sunday.

Since they were not there to confirm our attendance, we had to bring back proof. The all-important church bulletin. Not for the information, Mom was not a bake sale fan and supported the PTA by letting teachers associate with other parents. The bulletin was more than information for Mom and Dad. They really wanted evidence. Proof positive that we had our otherwise heathen butts in pews like good Catholic girls and boys. The Church Bulletin was the first thing Mom and Dad looked for when we returned from our time with Jesus.

With the many center aisle Catholics in Keansburg, there was a lucrative black market for Bulletins each Sunday in the small store just across from the church. Capitalism. Catholism. Merged in our great town. One enterprising youth went to the 7 o'clock mass and grabbed a bunch of bulletins right after Communion. He set up shop in the candy store across from the school and sold the Bulletins for a nickel a pop. The candy storeowners let him since kids paid for the bulletins and then spent the reminder of the offerings on candy and pinball games. After all, isn't God everywhere? Even in candy stores on Sunday mornings?

I knew today was a Church day though. Sis was in a mood and she was quite the little bitch when she was. With righteous indignation fueled from yesterday, she insisted we go to church. Sisters were like that. Especially this one. I was a kid brother and knew just how to piss her off. So I did. Quite routinely. So we had an understanding about our love for each other.

She hated me and I hated her. This mutual understanding was the catalyst for all our encounters. Love one another, my ass. She picked on me and I let her sleep in to wake to chores. Seemed fair to me. She won most of our battles so I liked winning even more.

Jersey Sure

Sissy had several advantages. She was bigger. She was stronger. She was vicious. I, on the other hand, was quicker and more devious. Together, we did our best to exist without acknowledging the existence of the other. It was not peaceful co-existence. It was war or denial and no point in between.

Sadly, my parents wanted us to play nice. Fat chance. She liked things like hula-hoops and hopscotch. While she could climb a tree with the best of the kids, it was not her first choice for activity. She was "developing". She was "evolving". I ran and jumped through life oblivious to all around me. We were at far different points in our youth, and the clashes became legend. As Sissy got prissy, her tolerance level for me disappeared.

The lowest point for this situation was on Sundays just like this. Headed for church like a loving family of orphans while mad at each other inside. Silence broken only with curses as we headed for words of inspiration by guys who knew Jesus first hand.

Mass was full, as was the kids' Mass each week. I sat with kids from class and we did Roman aerobics right on schedule. Stand. Kneel. Sit. Kneel. Repeat. The Latin of the service comforted. I actually knew a bit of what they said but that did not matter. It was like a mantra. A hum that took me places. I rode it to the beyond while moving in tandem with a congregation of locals. The Priest did his thing. The altar boys did theirs. The people followed along. All was right with the world.

The gospel that day was the Prodigal son. That one never made sense to me. The hard working kid got screwed. One off gallivanting and the other home working and the gallivanter got the party? Who was the smarter of the two? The priest talked about that in the sermon as well. He started out alright but then violated the rule of quit talking before the people quit listening. I yawned and fidgeted. Man, would he ever shut up?

The crowd fidgeted as well. Even the adults. One man had his head far down, in full nap mode. His wife nudged him and he snorted. I laughed. So did a few others who saw it. Then I saw Sis. She was smug and looked right at me. Seems she thought the Gospel was pretty much right on target.

The Communion was the usual pious march of people to taste the Lord. The Lord tasted a lot like flying saucers but without the little sugar beads inside. I let him melt in my mouth while I thanked Him for things. Even for my sister. The little bitch.

We headed home together. Bulletins in hand. We even talked a bit. Guess Jesus helped us from the inside out. Dinner was ready. Sunday Dinner was actually a late lunch. About two o'clock. Mandatory attendance. All of us around the table with meat and potatoes. Pork this week. Mom's favorite. We ate quickly, but it lasted a long time afterwards. Pop cut the meat as we passed plates and waited for our turn at the vegetables and potatoes. I took a little of everything. Even the sucky Sauerkraut. I had to. Mom was a stickler that we taste everything. She only took what she liked and what she wanted.

We talked at dinner. Light talk. Family stuff. There was a feel to it that made us all feel like things were alright. No one said it, but I knew they felt it as sure as I did. We did not stay mad at the dinner table no matter how hard we tried. All things were forgiven at the dining room altar. The bread of life cured things. Sis looked at me as I mixed my peas in my mashed potatoes. Green cherries amongst a mass of vanilla ice cream potatoes. Spuds made pod food

Jersey Sure

tolerable. She smiled and did the same. Dad saw it and did the same thing only he took it a step further. He mixed everything together. Meat. Vegetables. Potatoes. All in one big pile. Mom looked and disapproved but did not complain. She merely shook her head and smiled. So we knew it was alright.

Sis and I followed Dad's example. We whirled the meat with potatoes laced with peas and sauerkraut. Dad saw and proclaimed that it was good. "All going to the same place, right, Fat Boy?"

"Right, Dad."

We ate. We laughed. We talked. I do not remember what we said but I sure do remember that we said it. Dinnertime was good for us all.

Sis and I got to do the dishes. Like it or not. I cleared. Sis washed. I dried and put away. Mom and Dad went to the living room, turned on the TV, and settled in for a quiet afternoon of laying there. Sis washed and rinsed as quick as I could bring them to her. The small kitchen was not cramped. It was homey. I moved past her and began to dry the dishes so we could go onto other things. She washed the pots and pans last since they grunged up the water pretty good. I dried the dishes as the pots and pans filled the dish drain and then dried them. Sis finished her kitchenly duties and helped me put stuff away. Without even being asked. Pretty cool.

We headed inside. Dad and Mom watched TV together. Sis joined them but I didn't feel like watching anything, so I headed to the porch and the train set.

Dad set up a train set for me there. It was our Christmas set but it stayed up all year. My very own Lionelville. Courtesy of a piece of plywood painted green. It took up over a quarter of the porch with a little room to stand on one side to undo derailments. The transformer weighed a ton and powered the engine as well as the light on the engine and the smoking thing that sometimes worked but most time didn't. There were two switch tracks, not much good if there was only one when you think about it, and a Styrofoam tunnel with green and snow and everything. All in all, it was pretty cool to have a year round train set on the porch. I fired it up. The noise took me to trainland.

There is something about Lionel. HO trains had better detail and more writing and stuff but they lacked substance. Lionel made stuff that stood up to kids. The very train that circled the plywood today had been my brother's and took dart guns, attacks, and God knew what else. It still ran pretty darn good.

The porch warmed a bit as the train chugged about. Perhaps the transformer did put out some heat. I think it was more the connection with the station and the tunnel and the cars. It felt nice on the porch. The train chugged despite the weather. Woooo. Woooo. Pretty cool.

Somewhere between trip ten and trip ninety around Lionelville, the sun set. The train's light lit the way but only for a bit. For dark was cold on the porch so the train smoked to a stop in front of the station, and I headed inside.

Sunday lunches were scheduled and orchestrated. Sunday dinner was fend for yourself time. Dad made some Campbell's tomato soup and I had a bowl of that with crackers. That was a great Sunday evening meal after an afternoon on the rails. Tomorrow was school, and the weekend ended with the warm glow of canned soup in my belly.

Ed Sullivan entertained Dad and Mom so I headed upstairs to play. A train yard on the porch and a Western outpost upstairs, I had my own wonderland in the house on

Jersey Sure

Maple Avenue. The closet upstairs was not just the closet upstairs. It was Fort Apache. My very own full size model of Rin Tin Tin's home. It was not the only closet upstairs, but it was the only Fort Apache up there. The other closet was, well, it was basically a closet although it did have a really cool birdcage, minus the bird, on the shelf. The smaller closet was Fort Apache.

I set up the Fort and left it there. An out of site outpost for my use and my use only. Mom and Dad knew it was there, but they never played with it. Not while I was around at least. Sis never bothered with it either. It was right there, too. In between my room and hers. Part of me did not like that she did not bother. Most of me liked that she did not.

The Sears catalog had a real Fort Apache. Not real like out west with Calvary men who wondered what the hell they got themselves into and Indians who wanted nothing more that what they had before Fort Apache. Real in the form of just like on TV. About the same size too. Nineteen inches or so. Sears had the works when it came to Fort Apache. Lt. Rip Masters with the really cool name. Rusty with the turned up hat. The Fort itself with a full complement of soldiers and horses along with some Indians to be placed well outside the protective plastic walls of the Western base. The fort itself had gates that opened and closed, important during attacks. Fort Apache from Sears had walls with places for the men to stand to shoot safely at marauding multitudes. The Sears special had buildings too! A bunkhouse, headquarters, and the stable. All that in one big box for lucky boys and adventurous, trend setting girls.

I had Lincoln Logs, a hodge podge of plastic cowboys, horses, and Indians, and Lt. Rip Masters. It became Fort Apache without all the trimmings, the main boy, and the wonder dog. How Lt. Rip Masters came to reside in the closet at One Maple Avenue was a mystery to me, but I was glad he was there and dedicated an entire closet, at least the floor part under winter coats and miscellaneous clothing items, for his military career. Fort Apache, Keansburg style, smelled a bit like mothballs, but the men did alright thanks to good old Rip. As a plastic, looks like a person from TV, officer, there were few better. He led a ragtag but extremely interesting crew to several victories as well as a few massacres, both giving and receiving, while in my care. He was the big kahuna of this outpost.

Mom yelled up that it was time to get to bed so I got ready to do so. Pajamas donned, I headed downstairs to say good night. Mom first. She asked if I had my homework done and then checked my ears for potatoes. None there. I knew she would look, so washed them extra well. When I kissed Dad good night, he gave me a hug and asked how much I loved him.

"A bushel and a peek and a hug around the neck," I said and squeezed him tight. He liked that. I did too. Weekends were pretty cool. Besides, there were only a few more fifth grade weekends for me. Then it would be summer. Then it would be sixth grade. Man, I was growing up fast. Seems like fifth grade started only a few days ago. Weekends were cool. Sixth Grade weekends would be even cooler.

Summer Breezes
(Pets and Frog Fins)

Weekends were cool but were nothing compared to summer vacation when it came to coolness. Three months of no school, no homework, no nuns, and no standing in the corner. I did not get up to an alarm clock in the summer. Waking up was something that just happened. It was sleeps end versus some bell. Umm, umm good.

The sun eased warmly through my bedroom windows. Owls hooted in the day well after the sun started its job. I stretched and smiled at the welcoming light. The covers were nowhere to be found and that was all right. Underwear was more than enough cover in this heat. Early AM and the temperature rose faster than I did. Sitting up put me back in the race.

I was big on catty-cornered. There were two windows in the room. One faced Main Street and the other Maple. A catty-cornered bed meant cross ventilation. In a world where Air Conditioning was something that you got with popcorn at the movies, cross ventilation was vital. Breezes promised relief, albeit sporadic and short-lived. Humidity in New Jersey was as high as anywhere on the planet. In Science Class, Sister Chicken Little warned of air in big cities you could see because of pollution. In the Garden State, you drank the air. Especially summer air. Jersey Summer air tasted of humidity induced sweat and a putrid mix of aromas from the Fish Factory in Belford and the Perfume Factory in lovely Union Beach.

Even as a kid, I knew those places were not really factories. One was a cannery or something to that effect, the other a division of a company that made fragrances and flavors. It mattered little, both stunk up the air. In the winter, the cold repressed the smells so they were of little consequence. Background air almost. Subtle ewwws, so to speak. In the summer, it was an entirely different story. Between Memorial Day and Labor Day, summer heat cooked the smells. Nature's kitchen concocted something hideous. Nature also delivered this concoction in a way that defied the laws of physics. For in the summer, the signature smells of the Perfume Factory and the Fish Factory moved themselves to Keansburg. They had to. It was the only explanation. For the Perfume Factory was a few miles east of town while the Fish Factory was several miles in the other direction. Yet the two diverse aromas found each other in my hometown as sure as Romeo found Juliet. Two synergistically mutated stenches permeated the Keansburg atmosphere on summer days.

Those little stinkers. How did both smells merge and then drift in my window on summer mornings? Perhaps they walked. Just be bopped from their point of origin to our little town. Perhaps they took the train. Hopped a freight and jumped off near Keelen's and then spread through the 'burg. However those two rascals did it, they achieved a geographic impossibility. Two noxious aromas headed, salmon like, to areas around and adjacent to one square mile. A wonder of science worthy of Mr. Wizard.

Jersey Sure

The sickly smells marveled me to movement. First stop, the upstairs power plant, the bathroom. The house on One Maple Avenue was an old house. A house so old that electricity was not considered when it was build. As time progressed, and when there was no other choice, my parents' parents reluctantly installed electrical outlets on the first floor of the house. The second floor held only bedrooms so they skipped such a luxury for this level of the dwelling.

Luckily, I was the offspring to Handy Andy, aka Buddy, aka Little Will, aka Dad, who remedied that problem in his own indomitable style. Hence we had plugs in every room upstairs now, courtesy of a not very sophisticated but nonetheless complicated array of extension cords that weaved across every floor and into every room. All cords led to one room, the bathroom, the power source for all things in the upper regions. For in that bathroom was a medicine cabinet. Not just any medicine cabinet but one with a outlet on the side. A medicine cabinet rigged to the downstairs power source via an extension cord down the wall behind it. One out of sight extension cord that dangled mid air amidst plaster and board was good enough. Buddy considered half-assed well done.

One outlet for one plug limited most mere mortals but not Buddy. He purchased several magic devices that you plugged into a plug and transformed any single receptacle to one that held three. Plug one magic device into another of the magic devices and it held five. Do it again...... Perpetual power. In the Little Will School of electricity, one outlet energized a nation given enough magic devices and extension cords. Buddy masterfully powered everything on the second floor from this single outlet. The rest of the world could find their own extension cords.

The world had to look pretty hard for additional extension cords since an extraordinarily large number of them snaked in and out of all the rooms upstairs. Not to mention the one out of sight behind the wall in the bathroom. Each room had at least one extension cord and each extension cord had its own magic device. Here, in a twisted tribute to electricity, there was a rainbow of power. Brown cords led to orange cords led to white cords led black cords led to brown cords. Cords overlapped. Cords twirled together as if mating. Short cords. Long cords. Skinny cords. Fat cords. No skimping here. Buddy taught us how to modify plugs with that inconvenient third ground prong to fit into outlets with only two slots. He further demonstrated his technical prowess with first hand examples of how electrical tape ensured every extension cord lasted forever. Several of the extension cords were entirely encased in electrical tape.

Extension cords powered all for my sister and I as the same extension cords had for my brother a decade earlier. The radio in my room was my brother's prior and had the same cord tying it to the same maze of cords. As did the stereo. As did the clock. My sister's room was similar but had the addition of a hair dryer and those girly things she used to enhance her budding beauty. We had a road of cords that lead to Rome in the form of our bathroom. A Roman bath of sorts with a modern twist. Courtesy of Buddy and the wonders of extension cords.

While the weaved extension cords presented some obstacles and the occasional arching lightening bolt, we had power and that made us happy. I stepped over the cords and began the day as most days before or since. It was time to drain my bladder.

The bladder was the muscle of life. It ruled our entire cycle of existence. Early in life, the bladder let loose at will. For our first three to five years, the bladder ruled all.

Jersey Sure

It did not matter if we were awake or asleep. Perhaps we were dressed. Perhaps not. We could be on someone's lap or crawling on a brand new rug. The bladder decided to piss, and we urinated until we could urinate no more. Midday. Midnight. Mid-meal. Matters little. Midstream took over.

There were counter measures, but most were for mopping up, not much in the way of prevention. Diapers. Diaper bags. Kids held at arms length while the juices fountain all within spitting distance. Wipes. Towels. All just bided time and cleaned the spills until we mastered that particular muscle. First we learned to get the food into us correctly. Bottles. Sippy cups. Soon, we stop wearing our food. Then the priority shifted to getting it out at times we choose rather that the other way around. Onto potty chairs. Then we evolved to underpants. In time, we stopped wearing our food by-products.

The circle of life. Nourishment in one end in a manner we controlled. Waste out the other likewise. It took some longer than others but until we controlled the bladder, we do not move forth in the world. That was the very reason school started for most at age five. It took most five years to master the bladder. Those few kids who took longer received extra attention and shame for having failed in this civic duty. The bladder must be mastered!

Alas, the bladder was never really mastered. It let you think you controlled it. For a few decades, we transported the bladder to the bathroom should it need attention. We taught this pesky muscle to wait. The bladder succumbed to the body and the mind for quite a while. We moved from diapers to training pants. We learned to wait until bathroom break or recess to let the bladder loose. In worse cases, we raised our hands and then head for relief, one'ing or two'ing it embarrassed that we had to ask in front of kids we knew. As people got older, even this stopped. They sat in meetings and merely waited until they can go. Adults could drive for hours on end and drain the bladder only when they fill our tank. The bladder did what it needed to when the adult decided it was time. The adults were in control. Victory was theirs.

Or so they thought. The despot never really abdicated. A few decades later, the bladder ended its exile and resumed its place on the throne. If it let the adult get that far. The coup began slowly at first.

With military like effectiveness, the bladder targeted the rest cycle. A tired enemy was a weak foe. Adults no longer got eight hours of sleep because the bladder flexed them to the bathroom. Not every night. Just once in while. Then a few more. Then every night. Then a few times a night. Soon, eight hours of sleep was a used to be. All just foreplay. Training as it were. Conditioning. The bladder wore down resistance to ensure the return of the King was permanent. Adults get tired. Adults get embarrassed. Adults complained. The bladder eroded them back to the reality that it will soon, as it did all those years ago, operate at will. Back to the glory days when the bladder ruled all. It takes a while but sooner or later, the adults gave in. Diapers returned. Plastic sheets did as well and that accompanying smell that stayed with us every place we go. The bladder wins. Eventually. But on this fine summer morning, my bladder was in the dormant stage and waited its turn. So I tapped it at a time of my choosing and I chose now.

The day ahead was an untapped adventure. I jiggled a bit, flushed, jiggled the handle, filled the tub, and did the essentials in the mirror attached to the power plant. The big white house on the corner had many rooms but only one of them had bath in the title. Our home did not have that new fangled, state of the art contraption, most called a shower.

Jersey Sure

The tub monopolized the bathing options. It was big. It was old. It was various shades of what used to be white. It took a while to fill. After balanced and knowing turns of both faucets, confirmed with the standard hand test for temperature, I went back to my room to pick out my clothes, stepped over the extension cords as I did.

Selection was easy. Yesterday's jeans were still tolerable so I grabbed them. Socks were where they should be and the T-Shirt selection in my drawer was adequate, even if mostly hand me down. Underwear gave way to swim trucks since I never knew exactly when they would be needed. Back to the bathroom for bath time.

This was the morning, no nonsense bath. No boats or soldiers. No tidal waves. No bubble barricades. No Poseidon inflicting his wrath from on high. In and out. The day beckoned. Rather than wait, I used the few inches of water in the tub to best advantage. The arch to dip my limited hair was something Ed Sullivan would have on his show, just after the plate twirlers. The faucet spit but I finished bathing long before it finish filling. Plugged pulled, I dried quickly, put the towel back on the radiator/towel rack/clothes dryer, dressed, and headed downstairs.

The house was quiet. My sister was still asleep. Both my parents were at work. Our dog, JoJo, was out doing what he did in the mornings after my father let him out before heading to work. My father opened the door to let the dog out and did not even interrupt the flow of a conversation. It was as instinctive an act as stirring a cup of coffee or looking at the sky. Just another thing you did. Let the mutt out. The mutt would come home when the mutt was hungry.

We had many mutts over the years. JoJo was the current one. He was also one of the most important since he was mostly my dog. He was the Van Wagner dog but I knew he was really mine. Since I was the youngest in the house, JoJo was the only thing on the food chain lower than me. A pet was vital for the youngest child since it was something further down hill when the shit started rolling. Until I could beat up my sister, the dog was my source of relief anytime all hell broke loose.

JoJo was part something and part something else. Perhaps a third or so of something else as well. We were not sure where he came from nor what he was. He was a bar dog in that Dad brought him home from a bar one day and he sorta stayed.

JoJo went through a lot being a Van Wagner dog. I picked on him when they picked on me. Mom just kicked him as she walked by because he was there. My sister liked him but was too busy checking to see if her blouse swelled more each day to bother with him. My brother was already away so was a visitor when he popped in on those all too infrequent leaves from the Air Force. He never really knew JoJo and JoJo never really knew him. Then there was Dad.

Dad loved dogs. Alright, he loved them when he was drunk and forgot about them the rest of the time. But when he was drunk, canines were a major source of love and entertainment. He sang to them. He sang with them. He talked with them. His was a special dialect. Apple Jack tongue. Dogs seemed to like it. He embraced them. He laid on the floor with them. He put hats on them. He took them for walks, on a leash even, at 2 O'clock in the morning, just to piss off the neighbors. Dad bestowed on JoJo a dubious honor but an honor nonetheless, in that my father taught JoJo how to howl at the moon. It was a wondrous sight, worthy of mention on Mutual Of Omaha's Wild Kingdom. Man Teaches Dog to Howl at the Moon! JoJo seemed to like it. My father did as well. My mother......well, she did not share this monthly joy with the man nor the dog of the

Jersey Sure

house. This was not an acquired taste. This was something you either had or did not. She did not. He did. In spades.

My father was a lunatic in the truest sense of the word. He was in sync with the moon. The full moon. It called to him. It captured him. It took him to places he often did not remember. Not every month. Not in months that contained the letter "R". In months when the full moon occurred during that rarity of rarity, cash in hand. The effect of a moon fully aglow was tempered by cash flow, so he was not Lon Chaney each 30 days or so. However, if it was a full moon and a payday, we knew it would be a while before we saw him. He was a creature of the habit as well as a creature of the night. Full moon plus payday equaled Dad missing for several days. Doing things we wondered of for years. Some things we discovered and wished we wondered of for years. Dad ran amok with the moon.

JoJo was a souvenir of some full moon a year or so ago. He had some quirks, but they were good quirks. He slept under the corner table in the living room. This refers to JoJo, not my father. Although my father did indeed sleep under that particular table at least once, Dad was allowed on the furniture while JoJo was not. For JoJo, the furniture was a no-no. He only used it when we were not around. He drank from the toilet and ate from a different bowl just after dinner. He ate people food since that is what he was fed. When we remembered. When there were leftovers. He let you know when he needed to go out and then knocked on the door when he came back. A knock that began as a nudge but then intensified if we took too long to answer. We loved this clever canine but he came and went at will. Sometimes we forgot him. Sometimes he forgot us.

JoJo was a Keansburg dog. Keansburg dogs roamed. If people even owned leashes, they did not use them. Except during full moons and only then to piss off the neighbors. Most folks opened their doors and wished their pets well when they needed to go out. Fenced yards were rare so dogs just went where they chose. Dogs in town had the run of the place.

If Keansburg had a dogcatcher, he was inept to say the least. The dogs in town just chuckled when they saw the would-be dogcatcher. They lifted a leg to wash his tires as he eyed them with his net. A quick snarl later, and he moved on. The dogs went about their business. After all, Keansburg dogs were Jersey dogs. They left droppings wherever and they did not take shit from anyone. They thought the very concept of a dogcatcher quite amusing.

It was not unusual to be walking around town with the guys and to see JoJo headed in the other direction. Sometimes we greeted each other for a few minutes before parting company. Other times we merely acknowledged each other and continued on. Seems we ran in different circles. Perhaps I would see JoJo later today. Perhaps not. He was out and about and I just began. Fate would decide.

I turned on the TV and headed to the kitchen to grab a bowl of cereal. In the house on Maple Avenue, we had a few more options for cereal than we did for bathing. Cheerios was usually my preference, but today felt like a Shredded Wheat day. Thank God for the Chicago Worlds Fair and Shredded Wheat, Cracker Jacks, and the Ferris Wheel. Man knew how to make great stuff. The big cube of brittle wonder barely fit into the bowl as I poured milk over it, snatched a few fingers of condensed milk while I was there, and went for the sugar bowl. Even shredded wheat tasted better covered in sugar. The TV warmed and blipped to life by the time I made it back to the living room. I flicked the dial a bit. Our New Jersey selection was actually all the New York channels. There were many options. Channel 2 was CBS, 4 NBC, while ABC broadcast on 7. The three majors usually had

Jersey Sure

some sort of news in the mornings, except when Captain Kangaroo filled the screen with his great beard and welcoming nature. I was not in a Captain Kangaroo frame of mind that morning. Bunny Rabbit and Grandfather Clock were nice, but this was a day to be outside so I surfed past CBS quickly and rocketed passed 4 as well with a stop at 5 for WNEW.

It took me a bit longer on Channel 5 since it was commercial time. I let the advertisement ramble to see what show was on. The programming on WNEW was unpredictable. Sometimes it was a boring talk show but other times they reran shows as old as my parents. Things like My Little Margie and Oh Susanne. Gale Storm was quite a force in televisions early days. She and Topper topped the rerun cycle in the New York/New Jersey market. Not this morning. It was the news. Yuck! My hand blitzed passed the ABC option to see what Channel 9 held. No much it turned out. Joe Franklin talked to other old guys. The stop there was brief.

Two more channels but only one more real option. No need to head for the end of the dial. Channel 13 was the educational channel, which I avoided. After all, it was called the Educational Channel. If they wanted kids to watch, they should have called it the Chocolate Channel. Besides, I watched it a few times. The educational value of Jack LaLane doing strange things to chairs while in tights eluded me. There really was only one more choice for me. It was not Jack LaLane in tights.

I headed for Channel 11. WPIX was my place. Popeye lived there, courtesy of Captain Jack McCarthy. The Three Stooges resided there, introduced each day by Officer Joe Bolton. All that in the afternoons, but the morning usually had cartoons. WPIX did not disappoint me this fine morning. I settled in for some Courageous Cat and Minute Mouse.

Canine Crusader and Rodent Right Arm filled the void along with the Shredded Wheat. Breakfast over, I turned off the TV and headed to the kitchen before heading onto Greg's. After all, there were chores to do. Mom got home at 3:30 and expected the house to be cleaned so I did my part now on the off chance that the day would have me elsewhere when Katie swam in from the car pool.

The dishes were easy. A few coffee cups, the pot that filled them, and my cereal bowl. A quick rinse was enough. No one was looking. I left them in the drain for Sis. She had to do something. I wiped down the oilcloth that covered our dining room table. Linen be damned. We had oilcloth to withstand even industrial spills. The wipe cloth flew from the hand to the sink without me even re-entering the kitchen. A few things to pick up in the Living Room were all to challenge my resolve this morning. The sheet on the couch needed to be straightened and the 2x4 support had to be positioned directly under the broken part again.

My folks rarely purchased new furniture. Once that I knew of, so it was quite an occasion. Sadly, the newness of the furniture was short lived in the Van Wagner Household. A 2x4 propped up the center of the couch since it was broken and listed a bit if the accompanying board was not in the correct spot. The extra board was there right from the beginning. Thanks to Chucky Brown.

Chucky survived the model misadventure but steered clear of me since. I bet his Dad was behind that. Parents always blamed the other kid when their kid did something wrong. Even my parents did that. Bad influences were much easier on them than the very possibility of bad parenting. Whatever worked. Chucky's love for Army stuff went deeper than just models that charred the formerly lovely yard at his home. He liked to play army and a few

Jersey Sure

shorts days after my folks brought new furniture we played Army at my house. Folks at work, and the house became our playground.

Chucky chased me from upstairs, and I ran through the living room to the front door of the house and freedom. The chasing Chucky plummeted down the stairs and turned into the Living Room to capture his prey. Ah, but the prey had other ideas that day and Chucky caught a B.A.R. full blast when he entered the Living Room. It was the end of the line for Private Brown. Chucky may have been three years older than me and twice my weight, but he could not elude play death that day so he went in style. An Arrrrgggg, a clutch of the chest, and Chucky threw himself onto the new couch. All of him. Onto the new couch. A couch that was top shelf for our house but was not built for the demise of Private Chucky Brown. It died with him. Crack!

That was one of the few times I did not panic in the face of imminent death. A brand new couch broken and I did not panic. It was a case of plausible deniability. It was actually a bit surreal. I merely ignored it and hoped it would go away. It didn't. My father noticed it that night when he lay on the couch and it sagged a bit. He got that inquisitive, stir a bit, thing as he pondered why the couch felt so weird. I lay on the floor and watched TV, very, very intently. He stirred. He reached. He felt. He noticed. The reaction was pure Buddy. "What the hell? This damn thing is broken. A brand new couch and it is broken. What the..??" I looked in amazement, as if I sincerely wondered how that happened. He fussed a bit. He fumed a bit. I sympathized with him. Brand new and already broken. Of all the luck. He hit upon the 2x4 fix. Damn if you pay to have a brand freaking new couch fixed. Those Bastards!

So we adjusted it daily ever since. I made sure it was right under the broken board. Dad deserved a few minutes of comfort if he came home tonight. It was the least I could do since he had the misfortune of getting stuck with a defective couch. Then it was on to the Master Bedroom to make the bed.

The designers of the big white house on Maple Avenue had not intended the Master Bedroom to be a Bedroom at all. For the Master Bedroom had an outside entrance. Even Frank Lloyd Wright did not have an outside entrance to a bedroom in his designs. Hugh Hefner maybe. But Hugh Hefner was not a Jersey boy. Our house not only had an outside entrance to the Master Bedroom but that specific door was our major portal into and out of the house. From what we affectionately called the side porch. The Master Bedroom was the first thing visitors saw when then entered the house. An interesting first impression to be sure but we did not think much about it. It just was. I made the bed, as was expected, and completed my chores for the day. All while two cartoon heroes saved the big city in the Living Room. TV off, I headed for Greg's house. I took my frog fins in case we went swimming, which was very likely. After all, it was summer and we had beach passes.

Some kids had pool passes. Big bucks those Pool Passes. The Crystal Pool, the community's salt water filled entry in the pools for the ages competition, was cheaper than the Chlorined Belvedere, but both were beyond fiscal reality for my friends or myself. We had beach passes though and that saved 10 cents a day, or scaling a fence. Beach pass in the pocket, frog fins in hand, I headed out. Greg did not know it, but he awaited.

Greg lived one block behind me so I took the shortcut through the yard between us. It was one of the semi-official shortcuts that saved going around blocks in town. I could get from Maple Avenue clear to the boardwalk via shortcuts and bypass a half a dozen blocks. Kids everywhere used shortcuts. Kids were far more efficient than adults. Somewhere between childhood and adulthood, adults stopped using shortcuts. A sad but inevitable part of the aging process. I think it coincided with hormones and puberty but this was just a theory. Once boys noticed budding breasts, they walked right passed former shortcuts. Soon they sacrificed efficiency for whatever allure those budding breasts held and never used shortcuts again. They forgot the shortest distance between two points was a straight line. Or perhaps they just focused on two points and two points only and missed shortcuts as they walked and drooled. They let little things like houses; streets, property lines and the like herd them in courses far more inefficient than straight lines. I was pre-puberty so still used shortcuts. Hoped I always would.

This particular shortcut was the most frequented one since it linked me and Greg.. We wore a path with all the cut-throughs. That was tacit approval for the process if ever that was approval for such things. Sure, the old ladies that lived in the house that sat on the land of our semi-official shortcut scummed us off, looks wise, once in a while, but did not really protest too loudly. Not that we heard leastways. Not that we heeded for sure. If they yelled, they really didn't really mean it. I think. The option would have been to use the sidewalk and take a few extra minutes. Not likely. The old ladies must have understood.

The old ladies there were an odd couple. Two of them. Sisters or something. I never really knew, but they kept to themselves so what the hey. They had a dog named Boy. Boy was a Keansburg dog and roamed the neighborhood at will, as did all his canine brothers and sisters. Although he did not hang out with JoJo, Boy was one of those dogs JoJo knew. After all, dogs had a hierarchy of friends as well, although you sniffed the butts of folks on your hierarchy if you were a dog. I had a theory that dogs were in the Garden of Eden and ate the apple core that Adam and Eve dropped when God scared the heck of them with that booming, you're busted, voice from Heaven thing. After the Marshall of all of fruitdom took care of the wayward duo, he punished the dogs there by swapping their butts all around and placing them on the four corners of the earth. Hence, ever since this missing episode of Genesis, dogs quested to find their true butts. They walk up, sniffed, and pondered, "Is this my butt?" I shared this theory once in class, and the Nun did not agree with my approach to the pets of Eden. Go figure.

Bible stories aside, the two ladies with the yard with our shortcut called their dog in a very distinctive way. It was a sort of singsong thing that consisted of two words yodeled repeatedly until their mutt came home. Their voices echoed as they call, "Heeeeerrrrrrrr, Boooooyyyyy." "Heeeeeeerrrrrrrr, Boooooyyyyyy". Now, in Jersey, there was not a lot of yodeling. The yodeling duo might as well have painted a sign that said, "Goof on this". We often hid in the bushes and echoed back, "Heeeerrrrrrr, Booooooyyyyy." "Heeeeerrrrr, Booooyyyyy." Sometimes we mimicked them even when they were not canine calling. I never did see their reaction, but part of me thought they smiled.

Boy's ladies were nowhere in site that day when I cut through their yard. Mrs. Hallinan was though, so I paused by the fence and attempted to communicate with her. Attempted because the Hallinans were first generation Irish immigrants. The Hallinans rented the house on Main Street that shared a property line with ours. They were really nice people. They told me of picking potatoes and working the fields in the old country. On most days, I understood about half but enjoyed all of what they said. Their Brogues were lyrical. It was like listening to Opera. No matter the words

Jersey Sure

or language. It touched the soul. Gaelic was a musical language, and the people were hardy, happy folks. English was dramatically enhanced when interspersed with a touch o' the Irish. Less effective communication for sure but peaceful.

Mrs. Hallinan putzed about in the yard this fine day, so I greeted her. She smiled and came over the fence to chat a bit.

"Top er ta mornin to ya, Guilbert Ha ar ye this fin summer mornin?"

I translated and exchanged pleasantries. Odd thing was that I found myself doing a pitiful brogue as I did. If she noticed, she merely took it as a sure sign that my Irish roots surfaced when with brethren. She told me a wee bit about the weather and the news, but somehow always ended up talking about Ireland. It seems there was no place quite a good as where you just left or where you were going and no place quite as bad as where you were. Many people went through life wishing they were somewhere else. Sad state of affairs in my way o' thinking. She was happy as she complained though and that was an Irish thing. For the Irish smiled even when they complained. There was a light in the eyes as they told of the woes in their life. Nothing a wee bit of the scotch didn't fix, it seemed.

She told me of Old Charlie and how it sad it was about him. I agreed. Old Charlie was one of our local fixtures until last week when we found him dead in the gutter outside our house. Our initial thought that he was sleeping it off drastically underestimated the length of his nap. Old Charlie, never had his last name, lived down Maple Avenue in the boarding house on the corner of Maple and Braden. He was harmless. One leg shorter than the other, he was known for his special shoe that offset the missing 5 inches on one side of his body. He was one of many folks who lived from social security check to social security check.

That particular cycle of life was easy to spot. Three weeks of the Jersey version of sobriety. Drink only beer and only a few each day. Walk to the store for the day's food and walk home. Make the trip slowly since it was the highpoint of the day. Old Charlie mastered that walk and socialized with all on the route, if we did not see him first, that is. For Old Charlie was a time taker of the first magnitude. An ambusher. If he saw you, you were trapped and had to spend time with him. He had all day to get to the store and back so he had time to sit and talk and talk and talk. Old Charlie normally planted himself on our front stoop if he saw us. He liked company. We were one of the stops on his store route. He sometimes got you on his way there. Others times on the way back. Sometimes both. His leg may have been short but his eyesight was long. He saw you from many houses away. He paused, stood tall on his good leg, caught his breath, and waved. You were screwed. Nicely. His face lit up, and you knew he was happy to know you would be there for his visit. He expected you to sit and talk. We usually did. Sometimes we saw him before he saw us and dodged a bit until he passed. Usually, we just abdicated and waited for him to get to the house and mosey up to the stoop for a sit. An hour or so later, he shuffled to the next stop on the milk run. It was routine. For three weeks.

For one week, it was drink. He got the check, cashed it, paid the rent, and headed for the Main Street Bar. No loitering on these trips. There was drinking to do. If we were up late enough, we saw Old Charlie making his way home with less than all of his senses. Bob and weave with occasional stops for directions. Sometimes we helped him. He thanked us every five steps. Like it was the first time each time.

Last week was the middle of the cycle so we were surprised to see Old Charlie laying in the gutter in front of

Jersey Sure

the house. My Mother's car pool saw him and drove around so to neither disturb nor kill him. My father saw but let him rest since it was dark and helping him home meant being thanked every five steps. We saw him and gave him a while to wake up. A few tentative checks later, we determined something was not right about Old Charlie. We called the police and they showed up to wake him up. They did not succeed. Old Charlie had cashed his last Social Security check.

Some would say he died a broken man in the gutter. The facts may even support that theory. He drank to excess. He was addicted to alcohol. He had very few worldly possessions. If fact, his wardrobe was basically the same year round with the addition of a heavy coat in winter or a slightly battered suit jacket on cool days. From the outside, and based on traditional societal standards, he could be judged a failure. He left no statues nor much impact on the world. But sometimes the trappings of our legacy, or lack thereof, did not tell the whole story.

Old Charlie was a man with stories to tell and a habit that he indulged at the expense of few but himself. He was friendly and smiled with his entire face when he saw people he knew. Charlie was a gentle soul who made you feel good about taking time to be with him. How many people can say that about themselves and have it be the truth? The world would be a better place with a few more Old Charlies.

Mrs. Hallinan missed Old Charlie and commented so to me. Or so it sounded. She mentioned something about the fabric of the neighborhood and I thought that was a lovely way to describe him. She went about her putzing and I continued my short cut to Greg's.

For some people, you knocked on the door. For others, you rang the bell. For best friends, you yelled. I yelled. "Heeeeeeyyyy, Greeeeeggy". "Heeeeeeyyyy, Greeeeegggy". The family was used to it and actually looked forward to my distinctive sound. That was my story, and I stuck to it.

He came to the door and said, "shhhhhh. My Dad's home." I shhhhhed. Greg's Dad was a force to be reckoned with. He was Italian-Irish and married Italian so he was partially Italian by blood and all Italian by life style. Jim Smith was an Iron Worker. Some who knew him thought first of his size for he was a big man. He looked a bit like a prize fighter, a man who "…couda been a contenda." Some of his peers in the Main Street Bar thought him gruff, in a way that came from a life of hard work and daily struggle. Jim admired Miss Rheingold with them, and even voted for the sweetest sample of beer-girl in this annual blue collar Miss Sexy Suds contest, but he normally kept to himself when at the bar. His coworkers shared his work conditions of the long hours interspersed with long lay-offs and admired his allegiance to the Union, for he was true to the Ironworkers with each ounce of blood in his veins. Passers-by saw a man who spoke little but could intimidate with a glance. I knew he also intimidated by a shoe.

Jim Smith was a shoe thrower. He took a shoe off, pulled his arm back, and fired it at his target so quickly that the first time you knew he did it was when the victim was hit. When he lay on the couch in his living room, his shoes were on the floor within reach. His shoes were his weapons, and I never saw him unarmed. I saw him catch Greg with his shoe several times, no matter how fast Greg ran and dodged. Jim even fired at me a few times but missed. I think he missed on purpose. Fired for effect. It worked. Greg said shhhhhh. I shhhhhed. Not for Greg. For Jim.

Greg came out. A head taller than me, he already began lifting weights. He strutted like the older folks who flexed

Jersey Sure

while walking. A ten year old with egocentric attitude. Whodda thunk it?

Greg and I had history. We shared the same baby carriage and had pictures of us in the special pram to prove it. Perhaps it was an optical illusion but, although he was only a month and a day older than I was, he was a head bigger even in those pictures. Greg and I were as different as different could be. He was dark, I was burn and peel. He was very much the jock and I was very much not. He came from a family with kids all over the place while, with my brother away at the Air Force, my sister and I were the only two kids in our house. If we had not lived so close, we would most likely have not chosen each other for companionship. Yet we were friends, and that transcended all.

The Smith family was large. With six kids and all associated paraphernalia, the household was non-stop action. It invigorated me to go there, which I did a lot. For I was the Smith's alarm clock. Each school day found me there soon after my father departed. My face was as common at the Smith breakfast table as any of the kids there by blood. My sweetest thoughts of the Smith household were the ones centered around that table and its lovely chaos.

The Queen Bee of that beehive of activity was Aunt Flo, a very special lady. Not really my Aunt but we called adults either by Mr. or Mrs. or Uncle or Aunt. We never dreamt of calling an adult by their first name, so had Aunts and Uncles who were Aunts and Uncles, and Aunts and Uncles who were not really Aunts and Uncles. Aunt Flo was not really my Aunt, but I kinda wish she was. I loved her. She treated me like family and made me feel at home in a house that was not my home. An ability too few people really ever mastered.

Gilbert Van Wagner

Aunt Flo was woman of motion. This feverous force ruled the Smith home. Even Jim, the strapping, shoe throwing, ironworker that intimidated men, bowed to her when under the same roof. She was short but overpowered all with her pulse on all things done in that house on Seeley Avenue that became the place I started almost every school day for several years. She introduced me to coffee. Rare that kids drank coffee but she let us. I usually helped myself to a cup and settled in at the table for the show. Quite a show it was.

Flo moved from the icebox to the stove to the table in a cycle of supply and demand that had its own flow. Eggs cooked in mass quantities, sometimes accompanied by bacon or sausage. Depended on work or breaks in work. Union labor, or periods between, made for an unstable cash flow in this blue-collar household. Cereal boxes decorated the room. From vantages points everywhere it seemed. On the table, in the closet, and several points in between, Post and General Mills jockeyed for position. All props, since the real show was in the people. Kids came and went in various degrees of dress and undress. This was Aunt Flo's show, but the cast of characters made it quite the ensemble piece.

You can tell a lot about people's character by how they began each day. The Smith family was a microcosm of mankind in that regard. A collection of difference linked by genes and environment. Family. Flo was always there. Jim was seldom at the table for morning meals. If he was working, he was on the job already. If he was not, he was off stage but changed the entire feel of the set. An invisible presence. Jim was a volume control just by being there. The Paternal dampener. I felt it. Aunt Flo felt it. All the kids did as well. Jim days were quieter days. Not as good days. Subdued chaos days. But the kids were still the kids, Jim home or not.

Jersey Sure

The twins, two of them as was the norm, were as different as different could be. They were the youngest of the Smith children, having made their appearance about a year after Greg. Their different genders just one of the ways that eased telling them apart. Larry moved through life with a loose posture and motion. A kind of lop. That doh-de-doh thing some people had. Larry's face matched his stride. He had the inquisitive look germane to people with slightly bugged eyes, as if everything impressed or surprised him a bit. Larry seemed younger, as he was. His female alter ego, Diane, had neither the doh-de-doh nor the bug eyes, and that was a good thing. Diane, already empowered with budding looks, seemed a bit wiser than Greg and I in regard to certain things. The power of sensuality spanned age like a winged bird rode the wind. Effortlessly. Serenely. Confidently. It often flew ahead and waited for others to catch up. Diane soared. Dark hair and corresponding complexion, she had a doe like look that captured many boys in its headlights. She was a miniature version of her older sister. The older version of this dark beauty, Carmen was in full bloom and knew it. She usually was primped and ready when she made her entrance. She seemed a bit above it all and saw us all as bit players on her stage of life. I was young but saw them both with much older eyes. An "I don't quite get it yet but, when I do, it is gonna be nice" feeling. There were other Smith kids, but they were not players at the breakfast table. Boy, not the dog, the Smith boy called Boy from birth it seemed, did not normally join us at breakfast since he was older and on a different schedule. Robbie was grown and gone. He was their Jack. Boy and Robbie were family not there. I saw them sometimes and knew them but spent more time in their home than they did. Breakfast made for family. I liked being part of the Smith family, even if only linked by coffee versus blood. Besides, coffee tasted much better.

Gilbert Van Wagner

This was not a coffee morning. Breakfast was not a summer thing in the Smith household since each kid had their own schedule. This combined with the fact that Jim was home, Greg and I amscrayed. No planned route. Just somewhere. We stopped by the storage area adjacent to the house, basically the Smith Shed but part of the house itself. Greg looked for frog fins or the equivalent. Not much there in this tunnel like area, so we headed out. One set of frog fins between us.

The temperature neither overpowered nor hinted that it soon would. Our bodies sensed it and did not have us head for the beach. Instead we wandered. We rode the temperature as sailboats did the wind. Hot days steered us to the beach and the comforting coolness of the Raritan Bay. This was an outside day and our bodies headed for parts unknown. We just went, and the winds of the day guided us. Not far at the outset. A few yards actually but behind some hedges so out of range of Jim's eyesight and shoe. To the field right next to the Smith house.

Fields were wonderful things for kids. We owned them since no one else did. This particular field was our dirt fort field. The ground potted by well over a dozen remnants of our many forays into the science of dirt forts.

It always began with a hole. Not just any old hole. Our version of a foxhole. Just like in the John Wayne movies or on "Combat". Just like but different. After all, we never left things as designed. Kid foxholes had a few modifications. Requirements based on it concealing us from passers by on Main Street. Passers by who were German infantry one moment and marauding Indians the next. The passers-by were not the only magic transforming items. The dirt fort itself went from foxhole to headquarters courtesy of a ratty piece of plywood over the top. Viola! Albeit, a headquarters where no one could stand. In fact, all occupants, three at the most, crawled on their bellies to get in and then stayed on

Jersey Sure

their bellies to remain. A crappy headquarters by almost any standard, but it was ours. Masked from surveillance aircraft by plywood, some dirt, and a bush or two. Camouflaged against some unknown enemy. All ours. Complete with a flashlight, two candles, a can of green beans from my cellar, and four comic books, not the good ones. We could have survived there for months. Vic Morrow would be proud. Sgt. Fury would smile. John Wayne would, well, John Wayne would do whatever the hell he wanted. He was John Wayne! I thought the Duke would tell us "well done, Pilgrim" with that side stance, sorta hand thing combined with a glance that was exclusively his. He would have even hung around a bit with us since we were so cool.

Today we hung around a bit but never really got into it. A short linger, but basically we passed the fort/foxhole/headquarters. It was not a beach day, but it was not a dirt fort day either. We moved on as if we discussed it but, actually, it just happened. Our course had us drift. Not beach bound. Not fort bound. Not house bound. We ended up on Forest Avenue and heeded the call for grapes. Grape bound!

Grapes were not a passive fruit. The fruit of the vine somehow knew whenever we were in the neighborhood. The water full raisins planted the thought of hunger as sure as the aroma of Turkey on Thanksgiving morning. I was never really sure how grapes did it but it happened. A smell? Telekinesis? Photosynthesis? Subliminal messages? Grapes were extremely effective marketers. Greg and I headed for the grape vine just behind a house near the Water Treatment plant. Of the 17 grapevines in town, and we knew them all, this one was the most vulnerable. Joe and Louise also had a grapevine, the most protected in town, if not in state. Rumor was someone actually stole some grapes from the maximum-security vine, but no one believed it possible.

Gilbert Van Wagner

This specific grapevine was not a high-threat pillage run at all. The folks there were seldom home, picked the grapes they wanted, and just left the rest. They actually welcomed our pruning efforts. Although they never said this to us or anyone associated with us, we were confident it came from a reliable source. We made it up. Made the feasting a bit less guilt ridden. We came. We ate their grapes. We departed. Content and well hydrated, we continued our jaunt up Forest Avenue with the wind.

It was then we noticed we were not alone. I noticed first and let Greg know so we could decide what to do. Greg's little brother Larry serpentined yard-to-yard and tree-to-tree in a overtly covert attempt to follow us. Larry was a little brother and sometimes asked to hang out with us. It was part of his obligation as a little brother. It was in the Little Brother code of required behavior.

Little brothers are a pain in the ass. I know because I was and am one. Although my brother was 10 years older than me and gone from the house by the time I could really get on his nerves, I am sure there were a few times he did not want to stop when he strangled me. For little brothers want to be with big brothers even when big brothers could not be bothered. If they liked a particular sports team, the sibling did as well. If big brother liked some special musician, the littler version of him suddenly thought that music cool. The big brother did not merely dress, he set the standard for fashion. He did not merely make life choices, he shaped desires for his fledgling brother. Big brothers had clout because they were cool in all they did. Rest assured, Beaver did not just respect Wally. He wanted to be Wally as he grew.

Larry was Beaver to Greg just as Greg was Wally to Larry. Consequently, Larry routinely asked if he could

Jersey Sure

come with us, regardless of where we went. We answered as any bigger guys would to younger wanna-bes. No! It was part of our obligation as older guys with little brothers asking to come along. I took particular joy in saying no to Larry since I did not have any little brothers of my own. He was a surrogate sibling. A faux Beaver so to speak. Still, on occasion, Greg and I let Larry hang out with us. When we did, we made it painful. All part of the code.

We ambushed him. We picked up the pace and plotted. Right out of Roy Rogers or the Lone Ranger, we headed "round the bend", in this case on Forest Avenue in Keansburg rather than the high desert or the outskirts of Tombstone. Just like Roy or The Masked Man, we acted as if blissfully unaware of the stalker. If we had horses, we would have quieted them while we drew weapons and moved stealthily to the pass. Luckily, this bend in the road had hedges, natures camouflage. As if scripted, we dove quickly behind the hedges and laid in wait. The stalked became the stalkers. We waited quietly for the unsuspecting Larry.

He arrived and eased around the bend in the road. He sort of U'ed, akin to a cartoon bandit. Larry bowed his body so his head peered around the corner to see where we were. It seemed his neck telescoped a bit when he did. Impressive. So impressive, we almost giggled. First, because it looked funny. Secondly, because he did this right in front of us. Down scope, he cleared the bend and stopped. Larry tried to understand what he did not see. He did not see us. Larry pondered where the heck we could be. Only for a minute. Then the older brother propelled from the hedges and he and younger brother fell to the ground, limbs akimbo. Greg pounced on Larry because he was indeed a pain in the ass. But we let him stay with us that day. It was a good thing. Larry would make the day an adventure, although we did not know it at the time.

Gilbert Van Wagner

Fate drove us to the railroad tracks. Fate drove us there several times a year. It was usually not by design. It just happened. We ended up on the tracks just because. We were addicted. Hopelessly. Railroad tracks were the drug of choice for my friends and myself. For tracks offered adventure. Escape. They pointed away. As far the eyes could see, railroad tracks promised a path to places unknown. They drew our eyes and our spirits outward. Long. Straight. They linked us to people we did not yet know. Home yet grounded. A community chained together one tie at a time. Neighbors not yet met. People on our line. Railroad tracks beckoned us each time we saw them.

Of course, we were not allowed to walk them. This was not one of those implied, "you should have known better" things like licking light sockets. This was stated and restated with great clarity. It was too dangerous. Railroad tracks went well beyond any conceivable limit set by our parents. We knew the absolute perils they presented. Danger. Unknown places. Punishment waited for us should we dare to proceed. Our parents set defined limits and hiking the tracks clearly exceeded every one of them. There could be no right of appeal. No justification. Not explanation. A hike on the tracks resulted in severe consequences. That threat of punishment deterred us. At least a bit since we limited our hikes on the tracks to several times a year. Enough time for the appeal of adventure to overpower the memory of the last repercussions. The scales tipped, and we headed off on the iron beams. Today, we answered the call. Greg and I walked side by side. Larry brought up the rear.

There was a science to walking tracks. Railroad workers did not appreciate the symmetry of even spacing. The distance between ties ranged from several feet to nothing. Quality control in building railroads only mandated that the ties were actually somewhere under the rails. Consequently, hikes on railroad tracks demanded focus. To have the distance between each step vary yet not walk like a drunken sailor was a craft few appreciated until they attempted it. It usually took us about a mile to capture the rhythm, but it returned.

We headed out without direction or purpose but moved ever onward. The warm day turned into a hot one with nothing overhead to shield us. Railroad tracks were not big on shade. While forest and wood surrounded the right of way, the course itself was as open as open could be. The hot day eased into scorcher status, but it mattered little. The adventurers adventured.

Conversations shifted effortlessly from the mundane to the even more mundane. We bonded. Three of us. Two linked by blood. All linked by experience. We hiked the rails.

This particular hike took us to the East. Passed East Keansburg and Belford and well into Leonardo. All right, Jersey towns had shitty names, but you had to love a state with monikers like Hoboken, Weehawken, Parsippany, and Hopatcong.

Often, the hike was quiet. On hot days like today, it was extra quiet. Right up until what qualified as the single greatest conversation maker known to man, the trestle. Trestles offered adventure in their very existence. Here the rails were evenly spaced, with only air beneath them. New Jersey's name as the Garden State was fueled via the many waterways that cascaded throughout the land. Creeks. Brooks. Rivers. Bays. Jersey had an ocean on one side, a river on the other, and a slew of waterways in between. We crossed several on each hike and enjoyed the trestle over each of them. Trestles did not merely cross rivers, or streams, or creeks for us. Each one spanned an abyss. As soon as one came into sight, the energy level rose for the adventure increased in stakes.

We looked under the trestles before we crossed. What was down there? How long was this bridge over a massive, rippling waterway? Dare we? We scanned the horizon on each one just to ensure we had enough time to cross the trestle before a train took our only path away. The scanning was intense. It was to ensure we survived the crossing. It was as if there was a pre-crossing trestle safely checklist. Look in both directions. We did, complete with hand shield to block the sun. Check. Use eyes as well as ears. We all cupped hand to ear and audio scanned the air. Check Listen for vibrations, an addition to the checklist based on old Indian lore right from The Iron Horse and other historical documentaries. So we placed our ears to rail, akin to wise redskins like Michael Anasara. Check. When we were absolutely sure there was enough time to cross did we venture onto the trestle. After all, safety first.

Once out there, we discarded safety quickly. We laid on our bellies and looked down between the rails on each trestle. We admired the handicraft of the braces and struts that suspended the rails from one bank to the other. We spit. We dangled a few times but this was really kinda stupid by any standard, so it was not the norm. We balance walked to show off. We looked death in the face and smiled. Each crossing was a victory.

As the day eased into afternoon, the heat took a toll. In Leonardo, the heat drove us closer to the water under a trestle as we sat on the bank and let the moisture and the sound refresh us. Somehow things went awry. We went from boys on the banks to fugitives so quickly that we did not see it coming.

It seemed we sat near the edge of the waterway one moment and ran from armed guards and an armored assault group the next. Someone dangled a foot. It may have even been me. I remember being knee deep and swimming but the panic of running for my life blurred that portion a bit. We stayed under the trestle for a while, hoped against hope to see a train go by overhead. The sheer idea of it scared us while it captured us. A train. Overhead. In the air. With us underneath. Wooo hoooo. It did not happen. That day.

Larry almost drowned, although I loaned him my frog fins, and at least would have if Greg had not saved him. We swam around a bit more but never bothered to take off our clothes. The swimsuit under the pants was really a waste. We frolicked. We played. We moved deeper and deeper in to the water and up the creek.

Larry whined a bit since he was a crappy swimmer and was a bit shaken from having almost drowned. Kids! I even let him wear my frog fins since he almost died and everything, even though we were in water that was only over our heads at the very center of the waterway. Whiny kid. We ignored his pleas and moved into the waist deep water and up the creek, literally without a paddle. We went for miles. On a sudden quest to something. A few miles later, through the town but always out of sight in regard to civilization, we found it. The creek went from a wooded area to an open field. A vista. Open to the sea. The water current should have been a clue, and we saw the clue once all the evidence was in front of us. We had been walking with the current in the creek and headed to the sea. Explorers. Would be Lewis and Clarks. Bonded by the daring adventure of waist deep water to points unknown.

Then we saw the sign. It took us a few minutes to read it. A few moments more for it to register. After all, we were far away from civilization. In a place only bold pioneers dared to go. A first. Then this sign was there. Half a billboard size sign. Official looking.

Bold red letters opened it. Warning! Hmm. That did not sound good. Property of the United States Government.

Hmm, again. This was not headed in a good direction. There was some blahdy blah and something about a Naval Ammunition Depot or NAS Earle, but the one sentence that caught my eye was enough to get me in motion quick. Upstream. It read, and it read as if aloud and on a speaker, Trespassers will be shot. Whffffft. Suppressed in the water perhaps but I turned so quickly and ran that the Whffffft had to be there.

Greg followed. Larry was a bit oblivious to it all but picked on the hasty exit and herded after us. In my mind, there were sharpshooters with me in their crosshairs. A full amphibious force was ready to swoop on this group of intruders. I ran my fastest mile ever that day. The water did not slow me. In fact, if there was a rope tied to me, you could have water-skied behind me. If the wake was not too big to take you down. We made it back to the trestle in a matter of minutes and exited to the tracks and home to safety at speeds that set records in any book.

The escape exhilarated us. We thrived on it. Although Larry lost one of my frog fins, I was not upset. The image of him as we ran like crazy was worth it. For we escaped via our entrance route, only in reverse and a helluva lot faster. Running in water was a bit challenging even under the best of conditions. Add in panic. Add in boys who knew the entire US Army was after them. Then put Larry in some frog fins and you had an escape turned escapade. Frog fins made for good swimming. They really made for crappy running. At the peak of the escape attempt, I saw him. Eyes way, way out, our wakes almost knocked him over, and he lifted his feet clear of the water to try and move those pesky frog fins. If I were not scared shitless, I would have laughed like crazy.

I got away. Greg did as well. Larry did but cried by the time he caught up to us. Somewhere between a trestle in Leonardo and a recently invaded Military installation, violated without the knowledge of the US Army, was a half a set of frog fins.

We made it home but the brave episode of the boys against the military overshadowed the rest of the journey. We were late. We were grounded. We were alive and happy. Summer days had that effect on things.

Landfill Baseball
(Jocks and Those Itching to be Jocks)

Keansburg's version of sandlot baseball was landfill baseball. Named, appropriately, for the lightly-dusted-in-dirt pile of rubbish that served as our little league field. All the teams that played there were from the town since health officials in nearby communities allowed their trash to be imported but, for some strange reason, did not allow their youth to master the fundamentals of baseball on the same spot.

Playing baseball on hundreds of tons of garbage added a whole new element to the game. No soft, cushioning grass for kids in the Burg. We slid into second on dirt with the sponginess of industrial grade concrete. Most little leaguers across the US had the luxury of a level playing field. The privileged few living in Keansburg had a rolling field complete with tractor ruts. Ruts often several feet deep with surprises ranging from puddles to pet carcasses. We considered it lucky if the carcass was fresh. The sound and feel of stepping on a pooch that wintered death in the dump

Jersey Sure

was something few experience. Those that do, never forgot. No matter how hard they tried.

Landfill baseball made the game a true living history. We were connected with all those who played this sport before us. Linked with boys, now men, who cheered for DiMaggio and Ruth as we did for Mantle and Maris. We felt things new to us but common to the sport everywhere. Chatter that instinctively honored the unspoken but nonetheless sacrosanct "say everything twice" rule. "Swing, Batter, Batter." Way to look, Jimmy. Way to look." "Play's at second! Play's at second!"

This magical sport fostered a comaradie that bonded the "Bring it on" shortstops with the "Please don't hit it to me" outfielders like myself. Baseballers everywhere joined not just a sport but a ritual. A ritual steeped in history. Thanks to landfill baseball, we actually stepped on history. This being NJ, perhaps we even had a few prior players, or at least some of their body parts, mingled carefully with last year's newspapers and orange peels. We did not merely play a historic sport. We played on history physically. Sometimes history stunk.

This particular hot, July day, history reeked. There was no wind to save us. The infield smelled a bit. That "something's turned in the refrigerator" odor. Offensive but not "puke your guts out" so. Outfield was an entirely different story. Our warning track was the actual dump. The pre-landfill one. Home to rats and other less cuddly vermin. Out there it was just us crap players and the seagulls. We didn't just stink up the field. The field repaid us in kind.

I was in the outfield. Deep in concentration about the webbing of my glove. It had been my brother's. The glove and the webbing. A hand me down of significance. For a glove was far more than a glove. It was far more than a tool of the baseball trade. A glove was personal. It has stories to tell. Athletic feats to report. Letting someone use your glove, never mind actually giving it to them, was akin to letting someone have your girlfriend. At this stage in my life, I was about as effective with either. But at least the glove came home with me even after really, really bad outings.

Leather smells good. Especially in comparison to waste products in mass quantities. That was why my face was buried in the glove. Smelling. Analyzing the webbing. Hiding from the stink. Alas, a baseball glove on the face severely limits visibility. In fact, if you pushed your face in far enough, it also cut off hearing.

It was not the cries for my attention that made me take the glove from my face. It was not an intent to focus on the game and understand where the play was or how many outs we had. It was mere chance that had me return to the reality of this team sport. Mere chance that had me see that people pointed in my direction.

"SHIT". It was merely a thought but it was there. I assumed my stance. Patented by days of practice against imagined batters. Legs spread. A slight squat. Fist into the glove in a "ready for it" motion. I focused on it. This was my moment. I looked like a ball player.

A ballplayer who did not realize the ball had hit the ground behind him several moments earlier. A ballplayer who did not know that the ball laid there. Behind him. A ballplayer that preened, not knowing a double fast became a triple and a potential in the park homerun.

Finally, I realized the crowd pointed behind me. There was anger in their cries. The shortstop ran like hell towards me, and he did not look happy. I looked back. A seagull flew and distracted me for a moment. There was the ball. I moved towards it and planned my scoop up. I would turn

Jersey Sure

quickly and relay it. The play would be spectacular. Tinker to Evans to Chance be damned. This would be a relay of beauty. I scooped. I turned. I dropped the ball.

It was a quick recovery, though, since the ball did not go far. It settled in a small rut. My breathing was just short of requiring medical attention, and my pulse raced like a runway train, but still I scooped up the ball and lobbed it to the nearest player. Lobbed it as if it were a time bomb about to explode. Not the smooth relay I imagined but more of an "anything to get rid of it", desperation throw.

Unfortunately, I overthrew it. Not an especially hard feat since I threw it to the shortstop that was, thanks to the brilliant combination of his speed and my fielding ability, a mere 10 feet from me.

The shortstop was a good player, and it showed in the way he handled my relay. He ducked to get out of the way and rolled on the ground to avoid being hit in the eye at very close range. For my part, I was finished. The ball came to me, and I relayed it to another player. Job done. I was ready for a break. Time to enjoy the fruits of my labor as the shortstop did his job.

He recovered from his roll quickly and chased the ball back into the inner portions of the outfield. He would have been quicker if he had not come so far away from his normal position in shortstop. But I did not criticize. I watched his hustle. It was impressive.

He ran with passion. He reached the ball about the same time the second basemen did. Unfortunately for them, neither saw the other coming. They managed to dodge each other at the last minute, but the errant ball dribbled harmlessly into the in field as they did. No harm done though, since the runner who hit the potential double to me already passed home plate and high-fived his team.

Things quieted down then. At least eventually. Some folks yelled some things at me, but sound did not carry

Gilbert Van Wagner

well to the outfield. There was a few looks of disdain, but that did not dampen my feeling of success. I fielded one and remembered to throw overhand. Another successful outing.

The 4th of July
(Pyromaniacs and Earaches)

The 4th of July was the peak of summer. Memorial Day was well passed and Labor Day, the day that signified the end of summer, was months away. Summer heat was almost to the max. We had a whole month of summer under our belts, and now we got to blow things up. It was our right as Americans. The right to celebrate independence through the age-old glory of pyrotechnics.

Keansburg had fireworks just like other towns. We did the entire red, white and boom thing. Everyone in town was really American on the 4th of July. We suddenly remembered that we were here by birth and/or by choice and stopped being Irish-Americans, Italian-Americans, Polish-Americans, and anywhere else-Americans and just became Americans. For one day. A day a fireworks, and Americans in the Burg liked fireworks. Keansburg expected it along with the mayhem incendiary devices in drunken hands tended to induce. Consequently, Keansburg had rules about what fireworks people could have and those rules did not allow firecrackers. It allowed the wussy stuff like sparklers and that crackly ball things, but it did not allow firecrackers. The law was very specific, widely publicized, and very well known. It was also largely ignored. It successfully made firecrackers more desirable and slightly harder to get.

Sis and I got firecrackers from some friends and headed out to have some fun with them. The firecrackers that is. The friends were elsewhere at the time. Firecrackers amazed with all that could be done with them. They shot cans in the air. They were louder when ignited in trashcans. With the lids on. Hold-your-ears-and-listen loud. Bam! Plastic soldiers lost limbs to them. Firecrackers were lots and lots of fun. For a while. Then some big kids came and decided to do things that felt wrong at the beginning. Things that felt bad at the end.

They lit the firecrackers and threw them at each other. Playful danger in their minds. What little ones they had it seemed. They were bigger than us. They were older than us. They did what they wanted and basically ignored us. Two kids in the middle of a firecracker-tossing contest. Sis and I were merely bystanders on the battleground. Somewhere along the way, a firecracker went off near my ear. Everything changed as soon as it did. Somewhere between my crying and the intense ringing in my ears, the big kids left and Sis walked me home. It hurt like hell, and the 4th of July activities stopped for me that day.

At home, Dad and Mom were real kind to me. I cried a lot, and they let me. It hurt, so they let me cry a lot. They even made up the couch for me. Making up the couch was a big thing. We all had beds, although Mom and Dad shared one, so there really was not a need to sleep on the couch. But Dad made up the couch; a pillow, a sheet folded in half, and even the afghan Nana made for us, all prepped while Mom held me.

I laid on the couch and put my bad ear to the pillow. It helped to put my bad ear to the pillow so I did. The sun set slowly, but that was outside, and I was inside crying. Tears came. For a long time. Dad sat on the couch for a while and

Jersey Sure

said things intended to make me feel better. It still hurt. He scrunched me a bit, it was not a big couch and sagged due to the 2x4 brace, so he moved to the floor and sat so he could touch me while I cried.

Crying was an art, and I was in the zone that night. A good cry blocked out everything else. The sunset. The fireworks moved to memory. Mom went to bed, and Sis did as well, but my face in the tear stained pillow did not see. Night became real night. People asleep and the world gone quiet night. None of that registered. The art of crying became the art of sobbing. The ears rang on. A little bit less with each passing hour. The pain slowed to death as the 5th July eased to life. Slowly. Too slowly, but I noticed and slipped from wet eyes to sleepy eyes.

Through it all there was a constant. A hand that comforted quietly. A father's touch. A grown man sat on the floor and just comforted. An occasional murmur of reassurance. Ever present.

As I drifted to sleep, I thought Dad would get up and head for bed. The floor was a floor after all and that was no place to sleep. He patted my shoulder. He rubbed my head as if to massage the pain away. Between nods into sleep, I looked and he was there. Vigilant. Quiet. His glasses framed tired but opened eyes. Once he rested his head on the couch, but his hand rubbed throughout. It rubbed me to sleep. A sleep away from pain. Away from that humming in my ear. Away from sobbing.

The sun went to work while I was asleep. I opened my eyes to the daytime living room. Early daytime but daytime nonetheless. Birds chirped in the day. Owls asked who was up. All else was quiet. People somewhere else quiet. No ringing in my ear quiet. I noticed, and a smile bloomed. My ear did not hurt. The missing pain was as visible as the visiting pain had been. Pain gone was a heck of lot better than pain here. I was real glad it had only come for a visit.

Somewhere in the night, the blankets balled at the end of the couch. The pillow was still where it was but was pinned by a head that looked up to the ceiling now. I had tossed myself sunny side up.

I did the morning listening thing. The see if you can hear where everyone is thing. It did not work. My ear still worked but there was no sound to clue me to the whereabouts of Mom and Sis. Perhaps they were still asleep. Most likely. It was early. The day was new. There was carry over from yesterday though. A hand rested on my chest. A hand attached to an arm, attached to a man asleep on the floor alongside of a couch that held his son.

Dad was there. I looked down. Part in awe. Part in surprise. He was there all night? He stirred and looked up at me via sleepy eyes. I breathed deep and smiled. Happy not to be in pain. Happy to see him there. He saw I was alright and smiled. He patted my chest, and we both drifted back to sleep. Content. Connected. My ear did not hurt. Dad felt a lot better. I had a crappy 4th of July. I had a great 5th of July though. Thanks to that man on the floor by the couch.

It's All Relative (Cousins and The Sounds of Summer)

As Hoss would say, "Dad gum it!" Dad called up the stairs to get Sis and me up because company was coming. "Come on! Get up! You have to get ready and you have a lot to do!" No "Good Morning, sweetheart. Did you sleep well? How is my precious offspring this fine summer day?" Just a get-your-butt-outta-bed-you-have-work-to-do greeting for the day. All because company was coming. Not that company coming was all bad, it was just not all good. Especially the getting ready part. This was the last day of the getting ready part. It began last week, continued each day throughout the week, included an entire day of yard work and chores yesterday, and now invaded today before today even had a chance to get started. Jezze Louise. Gimme a break.

The house felt tense. As if the walls actually felt my Mother and Father's subtle panic and had for over a week. I think houses knew when things were up. Not all houses. Just those lucky enough to be homes. The others laid in wait. Our house was indeed a home and felt the anxiety

Gilbert Van Wagner

of the past week. Dad's sister, Eleanor, was coming, along with her husband, two daughters, and one son. Dad sure worried a lot about what they would think of us. I guess he wanted her approval or something. Who the heck knew? But whatever it was, it made the pre-visit a major pain in the ass. Mom was not as panicked but was tense nonetheless.

Mom saved her serious worries for when her brother Larry and his family came for a visit. Heck, we thought he was the Pope or something. Each visit was a major event with weeks of preparation, protocols, rules, restrictions, warnings, and directions galore for anyone who would actually encounter Uncle Larry. Seemed kinda silly though since folks like Uncle Larry and Aunt Ruth would like us anyway. Families were like that. But Mom and Dad worried, and we got to pay the price.

Dad and Mom made sure everything was ready. The house would be spotless. The yard would be freshly mowed and raked. There would be goodies in the house. A deceitful cornucopia of drinks, snacks, sandwich stuff, and whatever the guests may like. All props for a show that played only to visitors to the big, white house on the corner of Maple and Main. Backstage, Sis and I both knew we would do most of the work before show time. We did some of it each day this week and busted our asses yesterday with little thanks. Today? Well, today we would do the rest since company was due in the early afternoon. Lots to do. Ugh. Again.

Yesterday we were basically Dad's slaves since Mom worked a half-day. Today, Mom was off as well, so we had two Masters. Dad and Mom felt far more effective once Sis and I were up to do the actual work. Slave labor truly enhanced their overall productivity. I eased myself out of bed and headed to the bathroom for that whole bladder thing. A brush of the teeth, and I headed into the fray. Dad was up and ready to demand things of us. Mom most likely waited in ambush with chores for Sis and a list of items for me to get at the store.

I headed for the kitchen but Mom bushwhacked me before I got there. "Hurry up and get dressed. You have to get to the store for some things before Aunt Eleanor and your cousins get here." Mom had spoken! Not even a Good Morning. Just a get moving thing. I continued my trek to the kitchen for at least bowl of cereal. Kinda chuckled that Uncle Paul was not even mentioned. He merely sired Aunt Eleanor's children. He merely drove the car to get them here. It was all about Aunt Eleanor. The kids were mentioned because they were her's. Made me smile.

The Cheerios tumbled from the shaken box but Mom looked beyond my need for nourishment. She followed me into the kitchen least I think to take it easy or something. "Make sure you wash that bowl and then get upstairs and take a bath. Make it quick. There is a list on the table, and I need some things from the store quick."

I whined a little, but only a little since Katie was not to be messed with easily. After all, I couldn't let them win without a fight. A quick crack of the whip and she was gone. But not for long, I knew. I love you, too, Mom. No soggy cereal today. I ate standing up because sitting at the table implied a leisurely pace and Mom was not leisurely today so I would not be either. Not by choice, mind you. Just an instinct for survival.

I hid in the kitchen and ate. Time to read the cereal box. Some cereal boxes were better reading than others. Cheerio boxes were inconsistent in that regard. Too much of that health, eating this is good for you crap to make it a good read. But today was different since there was a giveaway. It was one in a series of cowboy figures. I already took it from the box earlier in the week. It was way cool. A free figurine. One of a set. It already was at home upstairs in Fort Apache. A bit bigger than most there but it worked.

That was old news. The torn lid evidence of the urgency in opening the box. It was slightly tilted ever since. It had been wrapped in plastic. The cowboy figure, not the entire cereal box. Health concerns required that it held minimum germs as my dirty hands and muddy shirtsleeve dove to the bottom of now crushed oats to retrieve it. It sure was exciting to get it.

Free stuff in a box excited us all. For me, it was cowboys and whistles in cereal boxes. For Mom, it was glasses inside of soap power boxes. The drinking kind, not the seeing kind. Glasses that went with the set of dishes you could call your own if you collected the entire series, one at a time, from one box of soap power at a time. If you ever got the whole set, you would have the cleanest clothes in the universe or a spare room full of Fab. The Van Wagner family had three cups, 4 glasses, a saucer, and some kinda of gravy thing so far. In only a year and a half. Wooo hooooo!

"Hurry up and finish that cereal. Make sure you clean up your mess. I do not want to walk out here and find dishes in the sink." I turned to see Mom but somehow she entered the kitchen, mortared an order at me, and left without being seen. Stealthy. Mom the cat. I washed the bowl rather than piss off the killer kitty.

A quick bath later and I was back at the labor camp. The song from the Wizard of Oz played in my head a lot at times like these. Not the "Off to see the Wizard" one. That was too lively. Not the "Over the Rainbow" one either. That was too sappy. The one with no words or at least no words anyone understood. The "Oh, wee, oh" song the guards sorta sang as they marched in service to the Wicked Witch. "Oh, wee, oh. Yoo, um" Repeat. "Oh, we, oh. Yoo, um." Ah, the days at the labor camp.

Sis and I passed each other, silently. We had a cellblock kinship as she headed for her chores and me for mine. Sis

Jersey Sure

had different chores that I did. My parents understood how to divide and conquer. Keep the laborers apart! They cannot plot our overthrow if we keep them apart! "Oh, we, oh. Yoo, um."

My chores involved errands. Gopher stuff. Gopher this. Gopher that. If I had to do chores, errands were good chores to do. Got me out of the line of sight. A trip away from the labor camp. I was a chain gang without a chain, without a gang, and without a boss man, overseer, with the shotgun and sunglasses on a lawn chair in the back of a pick up truck. "Oh, we, oh. Yoo, um." It sounded a lot better when you could skip or jump and touch a tree limb while you sang it. Sis stayed home with the screws, and I walked the streets like a free man. Alright, a free man with a list and orders to get his ass right back home, but we all dream. "Oh, we, oh. Yoo, um."

List in hand, I headed for our local store, CBS. Not to be confused with the TV network home for Walter Cronkite, Jackie Gleason, and Gunsmoke. Dad liked CBS a lot, the network, not the store. I do not think he ever actually entered the store. After all, the slave laborers went for him. Seems Mom may have gone to CBS, the store, not the network, a few times. Most likely to show me the way so she never had to go again. An investment of her time to ensure I was quick when dispatched later to fetch things. Kids in Keansburg started errands and chores early in life. For Blue Collar parents, kids had to earn their keep pretty young.

"Look! Dick took his first step."
"See Dick walk."
"Walk, Dick, Walk"
"Go, Dick, Go."
"Here is a list, Dick"
"Straight home afterwards, Dick"
"Yoo, we, oh. Yoo, um"

Gilbert Van Wagner

"Welcome to the labor camp, Dick."

CBS was used to it. It was the company store for the labor camp. There were a lot of young errand kids in the Burg. I was just one of them. My early trips to CBS were so early that I was taught to select the newspaper with the Camera in the banner thing up top. Why not just look for the Daily News as all knew it? Because on my early trips, I was too young to read. Hence, I looked for the Camera thingy. "Yoo, we, oh. Yoo, um."

I was also too young to count change and too young to read the list of items if Mom and Dad sent me for more than the paper. The process was pretty simple. They wrote a note and gave me the money and off I went. The lady at the store would take the note and point me in the direction of the items. She pointed. I fetched. She pointed. I fetched. Mom and Dad relaxed at home while the errand boy fetched. Good errand boy. Woof! CBS was close enough, and we only had to cross Main Street and dodge an occasional bus to get there. We were young. We were nimble. The buses had brakes. CBS or bust!. "Yoo, we, oh. Yoo, um"

CBS was our local store. Local in that we all used it. Local in that it was owned and operated by people that lived amongst us. Not like going to A&P and knowing some big company owned it. CBS was ours. I entered through the summer doors. It was dark. It was always dark.

The owner of this local market did not invest much in atmosphere. Ambience was not a word known to either him or most of the slave laborers with the list from the Massa's. Except me, of course, since ambience was a Wednesday word of the week. CBS did not have ambience. CBS was cold and dank. Outside light obliterated by stupidly placed butcher paper billboards that covered any and all windows. If they were after the cave look, they nailed it. CBS blocked windows all the time. It was not seasonal. The darkness of CBS eclipsed the seasons. Dark was permanent to CBS.

Jersey Sure

Today's shopping list was much different than normal. Milk, Bread, and the paper were daily items. Today the list included rolls, only if fresh, and some hot dogs and hot dog buns. Milk was on the list as well, so I headed there first.

The milk freezers were in the back of the store. They were not really freezers, but jumbo shrimp ain't really jumbo either, yet we called them that. I passed the standard row of canned goods. A quick flash of Campbell's color fought to freedom in the dark. Between the summer entrance and the milk freezers was the best thing in the store. The comic rack. A rack that held one of the best selection of Comics in town, bested only by Lehota's and that was clear over by the boardwalk. Today was not a day to, as Mom would say, dawdle. I really did not have enough time to stop and read comics. Company was coming, and I had other errands and chores to do. Mom would not be pleased. I smiled. Mom would not know. One run amok slave laborer paused at the comic rack.

I was a Dell person. Marvel was okay, but I gravitated to Superman and his many variations. Super Boy. Supergirl. That was one hot blonde and even the eleven year old me knew that. Justice League. It all tied back to the Man of Steel. The other Dell draws, Batman, Wonder Woman, although I did not understand why this Amazonian captivated so but sure knew she did, Aquaman, The Green Duo, Arrow and Flash, and others merely filled the void between the new Superman tales. He was the King of Comics. I scanned the rack, but only a new Flash was there for review. Review only, since my pockets were empty. At least of my own money, and Mom knew each cent she gave me and how much the items on the list cost so there was no hope of an extra ten cents for a comic from that source. So I just read.

"You gonna buy that?" Happy Harry, the owner of CBS, startled me and derailed my train of thought. His voice surprised me as he emerged from his surveillance/ reading dirty magazines hideaway just behind the comic display.

"Just looking."

"Well, this ain't no library. Either buy it or put it back"

I put it back. Slowly. Defiantly slowly. With a look at the jerk. I scanned the rest of the rack, pretended to be interested and able to purchase, and then completed the journey to the milk freezers. A meaningful glance over my shoulder dismissed the storeowner. I did not care for him much. He seemed sleazy. Although young, I was not naïve. Street knowledge of sex was not always accurate, but it was extensive. Hands-on learning, so to speak. I understood what Happy Harry was up to when in his so-called security booth. He hid in there with his Girlie Magazines. I had seen inside his Fortress of Solitude and felt like I needed a bath afterwards. The elevated, phone booth shaped cubbyhole was security central for CBS. The plywood, slightly bloated refrigerator shaped container stuck out like a sore thumb for all to see. It blended in like a Playboy Bunny at a Boy Scout Jamboree. First time visitors looked and said, "What the hell is that thing?" Harry was not known for his clandestine nature. No ambience. No clandestine.

The CBS security closet/container held a battered and bruised adding machine, some ledgers of questionable age, views to the mirrors in the corners of the store, and a lawn chair. Clearly the lower end of technology. It was more of a holding area for Harry's not so secret collection of dirty magazines. The adding machine and ledgers were ploys. Harry balanced other books back there. Usually one handed. Although he was an adult and I was a kid, I did not like him.

The milk freezers were next to the butcher case that helped all other butcher cases in the world look good.

Jersey Sure

There was nothing wrong with the meat here. Just nothing that made you hungry for the sandwiches later or the great hamburger the chopped meat would become. Mom brought her real meat at the A&P. She settled for Safeway or Shop Rite in a pinch but was an A&P devotee. It was only the occasional chicken that made it from CBS to One Maple Avenue. Sometimes, like today, hot dogs. After all, they were packed pretty damn good from wherever they came from, so we were most likely safe to eat whatever they were made of. We did not buy Hot Dogs from CBS often, though, because CBS charged a bit more than the bigger stores up on Highway 36. Mom was very select on what she made me go get at CBS.

Milk was an entirely different story. Milk was cheaper at the CBS than from the machine, and it was only a quarter of a mile or so, one way, to CBS so off to the store I went. "Yoo, we, oh. Yoo, um." Usually every day. I grabbed a half-gallon of Krauser's best, and headed for the bread and the Hot Dog Buns. The bread and buns were side by side but the rolls, surely related, were closer to the cash register. Distant cousins I guess. The rolls were loose in a bin, so I bagged twelve of the freshest. A loaf of bread, a dozen rolls, and a pack of buns later, I was at the cash register.

The lady at the cash register did her job but with very little passion. Seemed that when she dreamed at night or in the years of her youth, cashiering at CBS Supermarket in Keansburg New Jersey was not one of those dream come true moments. Minimum wage. Minimum effort. Even less satisfaction. I paid her. She made the change. She bagged the groceries. I watched and hoped to sense some emotion, but she was bland inside and it showed on the outside. I felt sorry because of that.

She was more than just a cashier. She was a person. A person with a life and a family. Albeit a family of one other. She had a daughter that looked a lot like her. They were distinctive in that they were always together, and the daughter looked like a carbon copy but younger version of her mother. They dressed alike, in old lady dresses, dress shoes, and socks regardless of the season.

A daughter that was with her this day just as she was every other day. A daughter who was today, as usual, engrossed in a comic book. A daughter as old as my brother but not as intelligent as me. I knew her because she was almost always here at the CBS check out line with her mother while her mother made change and bagged groceries. Her daughter has a look in her eyes that said child. I liked her. Almost always she looked from her comic book, and we smiled at each other. Somehow I knew that each time was a first time for her. She seemed innocent and pure, although outwardly old enough to be well beyond innocent and pure. Some would think her punished or limited. Part of me wondered if her so called disability was actually a gift.

The two of them rode bikes. Not right inside of CBS. That would result in canned goods everywhere and interrupt Harry's "alone time" before its climax. They rode bikes when not in CBS. They rode bikes to Church, which saw them at every 7 AM service. They rode bikes on Summer evenings for......well, it looked like they did it then just because that was a summer evening thing. Why bikes? I think part of it was because cashiers as CBS could not afford cars. Part of it was just efficiency. The other part was special. It was bonding.

Mother and daughter were connected. Old lady clothes. Old lady bikes. A old lady with a daughter who thought younger than she was and looked older that she thought. But when the daughter rode that bike, it was a site to behold. For she had the shape and muscle of her age but the innards of a kid. She rode with abandon. Not unsafe. Not dangerous. Not that kind of abandon. She rode like a kid. With magic. My bike rides were almost always an adventure. The bike

Jersey Sure

turned Trigger as we escaped. The bike turned cop car as I chased the bad guys of today. A Yahoo or two was good for the soul.

Adults did not Yahoo much. Too free an act. Too spontaneous. They were more mature than that. They rode bikes without abandon. She did not. The light in her eyes said so. Yahoo.

There was a smile but no yahoo today from the daughter. She looked up from her Little Lotta comic, she liked the Baby Hueys, Dot, and Harvey comics but occasionally snuck in an Archie, and smiled and went back to where ever Little Lotta was. I smiled and headed home. The labor camp would be on the look out for me.

Sure enough, Mom gave me that where-the-hell-have-you-been-look and I was sent out to "give Dad a hand". Giving Dad a hand was froth with danger on any given day. He was a klutz who thought he knew what he was doing. Today, it was twice as dangerous. His sister was coming for a visit, so he was stressed. Clumsy AND nervous. Volatile. Regardless, I was dispatched to help the accident waiting to happen.

He was out back, in the shed. The shed used to be attached to a garage but now stood alone. The garage was no longer. It was kinda like my grandma in that it was around for a while when I was first born but was gone so long I did not really remember it ever being here. Grandma and the garage were gone. I think they departed at different times though. Not sure, but they were both not around now except in pictures. The shed was still here though. The shed was the shed for as long as I remember.

The shed was a tribute to disorganization. Saw horses mated in wait atop the lawn mower. Coffee cans and mayonnaise jars full of anything and everything that might come in handy someday cluttered the shelves. Yubans, Maxwell Houses, and Hellmans of nails of all shapes and

Gilbert Van Wagner

sizes. Bent. Old. Ten penny. Finishing. It did not matter. We had them all. All but the one you needed, of course, since each jar contained a few of just about everything. Nails. Screws. Brads. Bolts. Washers. Arranged carefully based on the keep-it-just never-be-able-to-find-it system of chaos and disarray. Ah, life in the shed.

Dad loved the shed. He saw it as his place. He was the king of the shed and ruled without Katie's input. Katie did not ever enter the shed. It was old. It was musty. Usually, it was a wreck. She avoided it. That made it all the sweeter to Dad. It was his kingdom. His hideaway. His Fortress of Solitude. He loved it because it was his. I loved it, too. I loved it because it was his.

It was almost always cool in the shed. Even on the hottest days. It was musty too. Sometimes musty felt good. Today was one of those days. I entered the comforting dankness and waited to be told what to do. Dad did not take long to tap the labor pool.

"Fat boy," (that was his nickname for me although I was not actually fat) "take out the lawn chairs. Put them around the side of the house for your Aunt and her family." I stepped over the rakes and shoveled my way to the lawn chairs. Four of them. In different states of repair. The cloth, actually plastic strips, that formed the seats was pretty good on three of them. One had a few strips missing so the sittee risked a butt blow out if not balanced correctly. I lugged the chairs, two at a time, to the side of the house and placed them in a semi-circle facing the street. The show was the street. Passers by. Traffic. Pop-ins. Hopefully from the passers bys and not the traffic, although an occasional car or two took the corner too fast and ended up in the front yard of the big house on the corner of Maple and Main. Hence, we sat the chairs in the yard on the side of the house. No need to be speed bumps.

Jersey Sure

The chairs were not the only things Dad planned for his designated laborer. The grill needed to be set up. Alright! Fire! I grabbed the briquettes. That word always sounded kinda silly to me. Like baby bricks. Or a rock group that did Doo-Wop. "Ladies and Gentlemen, put your hands together for the one, the only, Briquettes!" Dad called them charcoal. Not the music group. That would have been a lousy name for a music group. Would be like naming a group after a city or something. That would be stupid. So I took the charcoal and dumped some in the grill. Right on top of the already powdered ones there. Hard to see if there was enough with all that powder flying around. It was about then that my chores ended. They did not end pretty though.

"Gilbert Joseph John!" Shit, I thought. Three names. Big trouble.

"What the hell are you doing?" I looked to my mother as she leaned out the kitchen window and yelled. I did the innocent face thing kids did as instinctively as a turtle hiding in the shell. "What?" It was actually a question this time since I did not think I did anything wrong but three names always meant trouble. Then Dad exited the shed, weighed in, and removed all doubt.

"For Christ's sakes. Don't you have the brains you were born with? Look at you!"

The dust settled but their anger didn't. Sis looked at the window and, in a show of support that I remembered later, laughed.

Dad told me to finish the charcoal and get my stupid ass in to the house to wash up, "....and for crying out loud, don't touch anything". Huh? No fire? No lighter fluid stuff and woooommmphf? That was the best part. Something told me not to argue. Perhaps the fire in their eyes. So I headed inside to wash up.

Alright, my hands were a bit dirty. The mirror in the bathroom told me what they were mad at and even I had to laugh. My raccoon like face was caked in black powder. Just my eyes were clear to see. I looked like someone in one of those minstrel shows from Shirley Temple movies. Not good. I laughed and washed up. My now gray shirt a mess for the day. I changed, washed, wiped the sink down with the towel, wrapped the towel so you could not see the charcoal dust, and headed back to time with family and visitors.

The cousins would be here soon. There was Dickey, about my age give or take a few months and two girls, Susan and Kathy, somewhere around the same age of Sis. We visited their place on the Cape last year. We were there for a week, and they were only coming for a day. We owed them a nice day. I knew we should be good hosts but, truth be told, I was a little intimidated.

They had stuff. A boat that we took out when we were there for a visit. A real boat. With a motor and everything. A boat Dickey drove as sure as he rode a bike. Basically his own boat. That impressed. I did not have a boat. Most likely would never have a boat. They had an extra bike I got to use while at their house. Alright, it was old, but it had good tires, and I got to ride all over Woods Hole, Massachusetts on it. I did not have an extra bike. That meant no bike for me today since it would be rude to ride mine and let Dickey walk. What the heck was I going do all day in Keansburg with cousins who had boats and extra bikes? If Dickey and I went to school together we would have run in different circles. Him with the Nifty Binders and a Roy Rogers Lunch box compete with thermos and me with my sister's old loose-leaf notebook held together by electrical tape and a brown bag for lunch. But we were related and would spend the day together.

Jersey Sure

I got along really well with my cousin, Dickey. I did not know nor really care how Sis got along with the girls. Sis could handle her own day with the girls.

Visitors meant I had to dress decent. Relatives did not visit a lot so when they did, we were on best behavior and had to look the part. A crew cut the week prior. A bath this morning even though I went swimming yesterday and couldn't have stunk too bad. Then another wash up after the charcoal incident. All that and it wasn't even school or church. My folks wanted it to be just right. Regardless of how much pain it involved.

There were some good parts. Slave labor stopped once the cousins arrived. No chores, although with three additional slave laborers the jobs would have moved a lot quicker. Once the visitors were there, Sis and I got to play and hang out with them. Mom and Dad acted as if play and fun was our job. "Yoo, we, oh. Yoo, um:" would have to wait.

Zero hour was almost here. Everyone was dressed and ready. Foodstuffs stuffed away for later. House cleaned. Lawn chairs out. I was the look out and sat on the stoop to look. Duty was short lived since they pulled up Main Street shortly after I manned my station.

I yelled to the house that they were coming. By the time the car turned onto Maple and made the quick right into our driveway, Mom, Dad, and Sis formed the front yard welcoming committee along with yours truly. The car eased into our yard with my Aunt and Uncle in front and a rear seat full of cousins. In unison, in the car and in the yard, the adults turned and said something the kids. I think it was for the same reason. Dickie and his two sisters took it in while looking out at my sister and myself as we took it looking at them taking it. All part of visiting tradition whether you were the home or the away team. The parental warning of "Behave yourself". "Yeah, Yeah, whatever," we thought in tandem. Everyone, car and yard folks, plastered smiles on their faces. The day began.

Reunions were odd things. Memories linked but not enough. There was the getting reacquainted period for all reunions. To take the reunionites from then to now. Updating each other. Physical differences were there to be seen and addressed, if it could be done politely. You did not comment that someone had porked up quite a bit. A bad haircut may draw a look but not comment. People mentioned the nice things. The looking great things. Not the, "Have you got some serious illness?" things. With cousins of the same age who had a year or so between meetings, it was adjusting to the new person they were as they adjusted to the new person you were. After all, a year plus was a long time when you are eleven.

We did the grip and grin thing with the adults. Then I greeted my girl cousins much like I would my sister. They were older. They were girls. They had little use for me or anyone like me. We smiled. Shook hands. Then dismissed each other as life forms and went our separate ways. Karen took the girl cousins since they had that gender and age link. I took Dickey so we could get to know each other again. We would most likely not see the girls much that day.

Dickey and I had a lot in common, so the getting reacquainted period was quick. We both were outdoors kinda kids but with different interests. Dickey had the boat and fishing thing going on, but I had neither a boat nor the desire to fish. Fish came in the form of sticks for me and only during Lent at that. But we liked just being outside. So we walked, talked, and tested the connection that worked each time we reconnected. That is a nice thing for we both knew it would only take a while, and we would be friends again. Nice when that works for cousins. Would make for hellishly long days together if it did not.

Jersey Sure

We putzed about the yard a bit while the folks and the girls mingled. My yard was old news to me but not to Dickey, but there really was not much to do there. Especially with the adults within line of sight. They settled in the lawn chairs, Dad got the potential butt blow out one, and enjoyed cold beer and warm reunions. Being Beer gophers was not our idea of a great time, so our time there was short lived. As for the girls, heck, who knew where the hell they got off to? Looked like they knew enough to stay away from fetch duty as well. Dickey and I headed towards the beach. Neither of us had suits but figured we could walk there nonetheless. Parents asked us where we were going so I told them. "...for a walk."

Dick was a year ahead of me in school but we had common interests. Both pretty good students but not geeky about it. Both liked TV, and westerns in particular, so we ended up playing a bit of Cowboys and Indians as we walked.

Cowboys and Indians translated well regardless of where kids lived. None of the kids I knew lived out West, but all knew how to ride horses. Make believe horses, that is. We all knew the Indians could, and most likely would, ambush us but loved Tonto at the same time. Bad guys, usually in black, routinely did things to thwart our efforts at a better world. We shot straight, rode hard, and were home for dinner. If we got bored, we became Army men or something else. Dickey may not be on his home turf, but he rode the range in New Jersey just as sure as he did in Massachusetts.

I showed him my town. Streets looked a bit different when you bragged about them. Main was a nice street. Houses pretty well kept. A few stores. Trees. A friendly look. I knew every crack of the sidewalk. It was nice to be tour guide to the world I knew. Dickey played along like a good tourist. I did the same when up on the Cape at his home. Although he had a few nicer toys and the neighbor hood had newer cars. His friends caddied for money. Mine did things I think Dickey's did not. Who knew?

We explored the town around Main Street for a while and reconnected in the process. Dickey was a pure spirit and easy to like. There was a naturalness to him fed by his own sincerity. I was impressed at how he balanced his life already. Although less than a year older than me, he seemed a mentor or advisor as well as a friend. He was confidant in who he was. It showed in a subtle way during our last meeting, on his home turf, Cape Cod. We had a great day, went home for dinner, watched the Rat Patrol, and settled in for the night. Out sleeping spot was cots on the front porch. Made for a nice summer resting spot. As with most boys, we joked a bit as we eased to sleep. Soon sleep enveloped me, and I eased into it. That feeling of a good day followed by good rest was sweet. Just prior to drifting off, I said good night to Dickey, partly in thanks for a great day together. Words I used many times to bid people Good Night, "See you in the morning." Simple words. Routine words like "How are you?" Sometimes asked even if the asker does not really care or even wait for an answer. "See you in the morning."

Dick heard but answered in the pure, insightful spirit of his that I grew to love. "If the Good Lord is willing."

Things that make you go hmmm. That was one of them. I drifted to sleep a bit slower but for the right reasons. Making it to the morning was indeed a crapshoot and a Higher Power owned the dice. Dickey knew it as sure as he knew breathing. I saw it thanks to him just being him. Hmmmm. Today's reunion was much easier because yesterdays like that.

We turned up Collins Avenue and took my shortcut to Center Avenue. Well, at least it was usually a shortcut. Today it was not really a shortcut at all since we looped right back to Main Street to get to the beach. But I wanted to show Dickey a shortcut that was mine. We galloped down Collins and turned at the opening to a well-kept secret of a shortcut.

Cement path. Houses on both sides. Shaded. A grape vine within striking distance. Good stuff anytime. Dickey commented and I saw it with fresh eyes. He saw the canopy of interlaced branches. Branches joined across the path like an answer to our prayer for shade. I saw it anew, even if only for that moment. We talked and bonded as we turned right on Center to get back to Main and then the beach.

They had beaches in Massachusetts, but they could not see New York City and the partially completed bridge that we could from Keansburg beach. So I showed off a bit. I knew the beach well. Beach passes made for in depth experience since I could come and go at will and not pay the dime each time. These beaches were less crowded during the week. I guess it was like that everywhere. Lots of Moms and kids pairings this day as was the norm.

We kept our shoes on and walked the beach just because it was a beach and beaches should be walked. Sand slipped into the shoes, I know they did on mine and I am reasonably sure Dickey's filled as we stepped as well, but it was either that or the shade hop thing. Sand had no place to hide from the sun and heated up a lot by midday. The shade hop thing would have us run from shadow, and there were not many, to shadow or blanket to blanket, and folks got mad when we did that, to make it to the water without blistering or crying or otherwise just not having fun in the sun. So we walked and let the annoyance of sands in the shoes just annoy.

The day was warm and friendly. Weather wise and company wise. My cousin and I got along. I sensed we would like each other even if we did not sorta have to since we related by blood and all. I smiled when I realized that and looked to him. He smiled back. He felt it too.

Gilbert Van Wagner

He saw the bridge being built, and I felt a bit special about getting to see it regularly. Just like he did when I went agog about his town, Woods Hole, having its own drawbridge. Right downtown.

We walked the beach all the way to the boardwalk but did not go on the midway. Too much distraction, too little money, and not enough time. Carr Avenue was not overly crowded so I guided us there. He jumped on Presto Lunch without even asking why.

Presto Lunch was not really Presto Lunch anymore. It was some other café, aka divey restaurant. But Presto Lunch lived on in the form a five-foot long welcome mat of tiles in the middle of the sidewalk. Tiles right in the cement. Whenever I passed those tiles, I jumped in the air, landed on them, and shouted "Presto! Lunch!" I did it for several reasons. It was fun the first time so I did it over and over. It was also a place where my mom worked before she was my mom. I heard she worked there back when Jackie was a baby, maybe even before. It seemed neat to "Presto Lunch" even though Presto Lunch was not there.

I jumped and said it. No explanation. Dickey saw it and did likewise. Neat stuff. We explored. My town was my town, but it was different when sharing it. We walked from Presto Lunch and stopped at Lehotay's for an egg cream. I liked egg creams. Chocolaty. Seltzery. No eggs. No cream. Not sure how they named it but it was a decadent treat. Dickey said they did not have egg creams in Massachusetts. That seemed odd to me. Why wouldn't they have egg creams in Massachusetts? Egg creams should be everywhere. I pictured a state with no egg creams and then remembered my visit to some cousins outside Boston a few years prior.

We visited them once and that was the only time I saw them. They owned a pizza place. That was way, way cool. We spent the day with them and they showed us around

Jersey Sure

their neighborhood just like I showed Dickey around mine. Just before we arrived, Mom and Dad gave us the standard, you better be polite and always say please and thank you lecture common on all pre-visits. We nodded and agreed. Even with Mom's personal, not to violated ever, rule of "do not ask for things". We knew to wait until offered a drink even if thirsty. We knew to die from hungry before we dared give voice to a request for food. On that particular visit to Boston, that rule resulted in a lesson on differences between places people lived.

The cousins in Boston were neat kids, and we got along well. But as we played in the yard and then the house, we got thirsty. My sister and I waited in hope for the offer of a drink, like good little offspring of Katie and Will. The adults there finally offered a drink when they turned to us and asked, "Would you like some Tonic?"

Tonic? Why the heck would we want Tonic? That was one of those things adults put in their drinks. Like Club Soda. Like Ginger Ale. Tonic Water? I declined politely. So did my sister.

The adults there were nice and offered us Tonic several times during the day, and we slowly and measurably died of thirst rather than accept. It continued throughout the day, and my sister and I felt like those folks in movies who needed water and saw only the cruelty of mirages. Mirages of Tonic.

Late in the afternoon, the adults dispatched the slave laborers, aka their children, to the store for some essentials. "Yoo, we, oh. Yoo, um." It pleased me that I was not the only kid treated as errand boy by the harsh adult folks. We headed for the store with the verbal list, "get some bread, a few tomatoes, make sure they are good ones, and some tonic." Damn, I thought, these people really like Tonic Water.

We got the store and it was like Joes and Louise's only in Boston and called the Polock's instead of the Guineas. Strangely the same while strangely different. The kids picked up the items, and I was pleased to see they also purchased couple of bottles of soda. Relief was in sight.

We got the counter and I noticed the kids had not purchased the Tonic. The ever helpful me reminded them. "Hey, aren't you guys suppose to get some Tonic Water, too?

They just looked at me. A quizzical, what the heck is wrong with you kinda look. "Tonic Water? No, but we had to get Tonic and here it is." They pointed to the bottles of soda.

Soda? That was Tonic? I had turned down soda all day while dying of thirst. My sister and I looked at each other and realized the uniqueness of Boston life. Tonic was soda here. How strange. We drank tonic as soon as we got back to the house and were offered some.

No wonder they did not have egg creams in Massachusetts. Any state that calls soda tonic most likely banned egg creams. Strange.

Dickey liked the egg cream. Chocolate. Seltzer. What was not to like? My egg cream tasted better since I knew it was Dickey's very first. We looked at the comic rack. Dickey said it was one of the best he ever saw.

We headed up Carr Avenue, past the school and church I saw everyday. Dickey pointed out the statue of Saint Anne and another of Mary. Hmmm. Yep, there they were. Just waiting to be seen every day. Dickey saw them so I did, too.

There were more bars in Keansburg than Dickey saw in all of Massachusetts. That did not make me smile, but it was indeed true. Dickey let me see my town fresh for a day. Company did that. We need that once in a while. Seeing stuff that somehow became background.

Jersey Sure

It happened in the house as well and that made us all a little better. The place was just a little cleaner. Some of the repairs that Handy Andy put off were done, albeit at the very last minute. Some of the glue that held the rungs in the Dining Room chairs was still wet when the company pulled up. We spruced up. The house spruced up. Places, everyone! Action! Sorta like the folks who decided to sell the house and made all those improvements to put it on the market and then ended up keeping it because it looked so damn good when they were done. Maybe we should invite company over just because we caught up on the chores just before they arrive. That and we appreciated things that we took for granted until they were here to see them as well.

Dickey and I returned the yard. The sun eased from the sky as if on an inner tube with a very slow leak. Sssssssssssssssssssss. Sssssssssssssssssssss. It took hours for all of the light to go away. We got back home in time to eat. The adults were still in the chairs in the side year. Had they even moved except to get more beer? Summer time in the Burg. Lawn chairs, cigarettes, and beer. The neighbors popped over as well, and the yard was a beehive of inactivity as they sat and talked. We entered, and they only registered it as a courtesy. Guess they reconnected as well.

Sis and the girls were nowhere to be seen and that was alright. Dickey and I hung around for a bit and then went into the house for a soda. No tonic this time. I took him up to my room and showed him my comics. He was a Dell guy too. We read a few, but it was not long before the folks called that dinner was ready. BarBQ!

BarBQ is good stuff. Burgers. Dogs. Sometimes chicken. This was one of those times. Company was here. The girls were back from wherever they went, and everyone gathered around the picnic table and grill. Food time! Chicken all around. Pssst, "you kids eat dogs and burgers just in case there is not enough", so Sis and I ate dogs and burgers. Smoke from the grill seasoned the summer air. There were chips and generic sodas. Good stuff. Generic colas sucked but generic Root Beer and generic Orange were hard to tell from the real stuff. I bypassed the cola. Based on the cans in the bucket with the ice, most others did as well. Colas floated in icy hope. Float. I didn't need them.

We ate with hunger. Hunger made things taste good. Liked you earned them. Then it was time for clean up. The folks headed for lawn chairs and more beer. They kids went to work. "Yoo, we, oh. Yoo, um."

Cleaning up was actually easy. After all, there were five slave laborers. Plus, we did not actually have to wash the dishes. Thank God for paper plates! Plates and stuff in the trash, a quick run to put the ketchup and stuff in the icebox, and we were done. It was quick.

Not quick enough to catch the sun. While we ate and cleaned up, it headed elsewhere to share its light. Dusk was here and night was coming. The adults drank beer and got that mellow, loving life thing going on. The kids played. All of us. Freeze tag. The girls cheated but still lost. Red light, green light. We played hard. We tried to beat the darkness. It did not work. Darkness came. With it came other visitors. A few at a time. Then many. Mosquitoes.

Mosquitoes did not like the light. They tended to stay away. Nocturnal, I guess. Bloodsuckers must be part vampire. These pesky bastards had the night shift. In New Jersey, the mosquitoes were a hardy breed and dared you to take a swipe at them. We sprayed that OFF stuff on and sucked it up as the sun disappeared. We played. We swatted. We muttered. We played more. Yell. Swat. Laugh. Swat.

Nighttime in the summer had sounds. Summer air carried sounds further and let them linger longer. Perhaps

Jersey Sure

it was just that we were outside to hear them, but I sensed it was something more. Summer air amplified it but to levels that pleased versus annoy. Sounds you heard above the hands that swatted mosquitoes to death. Crickets. Insects we did not swat. Crickets rubbed their legs together to entertain us. Background music. Insects were not alone in the calliope of sound. Owls made wonderful summer sounds. Hoots that reassured someone saw things in the night. Sounds abound. Noisy kids ran around in the growing dark A sound like a schoolyard at recess but more dispersed and freer. Meat sizzled on grills. Neighbors talked over fences to friends who were inside people for too many months. Sounds were very, very important to a summer evening. Especially one sound. One sound kids waited for with lust and abandon. Music to our youthful ears.

"Ice Cream Man!" The bells! "Ice Cream Man!" We scream. "Ice Cream Man!" It kicked up a frenzy. We heard the sounds and ran the other way. To home. To the money. To beg. "Ice Cream Man!" It was a question. It was a call for hope. It was begging for the cash to buy from the magic man of summer, the Ice Cream Man. He was always in Good Humor.

Scotty was our Ice Cream man. Is there a higher calling? Spreading joy everywhere you go. Refreshment to all with the money to taste of your goodies. A truck with bells. A white uniform and kinda neat hat. I ran home to plead for money. Pleading was easier when you used the moment. At the moment, we had company. Katie and Bud were good for ice cream money when there was company. We got the treats while we would not have other nights.

I chose the ten-cent ice cream bar rather than the nickel Popsicle. My father looked but did not argue. Other days he would have convinced me that I wanted a Popsicle. He was always wrong. I wanted the Chocolate Éclair Ice Cream. I settled for the Popsicle. For a Popsicle was much, much better than the dreaded alternative of no ice cream and a lecture on appreciating what we have. It was ironic that the "appreciate what you have" lecture normally came when they did not give you anything so you could appreciate it.

The ice cream tasted good. Perhaps because it was a summer night. Perhaps because I was tired after the exercise and laughter of freeze tag and red light-green light. Perhaps because I did not normally get an ice cream. Whatever it was, it worked. We sat for a while. Content. Quiet. We let the night grow dark and knew play was over. Until we saw a twinkle or two of hope.

Lightening bugs. They were mostly likely there for a while but ice cream was more attention getting than flying bugs with lights where their butts should be. We sprang to action to catch them. As soon as we finished the ice cream. As if fueled by greed.

Lightening bugs were the easiest bugs in the world to catch. They flew but not like a fly flies. More of a hover and at slow speed. It was like God wanted them to be caught. If not God, then surely the US Government wanted us to catch them. Why else would they offer a bug bounty?

If you collected enough lightening bugs, I think the number was in the thousands, you could send them in for cash! Every kid in the neighborhood had a stash of the cash convertible insects somewhere in their house. All you needed was an old mayonnaise jar, a little bit of time, and a lot of hope. We added more torch carriers to the stash nightly. I often wondered where we were supposed to send the bugs once we had them penned in a jar. Surely someone knew the address for the Lightening Bug Redemption Center. How long did they take to get the cash to the redeemers? What did they do with these bugs? Was it something like a spy effort? National Defense? Something dark? We collected to see.

Jersey Sure

Somewhere between lightening bug twenty-seven and twenty eight, the adults called. It took a minute to realize they stood near the car in the we are going now stance. Dickey and I looked at each other and felt sad in tandem. We were having fun. We laughed We played. Now we would not see each other for another long time. That sucked. We reunioned successfully, and now it was over. Too quick.

The good byes were real. Relatives and memories arrived. Friends and more memories left. None of us knew when or even if we would meet again. The car pulled out and diminished to nothingness at the bend on Main Street. So long, Dickey. See ya soon. If the good Lord is willing.

Boy Scouting—also with a Jersey twist (Eight Balls and Critter Patrols)

Summer ended as it usually did with the first day of school and with sixth grade came the big move to Boy Scouts. It always frightened me that the name for the point where young boys become young men in the Boy Scouts of America is pronounced, We Blows, but we handled the indignity and moved upward. Boy Scouts did not mess around. Seems we barely started when we planned our first hike. At least the first hike that had my patrol involved with the troop.

Cub scouts had packs and Boy Scouts had troops. Cub Scouts had dens and Boy Scouts had patrols. In the Cub Scouts, dens were numbered. In the Boy Scouts, patrols were named. This was a vital issue since the name often shaped the patrol. Boy Scouts avoided names like bobcats, tigers, etc, since many of these were actually ranks in the Cub Scouts. Instead they chose names of inspiration and awe. Panthers. Pythons. Cobras. Gators. Hawks. Titles

Jersey Sure

that spoke to their very nature and substance. I was in the 8-Ball patrol. We had a really cool flag and an attitude that scared the hell out of the critter named patrols.

Proper wear of the uniform was a very big thing in the Boy Scouts of America. Some folks got very, very serious about subtle nuances developed over decades of ritual and righteousness. Some scouts knew the regulations and had copies of the multi-volume manual that outlined the proper wear and care for uniforms of the Boy Scouts of America. We referred to these people as assholes, our own term of endearment for the would-be compliance Nazis.

Uniforms set the tone for fitting into the community of scouts, both past and present. Pants had to match the shirts. Neckerchiefs, by far the coolest part of the uniform since it could be used while playing cowboys and Indians, had to be worn evenly on the neck and rolled just right. Hats centered on the head. Belt without excess material showing from the clasp. Troop name and number sewn neatly on the upper sleeve of the shirt. Ropes of honor worn properly around the shoulder and under the armpit by select few, commonly referred to as the ass kissers. Merit badges, for those who actually earned any, displayed in the correct order of importance. Some scouts had so many merit badges they actually wore sashes to hold them all. Consequently, they looked more like visiting ambassadors than the anally retentive youth they actually were. Folks in the 8- Ball patrol were a little less stringent about uniform wear. I had a neckerchief and a shirt handed down from a previous 8-baller.

Uniforms be damned, the high point of my Boy Scout adventures clearly was the weekend camping trip/hike to Hidden Hollow, over ten miles away from Keansburg. It was the first time in the history of Troop 105 that 8-ballers

Gilbert Van Wagner

in mass supported a function other than the occasional monthly meeting. Our support for the monthly meetings was always noticed, and the ejection of one or more our patrol was as routine to the forum as the Pledge of Allegiance. Collectively, the 8-ballers decided it would be fun to see what this camping crap was all about. Hiking was easy, and our many jaunts on the railroad tracks made that portion seem second nature. We did the blankets over the clothesline thing a few times with mixed success and figured camping was like that only not in the yard. So we signed up for the weekend trip. The rest of the troop pondered what we would add to the mix. Rumor had it that at least one of the critter patrols backed out when they found out we would be there.

On the morning of the hike, ten 8-ballers arrived at the prescribed time with the other scouts. While Dads and/ or Moms dropped off the others, we showed up in mass in our hodge-podge of leftover uniform pieces in our own version of "prepared". Lou had a brown paper bag full of Devil Dogs and Yoo-Hoos. Joey had his Saint Anne's book bag complete with matches, lighter fluid, rope, a small ax, and knives; he rarely left home without it anyway. Tuffy, not his real name but I never did learn his real name, wore his leather jacket and French beret as usual, but brought a sleeping bag and put on his neckerchief on as a show of Boy Scout pride. I had my brother's backpack complete with baloney, crackers, water, shoplifted sugar wafers, and gum. United in non-conformity, the other 8-ballers completed the ragtag ensemble. Our adult leader brought some things like meat and fruits, so collectively; we were ready for the wilds of Middletown Township.

It was one of one of those crisp, clear Jersey autumn mornings, and we felt as one with nature. The hike itself was quite invigorating, even if far more structured that our normal impromptu excursions. There was only one fight on

Jersey Sure

the way, and it was minor since no actual weapons were involved. We cut through a few filling stations, and all used the opportunity to jump on the air hose that rang the bell. The gas jockeys raised their fist in habit but lowered them and smiled when they saw it was Boy Scouts. I made a note of that since it seemed we got away with things as Scouts. Could be useful in the future. Boy Scouts as an alibi. Hummm.

The roads were quiet. Even Highway 36 was sparsely trafficked. We crossed the border of Keansburg and journeyed through Hazlet and points beyond.

This hike, as with all hikes, took on a rhythm all its own. Chatter decreased in direct proportion to the distance traveled. Gentle games of grab-ass disappeared, and boys quieted. Even 8-ballers. Sounds changed. Thumping of feet eased into a tandem. An occasional fart generated short titters of laughter but little stink or fuss. Silence became a communication of spirit and purpose. Each scout found their own pace but complied with the herd. Each boy felt the same things, and each thought it unique. I was no exception.

I eyed the surroundings as we hiked but, truth be told, they were of little consequence. Laurel Avenue could have been the Bright Angel trail. The Colorado River could have marked the halfway point in lieu of Middle Road. Lily Tulip, the factory that had the big cup outside, could have easily been the South Rim of the Grand Canyon. For the effect of a hike on a hiker was universal regardless of locale. New Jersey or New Zealand, what we saw changed, but what we felt on a hike was the same.

My inner body spoke to me. As clear as indicators on the dashboard of my mind, my heart let my ears know it beat faster but was alright. My lungs pulled and pushed for air as my ego stifled the noise of the breathing. My muscles warmed with burning calories and flexed with increasing power. The backpack chaffed my shoulders despite the layers of protective clothing and I shifted it without missing pace. Movements seemed instinctive. Natural. Satisfying. My taxed body paid the sweet price of challenge. Each scout chipped into this kitty of self-discovery in much the same way. Singularly yet simultaneously.

Lined and hiking by patrol, the pieces eased into the collective. The Troop bonded as the miles passed. Even the occasional rest stops were uneventful. Scouts picked spots to sit without debate or discord. Some chose rocks. Others eased to the softer but equally cool grass. Without instruction or planning, Troop 105, even my own patrol of self-proclaimed misfits, honored an unspoken but nonetheless vital hiking tradition. We sat in a circle.

Water became the beverage of choice. Cobras shared raisins with 8-ballers. 8-ballers sat quietly. Adult leaders savored the tranquility of camaraderie. Peace reigned.

Peace crumbled as soon as we arrived in Hidden Hollow. The troop became a herd, and the herd stampeded as scouts jockeyed for the best campsites. The 8-Ball patrol immediately claimed the high ground and rallied together to defend their territory. Cobras, urged by the kicks and punches of my patrol mates, slithered from what became known as Ball Ground. Gators ran after their backpacks, skinned and hurled with Olympic efficiency by turf driven 8-ballers. Hawks found hats plucked from their heads and thrown far from the nest of hooligans. Adult leaders comforted the displaced but moved far from the seemingly rabid odd balls.

We set up tents provided by the Troop. Two boys to each tent. Each patrol grouped together, albeit the other patrols were clumped a bit closer based on the Neutral Zone that surrounded Ball Ground. The 8-ballers completed set up first, aided by our tolerance for crooked tents filled with thrown versus stowed gear and a ground littered with extra

Jersey Sure

tent pegs. After all, why use all twelve when six did the trick? We filled our pockets with some goodies and ran to explore Hidden Hollow.

That was when the Boy Scouts of America rained on 8-Ball expectations. The danger of fine print reared its ugly head. The Adult leaders corralled us for *structured fun*. The bane of free spirits of all ages. There were lectures. Yuck! Group instruction on flora and fauna. Boooooring! Classes on converting yarn and Popsicle sticks into God's-eyes. Geek-heaven!

Their safety spiels took the cool out of starting fires. They coached, cautioned, and controlled the enjoyment from using bows and arrows. Their fun sucking ability was unparalleled. Where we would have played Jungle Jim with his machete as he fought his way through the jungle, they stooped to describe the sacredness of the ants and other insects. We were made to sit beneath trees that screamed to be climbed as a Wally Cox look alike droned about species and habitats. As sure as the humans who happily walked onto the Twilight Zone spacecraft before the translation of "To Serve Man", we were cooked.

Proud and free 8-ballers captured and tortured in the very woods that promised freedom but delivered regimentation. Scout leaders turned guards and wardens methodically executed our hopes of joy and happiness. We 8-ballers did as all prisoners did. We plotted our escape. While accepting we would serve our time, we looked for parole from this Death by Boredom. Structured fun caged us. As sure as Steve McQueen, one by one, we broke free from that insidious cage.

Ten went in, but only some of us made it out. I was one of the first two. It began with eye contact and sign language during "The Wonders of Wood" punishment session. After knowing exchanges, a pair of us 8-ballers nonchalantly rose for a trip to the "facilities". We knew even the most heartless guard would not deny us that right. Nature duty done, and after a quick scan to ensure no adult looked in our direction, we crouched behind the porta-potties, a blind spot to the BSA screws. Step B in our plan yet to be determined, we wondered what the hell we were going to do next. It was case of "Death before Drudgery". A few psst's later, and five of us chose stagnant air and discomfort behind the pungent potties over a merit badge for whittling. One watched. Four planned. Then we moved. We made a break for the rise that formed the outer perimeter of Hidden Hollow Promises, camp for the misfortunate and uninformed.

We ran with an urgency that surprised us. A longing drove us in ways we did not understand and could not appreciate. Freedom laid over that rise. We could almost taste it. Then we heard the sound that threatened to deny us the sweet taste of fun. Footfalls. Running ones. Not animal. Two legs, not four, pumped through the woods just behind us. Someone chased us! The Screws! I thought it, as did all the escapees. I alone gave it voice. "SHIT!"

Like animals in season that felt cross hairs on important body parts, we serpentined through the forest, leaped felled trees in a single bound, ducked low hanging branches with a graceful bob and weave, and felt a surge of adrenaline seldom experienced in nature and survived. Our running was for life itself. If caught, more than mere lectures and boredom would be our fate. They would disband the 8-Ball patrol for sure.

If captured, our escape could be the Holy Grail of excuses that eluded Troop 105 leaders for a long time. The humdrum adult leaders may be boring, but they knew the premise of Divide and Conquer and hoped for exactly that opportunity for decades. Most of us would be banned from the troop. Those that remained would be dispersed among the critter packs for brainwashing and assimilation. For

Jersey Sure

our break from Hidden Hollow Promises was just another in a long series of 8-Ball adventures. We were not the first generation of 8-ballers, but we were steps away from becoming the first batch caught in the act.

The 8-Ball patrol's long and sometimes sordid history, shaded in controversy, was known throughout the New Jersey Scouting community. Three generations before us wore the numbered black orb patch and set precedents rivaled by many and studied on high. We were part of a legend. As with legends, fact and fiction blurred. Was it really an 8-baller that replaced the chocolate chip cookies with Ex-lax treats at the Jamboree? Could one lone 8-baller have single-handedly short sheeted every bed at Willowbrook all those years ago? Was it, as all suspected, a highly creative 8-baller that carefully drained gunpowder from hundreds of firecrackers, dusted twigs with that same gunpowder, methodically placed those gunpowder laden twigs in every fire pit in Hidden Hollow, and then savored the shocked and blackened faces at dinner time? The Boy Scouts were not sure but credited these and many, many other feats to our 8-Ball ancestors. We took the credit and did our best to uphold it. It was our heritage so it was our duty. We were part of a legacy.

It was no accident that Troop 105 had the only 8-Ball patrol known to man. Key leaders in the Monmouth County Boy Scout Council, a collection of adults firmly entrenched in the way it was when they were ten years old and wearing the uniforms to prove it, mandated there would be no other 8-Ball patrols. Sure, they carefully couched it in language that required patrols to select names from a pre-approved list or to justify any hoped-for exception but we knew it was all part of the anti-8-Ball movement. We saw the ploy just as our 8-Ball ancestors did. The annual "what if we were named something else" initiative was all part of the some plot. Did they really think we did not realize this review of names was unique to our patrol while the critter ones never experienced it? Each year they tried. Each year they reviewed our list of possible replacement names in disgust and frustration. "Killers". "Jackals". "Hellions". "Devils". "Mercenaries". "Thugs". "Bums" (My personal favorite). Annually, they tried. Annually, they failed. Annually, we laughed. They drastically underestimated us.

On that faithful day in Hidden Hollow, we were within feet of losing the legend. On the doorsteps of ignoble defeat, we ran not just for ourselves but for all those 8-ballers before us. I ran faster that day than at any time before or since. Alongside of me, the others kept pace. But sadly, the chaser did as well. We sped, but the gap closed. Still we ran. Up the hill as signs of autumn crinkled and crushed beneath our feet. We ran with a common although unspoken hope. The crest of hill was sanctuary. Somehow, we assumed that the other side the hill was more than just out of sight. It was the finish line. There, we were free even if the chaser was right behind us. However, if he so much as touched us prior to the crest, it was the end for the 8-Ball patrol. Forever.

Yards became feet. Feet became inches. Freedom raced into the realm of distinct possibility. Five ran as one and crested the hill as if linked physically as well as spiritually. The chaser right behind. All ran out of steam in tandem just as Hidden Hollow became that place on the other side of the hill. We slowed, stooped, paced, and panted like horses in the paddock of Churchill Downs after the Kentucky Derby. Only there were five winners this time and one lone loser who qualified for neither place nor show. Five 8-ballers who kept the tradition alive. Five proud misfits that raced for generations of misfits and won. It was the sweet taste of victory.

We turned to see who was so close to ending to legacy. Which adult almost succeeded where dozens had failed? Who was the one within arms reach from becoming legend

Jersey Sure

himself? For he was Holmes; we were Moriarity. He was the Lone Ranger; we were Butch Cavendish. He was Elliot Ness; we were Frank Nitti. Between panting breaths, I looked to identify him.

Tuffy!? I was stunned. Tuffy?? He was the one that chased us up the hill? The other escapees were as shocked as I was. We were livid. Tuffy?? We ran like that from Tuffy?? Anger first. Amazement soon thereafter. Laughter followed. We rolled. Belly laughed. All but Tuffy. He looked at the five of us like someone left out of the joke. He had that fake smile, lame chuckle, and slightly hurt look germane to one not quite sure what is so funny. Between his own gasping breaths, he asked "Why'd you guys run from me?" "Where ya going?.

Eventually, we composed ourselves enough to answer him. Tuffy feigned getting the humor, but he and we knew he did not. Some things are like that. For the next hour we wandered in the woods. Sat. Walked. Talked. Sat. Walked. Talked so more. We eased back into the campground later, retrieved Tuffy's fallen beret enroute, just in time for dinner. We were hungry and tired. Refreshed and victorious as well. We slept well that night. The sleep of confidence, having added to the legacy of the 8-Ball patrol.

Movies, big screens and little screens
(Matinees and Grate Popcorn)

I loved movies. At home. In theaters. Movie time was special time. A trip to the movies was a Saturday afternoon thing. Sometimes a Sunday afternoon thing. It was an air-conditioned summer thing in a town of electric fans for some and hopes of breezes for most. It was better as a winter thing as an escape from the cold and elements in a bay-wind bitten building. Movies worked well almost any time of the year. I was a movie kid and hoped to be a movie adult.

Movie curtains were part of the fabric in the Van Wagner household. Our parents, especially my father, watched movies at home, so we did as well. My sister and I did not choose the movie to watch at home. We got to vote though. Watch what my parents, usually my father, wanted or go elsewhere. I usually voted to watch the movie.

Movies on the television were not the same. Commercials sucked the life outta them. Dad watched a lot of movies on TV. In fact, I do not remember him ever going to the theater, but I guess he must have gone at least once or twice.

Jersey Sure

Didn't everyone? He liked movies on television though. I liked them, too, but not as much as movies at the movies. There was something special about the theater. Theaters enhanced by not having Dad there to make us fetch things or change the channels during commercials so he could see what was on the other channels. Movie theaters were dadless so they had a leg up on the boob tube.

There was a feel to a movie theater. Not just the place. The experience. That is why we talked about movies we have seen. It bonded us with all who saw the same movie even if we saw it at different times in different theaters. We all saw it and the experience was as important as the film itself. From the time you decided to go until you were back home again. The trip to. The trip from. The movie, usually movies for us double feature kids, between. The sights. The sounds. The smells. All part of the package. A package that almost always included popcorn. One word. Movieandapopcorn. I was sure there are people who could eat popcorn without watching a movie. They are sick, sick people with no sense of importance. God and the American Indians invented popcorn to be eaten while at the theater.

Good movies. Bad movies. Popcorn made them all good. Alright, some never qualified as good but popcorn made them all better. We munched it quickly during horror movies and smiled as we ate it when we danced with Disneyish cinema. Eating popcorn during comedies was messy and even potentially dangerous. The highest compliment for a comedy was how far you spit your popcorn during the funny scenes. Choke to death on your exploded maize, and the movie was headed for an academy award. Older people risked cooties as they shared popcorn during romantic, sappy flicks. Sometimes they touched hands in the very same bag of kernels. They usually wed soon after such intimacy. I think it was some church rule. Popcorn was as much a part of movies as sticky floors and gum under the seats. I liked popcorn. I had to. I was a movie kid, and a movie kid that does not like popcorn is not a movie kid. A movie kid that does not like popcorn was a critic-embryo. A sad, lonely creature that just sat there looking for things that were wrong. Me? I ate popcorn by the fistful and enjoyed the show. Buttered and prepped for a bucketful of emotions in all shapes and sizes as films popped to life before my very eyes.

Sometimes the movies scared me. Like that one with the guy who had the mask that made him see scary things and whenever he put on the mask in the movie, we put on 3D glasses in the theater to see the scary things right with him. Creepy to see folks from the movie walking over folks in the theater. That one stayed with me for a while. Long after the popcorn moved on to other things. That 3D low budget foray even came back to visit once in while in the dark of the night. Fear, the gift that keeps on giving.

Sometimes I laughed with the movies. Abbott and Costello always made me laugh. I hated to admit it but Bob Hope did as well. He was a Mom and Dad kinda guy, so I kept the fact that I like him quiet. Disney I publicly liked. Disney sometimes made me laugh but other times made me feel all good inside. That sappy, everything is right with the world feeling that made kids want to play nice. At least for while. Then it was back to suck eggs you bastard and every kid for themselves. It was nice while it lasted, though. Disney made great Saturday afternoon stories. Shaggy Dogs. Absent Minded professors. Cartoons as real as real can be. That Walt guy did it all and did it well. He was big on TV as well. Someday I hoped to see that magic place he built out in California. He had like a whole Frontierland out there. Way, way cool. Meanwhile, I enjoyed his movies. Disney anything was good. It would have been great to have Walt for an uncle. I bet he gave great birthday presents.

Jersey Sure

Disney aside, I was a sucker for Westerns. On TV or in the movies, cowboys ruled. John Wayne was big and bad. Roy Rogers was cool even if a bit preachy. Heck, every one but Wally Cox types looked good in cowboy hats. Westerns were predicable and I liked that. Even when filmed in color, Westerns were black and white. Good guys overcame bad guys. All was right west of the Mississippi, partner. Everything was a-OK around the corral. I rode the range and spoke with a drawl for days after seeing Western shoot em ups. It helped that seventy four percent of all television shows were Westerns' but TV shows did not touch me as much as Texas and parts out there in the marvel of Cinemascope. The wonders of yesteryear made for marvelous matinees.

Westerns were awesome, but Saturdays were made for adventure movies. Journeys around the globe. Travels into space. These yarns captivated me for hours on end. Flights of fancy with thinkers of things not yet and perhaps never. HG Wells was good all the time but Mister Verne was the master. Beneath the earth, under the water, and into the cosmos, he shared his imagination, and I savored each step of the joyous way. Ahhhhh, Jules Verne and his Mysterious Island. Put Captain Nemo on the screen, and the time went by in flash. Men with giant seashells on their back looked like shrimp as mutant squids tried to turn them to crushed Asians. I could watch that one over and over. That worked out kinda good because we only had one theater in town and their policy was show old movies until the film wore out.

The one theater was The Casino. The Casino got the movies well after they played everywhere else in the world but they usually had double features. Quite a gimmick. Alright, step right up! Yowsa, Yowsa, Yowsa. See not just one, but two, old movies for the price of one. Yowsa, Yowsa,

Gilbert Van Wagner

Yowsa. Come one. Come all. To the Casino and our double feature of movies everyone else has seen. Yowsa.

The Casino was located on Beachway, just across from the Heidelberg Inn, the place with the hot dogs grown ups liked. It was an old theater, but it was ours, and I liked it. In the winter, the place was all locals and that reassured. In the summer, the house was fuller and less personal. Nice, but not as homey. Like sharing your room with a visitor. Neat. For a while. After all, fish and company go bad in three days. Summer visitors to Keansburg came for three months at a stretch. Overripe, approaching stenchville in fish terms. But this day was pre-summer and I knew the Casino would be homey. Mom and Dad felt safe letting Sis and I walk across town to the Casino for an afternoons' fare. They opted to stay home, kidless. An opportunity to see two movies with their kids, and they decided to send us on our own. Parents missed out on some of the best opportunities at parenting.

It was not without a fight, though, since movies cost money. Sis and I were dispatched together, along with a quarter for admission and a quarter for snacks. Fifty cents each! Mom gave us the money. Reluctantly. Very reluctantly. The buffalo felt the pressure as soon as we started the run for the nickels. Each time we got money from her, she made us work for it with pleading and begging, and even then she hesitated. Damn, she was tight. Dad gave her a look when she tried to give us just the money for admission. No candy??? That bitch. Although I only thought it. Dad gave her a look, part correction and part pleading. She scowled as she forked over the extra cash. I didn't care. Just give me the money.

I savored the victory. Fifty cents was big money. Sis and I knew how to make the most of it. We smuggled. Popcorn was undeniably a movie thing but really tough to smuggle. Popcorn filled pants was an uncommonly strange

Jersey Sure

feeling and not worth the cash savings. Butter the popcorn and the feeling was out-and-out scary. All in all, it was a feeble attempt to circumvent some good old American price gouging. Candy was a different story. Easy to smuggle. Cost effective as well. Movie candy was double the street rate, so we purchased our candy bars and goodies before hand and smuggled them into the movie house. A Nestlé's bar tasted better when I paid a nickel for it and the kid next to me paid a dime. Heck, the movie house did not even have penny candy. My pocketful of red-hot dollars, slightly smushed and warmed, tasted all the sweeter when smuggled. So Sis and I smuggled. So did the other, pre-matinee kids at the candy store less than a block from the Casino. Youthful black marketeers stuffed their pockets with twice the sweetness and tasted victory with each extra bite later.

A Yo-ho-ho and a high five or two with kindred pirates, Sis and I headed for movies. A double feature again. Abbott and Costello versus someone or another and a Western. Wooo hoooo. Laughter and adventure. Pockets bulging with smuggled booty, we took our places at the end of the line. It was the end of the line for our togetherness as well. There were other kids there and hanging with a sibling was very uncool. Even at eleven years old. We parted company as if rehearsed.

The Casino was a gathering spot. Matinees meant kids. Public School kids. Catholic school kids. Reform School kids. They were all there. My sister stood with her friends and pretended I did not exist. Not a problem. She did not exist for me either. Older sisters can be yucky. Especially when they hung around with their friends. A bunch of budding bitches.

I stood with five kids from my class, school friends but not everyday friends, and got the tickets. The bond of standing in line to buy a ticket was neat. We looked at the

Gilbert Van Wagner

posters. Spoke of what we knew of the movies we were about to see, which was usually yarns about what we saw on the posters. One picture. A few words. We filled in the blanks. There was talk of last week's movies, as well as next week's. Movie line talk before we realized there was movie line talk, just like there is porch talk or beach talk or dinner table talk. We spoke, linked by smuggled candy and parents home happy that we were about to attend a double feature. Shuffle. Speak. Shuffle. Speak. The two step process to change from audience wannabe to ticket holder. A quarter away from full admission.

The money-taking person wore one of those old fashioned hats just like in the theaters in the movies. The same hats organ grinder monkeys wore. That was kinda cool. Stupid but cool. I gave him my two-bits, and he gave me my ticket. I did not hear any organ music. Maybe he did. I smiled. He smiled back. Seemed like a nice guy for someone in such a silly hat. Golden ticket, actually red but it felt golden, in hand, I moved from the buying line to the handing it over to the next person line. Musta been a union operation. "Hey, sorry but I just sell the tickets. You gotta go over there to hand it in. Just doing my job here. Move along. Move along. We don't want any trouble. Move along. Don't complain to me. I just wear the silly hat and smile. Move along." I moved along and left monkey hat man to his happy state as our very own indispensable movie ticker dispenser.

The ticket taker was an entirely different story. She was born without a personality. At least that how it seemed. She scowled. She had her flashlight at the ready since she was the "get your feet of the seats" lady as well. She did not just take your ticket. She evaluated you. She reviewed you. She questioned silently. Is this one of the ones I will have to get mad at later? Are you a problem? She took the ticket, squinted into your soul, evaluated, slowly tore the ticket in two, and handed back the stub, with a jab. A mean jab. A threatening jab. Must have been a lot of work to be mean all the time. She did her job well. She still let me in the lobby though. Must have sensed I was a Boy Scout and would be good. Ha! Ha! Fooled ya!

Ticket stub souvenir in hand, I headed across the lobby on a mission. The lobby of the Casino was like most theater lobbies. The limbo between out there and in the movie. Posters of films to come. A candy counter. The come hither aroma of popcorn. I was not impervious to the smell. It called to me like sirens of yore. If popcorn tasted as good as it smelled, I would rarely eat anything else. Based on the line at the candy counter, most there would agree on the general appeal of buttered joy. I forced my nose past the counter and headed inside the theater. The Casino had popcorn from a machine, and popcorn made fresh at the counter. The popcorn at the counter was available, right along with the overpriced candy, in the lobby. The machine was inside the theater. I guess it was so folks could buy popcorn without ever leaving sight of the movie itself. There was a candy machine near it as well. No going to the lobby if you were in the middle of movie at the state of the art Casino theater. The rationale for placing the machines inside the movie part of the place really did not matter to me. I did not buy the popcorn from the machine. The fresh stuff was better. But the popcorn machine was always my first stop. It had free popcorn.

That was not the intent of the popcorn machine people. However, their vending concept had a design flaw. Popcorn inside the machine, guaranteed to have been popped this century, was dispensed into a cup that dropped and sat on a grate while being filled. The designers, probably the same geniuses who created the milk machine, knew some of the kernels would fall so they designed a special bin below the grate. A holding area of sorts. That grate drew me and several others who knew the secret. We thought of it as the free popcorn bin. At least after some considerate delinquent modified one of the bars with a Herculean bend. A bend that created an opening just big enough for a youthful hand to slip in and get some popcorn. Free. Once you knew it was there and remembered some fundamental physics. A fist was bigger than a hand and a fist was bigger than the opening. Slip the hand in and grab but keep the fist full of popcorn and the same hand that slipped in now trapped the popcorn getter. I always imagined a kid trapped there. Fist full of popcorn as he died or was arrested rather than open the hand and let the free popcorn go. I was more clever. I pitched the popcorn.

One hand in the bin and another above in wait for free popcorn. I pitched the pinched popcorn with the hand through the grate and caught it with the other hand. Flick. A few kernels. Flick a few more. Stuff some in my mouth. Flick. More kernels. A slow process but good for quite a bit of popcorn. Sometimes only a few nuggets. Sometimes none. Most times about five. My record was eight in one pitch. Stale popcorn. Cold popcorn. Crushed popcorn. Free popcorn. Umm, umm good. I munched sneakily but did not dally. There were two kids behind me in line. Not popcorn machine customers. Flickers. Like me. Come to think of it. I never saw anyone actually buy popcorn from the machine. Hmmm. Oh well, one last flick and I headed for the lobby for the good kernels.

Popcorn in the magic machine made the fresh stuff taste so much better. Plus, the line for the fresh stuff was shorter now, so I paid my dime and headed inside to the movie. Stocked and ready, I eased down the aisle. It was noisy. It was chaotic. Kids jumped seats. There were at least two popcorn fights. Yells echoed in the space soon to be filled with the rays of movie light. I bobbed and weaved the bundles of energy that charged up the aisle and down the

Jersey Sure

rows randomly. Candy zinged to the screen. Carnage in the making. The word for it all was frenzy. Pure, unadulterated frenzy. Sunday Matinee at its finest.

Candy in pocket, popcorn in hand, and ticket stub in pocket, I settled in for the show. An armada of crappy candy sailed overhead. I carefully selected a few unpopped kernels and lobbed them at the screen, just to join in. Just because I was a smart ass did not mean I was not wise about what to throw. Waste not, want not. The candy barrage worked. The curtains opened. Time for the best part of the movies. Previews!

Previews hinted of things to come. Literally. Foreplay before we understood what that meant other than something adults talked about in hushed tones. At least before most of us understood but a few seemed to have a better idea than I did. But I understood previews. The good parts that could be yours. The parts that made the rest of the movie tolerable. There were previews for movies we could not see since they were on the Church's list of surefire ways to hell. Even the previews were naughty. Probably time in Limbo for even looking. Previews that hinted at adult stuff. Previews that teased juvenile libidos. We let it. Not that it was hard. Perhaps difficult is a better word. Juvenile libidos are, always were, and always would be, cheap and easy targets. Hint of cleavage and oo-la-la's and whistles followed. Most of the oo-la-la'ers and cat callers did not really understand why they oo-la-la'ed or whistled for felines at those particular preview parts. But they did it with fervor and authority. Oh, yeah, baby. Oo-la-la. Like dogs chasing cars. If they ever caught one, they had no bloody idea what to do with it. So they let it go and chased another. Previews were like that. Oo-la-la. Knowing smile. Blush. Juicy, baby. Oh, look, Disney. Whew!

Previews for shows next week. No cleavage or women tied and moaning. Kids stuff on these features of coming attractions. Another double feature. Loved that "And on the same bill!" thing. We hadn't even seen today's movies and I was ready to come back next week. Previews worked well on me. Oo-la-la.

Previews were also the quiet-down now, the movie is about to start time. Last minute runs for snacks. Quick stops in the rest room to ensure bladders made it through the first movie. Time to throw the last few crap candies or popcorn kernels at the screen. Basically, settle in for the show time. I used previews to prepare. Previews basted my mind for the journey ahead. To ready. To transition. From movie seeing hopeful to the main event. Time to ease the cheeks into a comfortable numbness. I suspended disbelief and walked willingly into someone else's story. Time to focus. Previews warmed me up. Not just hints of future tales but prep for tales about to unfold. God, I loved previews. Got my mind right. Just right. I hoped previews would work this well on me for a long time to come.

The curtains closed and then reopened. Theatrics. Previews over. Show time. The first feature began. Only a few people wandered the aisles. Then all was ready. Credits ended and the darkness urged me into the light of actions on the screen. The rest of the world eased from my mind as the movie took residence. Outside was outside. Inside was dark. Inside was wherever the movie took me. Only the screen mattered. Characters spoke to me. Scenery touched me. In a far away place, a whole bunch of people did a whole bunch of work so I could enjoy my popcorn and candy and forget about school, bullies, nuns, homework, chores, and the issues of life for the span of two movies. All that work. For me. My rapt attention honored them and all their hard work.

I feel asleep during the lovey dovey part and woke up at intermission. Intermission? How the heck did that happen? I headed for the rest room. During intermission?

Jersey Sure

I had to be nuts. Plumbing has its limits. Not just my own but the Casino's. Two stalls plus two urinals during one intermission equaled a problem. I had to go so there was little choice.

The line snaked outside the restroom door and back towards the popcorn machine. The smell was not popcorn though. It was of limited plumbing at peak periods. The smell was real. Real bad. My need was more real. The smell lost. I waited my turn but sentried the screen to ensure the dark had not returned. Wanted to be settling in my seat for the second feature. Had to get the mind right for the second show after getting the bladder right.

Urinals are strange things. One purpose and one purpose only. To piss in. No number two unless winning a bet. Just urinate. Home bathrooms did not have urinals. But outside bathrooms did not have bathtubs. Hmmmm. Thanks to my time tracking down Dad in bars, I saw a lot of pissers. They came in all shapes and sizes. The adult size hung at eye level for little kids. Disturbing in that they did. Kid sized was much lower and much smaller. Made kids feel just like Dad as they pissed on porcelain just like the big people. Some of the bars had the pissing trough. Not sure who the heck thought up community urination and did not really want to meet him, or her. The Casino has the one size fits all urinal. The five-foot tall, all the way to the floor, kind that even blind epileptics in mid seizure could use without missing. It was old. It was worn, and that took a lot of pissing over the years. It was smelly. It was tarnished. It was the shortest line. One hand on my nose and one further south, I let nature run its course all over a wide porcelain wall. The little yellow mint at the bottom made a great target so I practiced by precision pissing but did it quickly because the second feature, movie wise, was due any minute.

Gilbert Van Wagner

I made it just at the lights went low, and the curtains opened. It was nice that they did the curtains like that. Closed until time for the show. Opened as the lights dimmed. Theatrics! Just me and all those lovely people in the dark.

The second feature always had a feel to it. One movie down, one to go. A few people actually did not stay for the second feature. Stupid. It was like paying double for the first show since you did not get any money back if you left early. Why the heck would you leave after paying and all?

My nap during the first movie recharged me. The second one, the movie, not the nap, went quicker because I went where it wanted me to go. Slipped out of Keansburg on the images of places shot across the theater on beams of hope. Stories told. Stories heard. On good days like this, stories felt. It passed quickly and I had that, wow, is it over so soon feeling that most movies wished for but few achieved.

The crowd stirred and eased from movie land to reality as if shaking off a web of resistance. The bodies pulled from the chairs as if bonded and breaking free. Slowly. Reluctantly. Even kids walked to the exit. The smarter of us headed for the side doors to beat the crush of people funneling through the lobby. There were doors galore in the Casino. Four down each side, but they were exits only since they did not want to have ticket booths at each one. That would require way too many organ grinder monkey hats. So we used the doors as exits only. They exited into an alley. Functional, but not attractive. Three foot of space tunneled between the Casino and its neighboring building. Alleys were scary at times. Usually at dark times. This was a dark time.

Dark was. The day went somewhere else while we watched movies. That was always a neat feeling. Even if we first noticed it in an alley that made me glad others were

Jersey Sure

around. If it was just me, I would have used the lobby doors and stayed with the crowd. As well as the light. But we exited in small mass and blew through the alley like the down of a thistle. We dashed away home.

My sister walked with her friends and me with mine, but we kept each other in eyeshot. Once closer to Maple, we reconnected so the folks would think we were together the whole time. That seemed important to them for some reason.

My parents liked when we went to matinees. They were cuddled on the couch. We did not see them cuddle like that often. They seemed happy that we were back safely. We enjoyed our times at the movies. They enjoyed them even more.

There was sandwich stuff so I made a boloney sandwich and settled in for Lassie. Timmy was most likely stuck in a damn well again but Lassie would save the day. Lassie was a TV dog now but started out as a movie dog. Must have been cool to be a movie dog. Movies were better than TV shows anytime. Sad that Lassie was now limited to bailing out the bozo boy in a half hour of adventure. She would have been happier in a full-length flick like the old days.

Our family was a movie family, even when the movies were on that little black and white box in the living room. Movies were togetherness whether we were in Oz or Tombstone or someplace not as real. Places we may never be but that we enjoyed at the moment. Together apart. There was light in that darkness. Sometimes the light of enlightenment. Sometimes the light of entertainment. Sometimes the light of laughter. Sometimes the light of dark feelings. We watched movies together but entered the movie alone, free to go where we needed to at the moment. Some people laughed at movies. Some people cried. Some people looked away, fearful of what they would see but seeing in the fact that they looked away. I liked that about movies. One of the best was the Wizard of Oz.

Oz was a special movie for so many reasons, one of which is that we never got to see it at one sitting. My Dad did not like Oz, or he had seen enough. Whatever his reason, he was definitely not pro-Oz. Dad said the flying monkeys could take a flying leap. We begged and pleaded and whimpered to the very best of our abilities, and Sis threw a mean hissy fit. So Dad gave in. In a fashion. The flying monkeys got to come around. In bits and pieces. Like the scarecrow. A bit of over there and another bit over there. Sometimes Dad did not give in until well after the movie started. Other times he gave in and then decided, with great bluster, and he was a great blusterer, "That's enough of this happy horseshit." Each year we begged. Each year he gave in. But not entirely. We saw about a third of a bit of Oz, and Dad decided that was enough of that crap. Next year came and we saw another bit and then Dad pushed Oz away for an annual break. In four years, Sis and I got to see it one and a third times. Loved it all the same. Like Christmas spread out for twelve days. Twelve flying monkeys a leaping all over our black and white TV. I loved Oz.

In our house, Oz was the same color as Kansas. I did not know Oz was in color and that Kansas was in black and white until I saw it on color TV at my brother's. That year, I got to see the whole thing. My brother let me, and Dad had no control over his TV, and his TV was one of those brand new, RCA Color jobs. My mouth dropped when Dorothy stepped out of her messed up bedroom and saw little people in primary colors. Magic. Cinema at its finest. I saw Oz before but missed it. Color made it even more vivid. Tears do not have color. But color sure had tears. Good tears. Everything was alright tears. The witch is dead tears. Damn, Kansas even looked good at the end. Jersey was not

Jersey Sure

Kansas. That was a good thing. Farms smell and the little man behind the curtain was full of shit but I liked him in the movie. He lied to them but made them happy. He would have been a good car salesman. Hot air and all. Seemed fitting.

Dad may not have completed the tour of Oz, but he stayed the course for almost any other movie. The Big Preview on Channel 9. The Early Show on Channel 11. The Late Show on Channel 5, followed by the Late, Late Show. Movies. Black and White. Cops and Robbers. Cowboys and Indians. Laurel and Hardy. My dad liked them all. He knew Cagney better than he knew our neighbors. Dad was a movie guy.

I watched a lot of movies with him. Dad on the couch eating thin mints or Milky Ways. Me on the floor wishing for thin mints or Milky Ways. I did not always get thin mints or Milky Ways. I always like the feeling though. Movies at home were nice.

Movies at home were nice, but movies in the theater were better. The ultimate in entertainment satisfaction was a movie in the theater in the middle of a school day. With permission! We had that. Once, but it was awesome even if just once. It was called "Gone with the Wind". "Gone with the Wind" was not just a movie, it was a school trip. All the way to Red Bank with kids from other classes in Saint Anne's. On a school day, to see a movie. Woooo hooooo. A different theater. A whole new thing. This theater had a balcony. With seats and everything. We did not sit in the balcony, but there were people up there. Seeing a movie. In the middle of a school day.

Is there anything better? Just about any movie was good. School day escape. Every one of those was cool. So here we were seeing "Gone in the Wind" on a weekday.

Gilbert Van Wagner

Sure it was old. Parent old they said. I knew that even some of the old movies were good. Old did not make me worry, but the nuns felt the urge to ensure we did not worry that it was an old movie. They said things to make it sound better. When would they learn? That never worked. It did not work for Doctor visits. It did not work for shots. It did not work for visiting relatives. The harder the adults sold, the less kids believed it. When would they learn? Things adults said to make it sound better actually made it sound worse. With "Gone with the Wind", the Nuns, and they counted as adults even if they never had kids, said something to make it sound better that failed miserable. They said Epic. That is a shit word for something really, really long. Usually really, really boring. Shakespeare was epic and he did not even speak English. Not our English anyway. Who the heck is Ye and Thou? Old Testament surely. Get with it, Willie. Willie was epic, and epic was a yawn. The nuns did not stop there though. They said the sure killer. According to Sister Constipated and the other penguins, Gone with the Wind was "educational". Danger! That is the kiss of death to kids when selling something. Educational sucked.

But it was a school day, and it was a movie so I went. I knew it would be fun since I would be with kids and all. Sixth graders from all over Monmouth County headed for Red Bank. A gift of sorts for making it to the sixth grade. Regardless, a ride on a bus instead of grammar drill was alright with me. The movie really didn't matter. Epic. Educational. Or even both.

"Gone with the Wind" screwed up and was good. Very good. War stuff with all the carnage that touched me like John Wayne beating up Black Bart. But there was other stuff too. I liked Rhett. He loved that little kid, although she was spoiled and all with the horse and silly blue outfit. I liked Scarlett too. She had guts. Scarlett could been from New Jersey. Attitude wise. She never let them get her

Jersey Sure

down. She was a bit of a bitch and used people, but I think she was alright underneath it all. I ended up giving a damn about Rhett and Scarlet.

So much so that I decided to read the book. The very next day. The movie was that good to me. They did not have the book in the school library. That seemed kinda odd to me since they just took us to the movie and all. But what the hey. So I headed for the other library in town. The public library. The Keansburg library was in the Borough Hall. It was bigger than the Saint Anne's library but had a whole different feel to it. Not as pure. Not as safe. Not as homey. But I went and asked the librarian for the book.

She did an adult thing that sucked. She talked me out of it. Said it was too big for me and that I may want to consider something else. She thought epic was too much when it came to books for kids. She did not see the educational value of kids reading books that told of wars and love and all the stuff the movie I just saw had. She advised that I may be better off reading something else. Something easier. I did a kid thing. I agreed and left. Should have gotten it anyway. Should have conquered it and stretched myself. But she was an adult and a librarian to boot so I just agreed. Stupid librarian. Probably didn't like movies. In theaters. At home. Even in the middle of a school day. Epic or educational or not.

She was a pretty crappy librarian. Should have worked at the Casino and wore a organ grinder monkey hat. At least she would have let me see the movie. She kept a book from me as if it would prevent me knowing things about life and death and stuff. Stupid bitch. Life came at kids just like it did adults, and she could not prevent it. This was Keansburg, not Frontierland. Get a grip on reality, lady. Better for me to read about it rather than be surprised when stuff happened. La-la-la'ing through life as if no one ever got cancer, died, or went to war. Except in movies. Yeah, right. That was good life preparation. Censorship made no sense to me. Hoped it never would. Some librarians sucked. This one sucked big time.

Death
(Dead Tommies and the kid down the street)

Death sucked. My friend, David, knew it first hand since his father died last Thursday. They had a viewing at the Funeral home, and I really should have gone but didn't. If I mentioned it to Mom or Dad, they would have taken me. I could have stopped by on the way home from school. The funeral home was right on Carr Avenue, and I passed it everyday on the way to and from school. It would have been easy to pop in. It would have been right to pop in. I did not pop in.

The idea of a viewing was strange to me. The man was dead and in a box. Why would we want to see that? It was a dead body. I knew David's dad. He was a guy who wore his work shirt all the time. He worked for Esso and rode the bus to and from where ever he went to do whatever he did for Esso. He walked kinda ganky. That swinging the arms too far and too loose thing some big people did if they were not too well coordinated. David's Dad was not too well coordinated. Hoped his job for Esso did not require that he be coordinated because he was not. Not that it mattered anymore now. He was dead.

Death was strange. Gone. Where? Forever? In church, they told us about heaven and clouds and stuff, but they also told about hell and fire and all that pain. David's Dad was up close and personal to whatever the real thing is after we die. Where was he? Was he? Made me wonder and hope that wherever he was he was happy. David sure wasn't happy. His Dad was dead and, although they were not really close, not in the dad coaching softball kinda way, that guy in the box in that funeral home I should have popped into was his father, and David hurt.

I heard about it on Friday when David did not come to school. Seems you get to take off when your parent dies. Nice that it was in conjunction with a weekend and all. On the way home from school, I saw David and we talked a bit. He lived on Maple Avenue just like me but closer to Carr. Just a few houses from the funeral parlor that I should have popped into to see his dead dad. David was in his front yard. He was just sitting on the stoop. Stoop sitting could be good or bad. We sat on stoops to watch the world go by. We sat on stoops to get our balance when the world spinned too fast. David's world must have been spinning real, real fast that day. He sat on the stoop with his head down. Way down. Like he was somewhere else. Somewhere less painful. Stoop sitting could do that if you stoop sat right. David stoop sat right that day. Part of me wanted to ease on by. David may not even see me. He was on the stoop but somewhere else as well. But I could not pass. He may not have seen me, but I sensed him. His pain reached from where he was to where I was, so I walked to the stoop and stoop sat with him.

He saw me sit and greeted me wordlessly. His head went back down. Kinda like he wanted to be alone. Kinda like he wanted anything other than to be alone. He did not

Jersey Sure

know. Neither did I, but I stayed. It felt like the thing to do. I did not know what to say to David, so I sorta said I was sorry about his Dad and then hoped we could talk about something else. Or not talk about anything at all. Just stoop sit. It did not work out that way. David wanted to talk about it. He wanted to talk about the fact that his Dad was in a box around the corner. In fact, it was not really that he wanted to. It seemed he needed to talk about it. We did for a while and then he upped and cried. I saw it coming. Hoped it wouldn't, but it did. It simmered, but then burst forth like a puss from a body-sized blister.

I had no idea what to do. So I held him. Two boys sitting on a stoop. One crying. The other one hoping to ease his pain. Holding a friend while they cry about their dead Dad is a strange experience. There was no guidebook. There was not a class to prepare. You hadda wing it. So I winged it. I shut up and held David. No assurance that it would be alright because I was not sure it would be. No remedy for it since death was one of those things we could not just undo. His dad was dead today and would be tomorrow and the day after that and the day after that. Death was not a passing thing. It did not pass the one who left. It did not pass the ones left behind either. So I held David, and he cried. He cried a lot but gradually slowed to sobbing and sniffling. There are only so many tears in a human body, and he used up today's stock and the ones built up since the last time he cried. I was pretty sure he would be using up more real soon, but he spent his reserve at the moment and sobbed in place of crying. I held him as even the sobs slowed.

He pulled away gently and wiped his eyes and face as if to hide the fact that he cried. He was embarrassed, I guess, but I know I would cry if my Dad had just died. He pulled away from my arms and got real quiet. It felt like he needed to be alone again, but I felt like being there at that moment had been good. Now it was time to leave him alone with his pain. I said I hadda go. David stayed on the stoop as my feet escaped down the avenue we both called home. Like Lot's wife, I looked back that day to see the salty faced boy on the stoop. His head was so far down it looked like he was about to puke at life. His face was nowhere to be seen, but his spirit was clear to any who dared to look. He reeked of loneliness. Loneliness that would be worse when he got up from that stoop and went into the house attached to it. The house just a few feet behind him. A house forever changed. I knew what he would see when he went back inside. He did, too. He sensed it even on the stoop. He sensed it when he cried in my arms. He sensed with every breath since the moment he knew his father died. David would see the emptiness.

Emptiness like a hole that got bigger the more you took out of it. David had a Grand Canyon sized hole of emptiness in his life now. Emptiness that jumped right into his face from every nook and cranny but especially in the place he called home. His Dad's chair. His Dad's unread newspapers. His Dad's glasses. His Dad's coffee cup. Later, his Dad's Christmas stocking. His Dad's unpurchased birthday cake. Reminders of what was and would not be again. Reminders he would see today. Reminders he would see tomorrow. Reminders he would see years from now. Landmines of memories tripped when he least expected it. David's life walk just got a little harder. He sat on the stoop, fearful of the trip. I walked from David's stoop of solitude and headed home. Death sucked.

Death put a damper on my mood. I knew of dead people. We studied them in class. All those dead Presidents. Leaders. Good people. Bad people. All now dead people. I knew of relatives who died. Grandpa O'Connor took the big dirt nap before I took my first breath. Grandma O'Connor

Jersey Sure

laid down next to him when I was a year and a day old. Hope the heck it wasn't the cake. My memory of her was basically non-existent. She was someone from pictures and not a real person I knew. Guess my focus was on walking and learning to poop after the pants went down. Whatever had my attention, Grandma was just one of the dead people I heard about versus ever knew. Death was not a big thing if the people who were dead were dead for as long as you knew. That was how they were. Death was different was the people who joined the ranks were someone who used to be alive based on your dealings with them. David's Dad was alive to me right up until I heard he was dead. That sucked.

Death sucked when the person is old. It super sucked when the person was young. Like the two Tommys I knew who died. I thought of them as I walked up Maple with David still on the stoop, his dad in a box, and me thinking of people who used to be alive and young and were now dead and would never get any older. Like the two Tommys.

The two Tommys were not related. I do not think they ever even met. But I knew them both. One was Tommy two-doors-down on Maple Avenue. The other was Tommy from class with the disease that made him go bald so he got to wear a baseball cap right in the class. He was Yankee fan. At least he had been. When he was alive. But both those Tommys were dead now.

Tommy two doors down went to Vietnam alive and came home dead. His brothers and Mother and Father were still alive, but they seemed a bit dead now too. Like part of them died in a place they never visited. A place that came into their home and took their kin. Every time I saw them, I thought of Tommy. They worked in the yard and I waved. They waved. They looked sad. I thought of Tommy. They walked to the CBS and waved when they passed. They looked sad. I thought of Tommy. They did, too. He was

Gilbert Van Wagner

everywhere they looked because he was nowhere to be found. They really missed Tommy. Vietnam was more than a place Walter Cronkite talked about on the evening news for them. It was for the rest of us as well now because we all knew Tommy, and Tommy died in that place on the news. It crossed the ocean and entered our neighborhood on the back of a body bag that used to be Tommy.

He was about as old as my brother. I think. He was old enough that they drafted him so he could die. He was more present in the neighborhood since he died than when he was alive. My folks sighed when they thought of him. They kissed me sometimes just for no reason when they finished talking about Tommy and his family that got left behind. Tommy played ball with us sometimes. Back when he was alive. He swung a mean wiffle bat. Tommy told jokes sometimes. Pretty good ones. Tommy was just a kid who lived two doors down. Well, he was. But now he was one of those dead people.

Like Tommy from class with the disease. The Nuns never really told us outright what it was. But we knew it was not something good. Tommy with the disease was absent a few days at the beginning of fourth grade. As the fourth grade progressed, he was absent for a few more days. Then a week or so at a time. We knew it was not good because he was not in trouble for being absent so much. As if school attendance was not really a priority for Tommy. Like he had some special permission to miss school. Then he came to class with no hair and got to wear a baseball cap, even when we did the Pledge of Allegiance. Tommy had something, or else he would have been in big trouble for missing class and then wearing a baseball cap to school.

Tommy was a really neat kid. Even before he got sick. A bit of a jock but he played with all the kids when we

Jersey Sure

played stickball on the playground. He was smart, too. We were on the same level of SRA although I passed him up when he started missing so much school.

When Tommy went from regular Tommy to Tommy with the disease, he tried really hard to just be Tommy. Everyone tried really hard to treat him just like Tommy of old as well. It never worked. Tommy was not Tommy of old. He knew it. We knew it. He did not run as fast. Heck, after a while, he just sat on a bench and watched the games if he came to school at all. A few times, I sat with him rather than playing. I pretty much sucked anyway, so it was not a big impact to the team.

I thought of the times we sat and watched games in the playground. The kid that remembered what it was like to be a good ball player and the one who never knew it firsthand. Those moments with Tommy on that bench were kinda neat. He wanted to play, yet enjoyed the beauty of motion as others play. I was like that, too. For him, it was a memory. For me, a wish. So we cheered and kibitzed as others played. We both knew what it should look like when played right, and it was as if we were actually doing it while watching others who were really doing it. Sorta like being at Yankee Stadium. Mantle would hit a ball to the upper deck and thousands of wannabes felt the sting of the bat and the confidence of his hands. Tommy and I watched together and enjoyed the moment.

But that was last year, in the fifth grade. I never saw Tommy over the summer vacation but I thought of him now and then. When sixth grade started, Tommy came to school once or twice and he looked really, really tired. A bit sad too. I don't think he had a good summer. Not even a good weekend. The moments Tommy had in sixth grade were fewer and fewer. His desk spent more time empty than otherwise. Emptiness that become more than a temporary thing each day. One day, the Nun announced that Tommy would not be coming back to class.

We all moved desks that day. Upset the routine as each of us adjusted to a new seating plan. Tommy's desk was taken from the room. As if it would not be nice for someone to use after he was dead and all. So we played musical chairs. But for us, life's music went on. For Tommy with the disease, the music stopped and his desk was nowhere to be found.

Death sucked. But life went on. So I headed home. A little happier to be on this side of the unknown. Eleven years old was a good thing to be.

Epilogue
(Jersey, wherever I go)

The people are gone now. Some to other places. Some to other dimensions. Connections weakened or even severed by the ravages of time. Eroded by life's other priorities. Days became years and years became decades. Life's twists and turns changed us in many ways. It happens. Boys morphed to men and girls transformed to women. The child in us looks out at our own offspring and ponders how it happened so fast. Bittersweet. That's the word for it. All part of life.

The intensity of youth is seldom matched again regardless of who we were and where we lived. Friendships then shape relationships and their very nature for our entire span of time on this planet. From boardrooms to nursing homes, there is a truth to be found. Inside all of us is a ten year old. Perhaps not thriving as well as they should but in there nonetheless. You are no exception. Nor am I.

Some run from their past. I know I did. For a while. It did not work. A futile escape from something that is within them wherever they go. It is stuck to your soul with God's own version of superglue. Shake it. Rub it on the ground. Pick at it with a stick. It will not come loose. You then shaped you now. Your past is with you. Everywhere you go. As they say, everywhere you go, there you are. Your past is there with you as well. Deny it at your folly. However, dwell in it excessively at your own folly as well. Carpa Diem extremus. Forge the memories of tomorrow with each passing hour. Embrace the memories but hold today dearer. This book is my hug of a life that is quite wonderful. Each day. Yesterdays included but not exclusive. I celebrate today, and let the yesterdays in more each and every day.

New Jersey is my old country as sure as Ireland and Holland were for my ancestors. They remembered potatoes for every meal and dikes before a different spelling changed the entire idea of where fingers went. For me, the state of exits and industrial parks is my touchstone. Paid beaches and all, the third colony to declare independence from not-so merry old England, is part of me wherever I roam. It as vivid today in my very being as it was in the days of my youth. Decades after actually living in the Garden State, I am still a Jersey boy at heart. Occasional trips back to a place that is no longer my home but remains an essential part of my life. Trips not just to see the loved ones still there. Journeys into my own yesterdays. It is what I was as well as what I am.

In today's society, most, if not all, of us are from somewhere else. For me, my home and family are now in Utah. Bizarro world in comparison to the land of my youth. Quite possibly as far from Jersey as one can be. But Jersey is still there because, wherever I go, there I am. My heart carries the Old Country with me. Drop the New. Say it with an attitude. I love it and all the people in it and from it. Jersey. Fuckin' hey!

About the Author

Gil Van Wagner is, first and foremost, a story teller. Born and raised in New Jersey, his career in the Air Force and corporate America gave him plenty of tales to tell. Plant this Jersey boy in Utah and the material for stories is virtually limitless. "Jersey Sure" is not his first book nor is it the last. Gil is married and has one wife, one son, two daughters, two sons in law, one daughter in law, and two grandchildren. Each day is a treasure trove of stories to tell and Gil enjoys them in the making as well as in the telling.

Made in the USA
Coppell, TX
13 December 2019